WHAT'S FOR DINNER?

{ CURTIS STONE }

WHAT'S FOR DINNER?

Delicious Recipes for a Busy Life

Photographs by Quentin Bacon

BALLANTINE BOOKS   NEW YORK

Published in the United States by Ballantine Books, an imprint of
The Random House Publishing Group,
a division of Random House, Inc., New York.

BALLANTINE and colophon are registered trademarks of Random House, Inc.

All photographs by Quentin Bacon, reprinted here by permission of the photographer.

ISBN 978-0-345-54252-6
eBook ISBN 978-0-345-54253-3

Printed in the United States of America

www.ballantinebooks.com

2 4 6 8 9 7 5 3 1

Book design by Liz Cosgrove

*I would like to dedicate this book
to my gorgeous wife, Lindsay.
You are the most beautiful mum
in the world and watching you
with our son, Hudson,
is simply the greatest gift.*

CONTENTS

INTRODUCTION

" What's the best thing you've ever eaten?"

This is my favorite question to ask everyone, from friends and fellow chefs to people I've just met. The answer always starts the same way: "My mother used to make . . . " Whether it's chicken pot pie or meat loaf, the dishes we grew up eating, the ones made with love and shared around the dinner table, are the ones we seem to cherish the most.

For me, it was my mum's roast pork. It wasn't just the savory-sweet flavor and crispy crackling that I loved. Dinners at my house were all about being together. Whatever had happened during the day, you could always count on the dinner table to be a place to share experiences, dream about the future, talk over your worries, and connect with people you love. It seems so simple: A happy family starts with a home-cooked meal.

As a chef, I was lucky enough to cook in some of the best restaurants in the world, and I always thought I could easily write recipes for home cooks—that is, until I actually met some home cooks. While I understood that people have limited time and often need a bit of inspiration, I didn't account for family members coming home late from work, the whirlwind of soccer practices and dance recitals, different taste buds around the table, tiny kitchens, blunt knives, and the mass exodus after dinner that leaves Mom with a stack of dirty dishes.

I have now cooked in hundreds of different homes around the globe. And while the challenges vary from house to house, one is common to them all: Everyone has a busy life. My test kitchen creates four hundred recipes a year. I travel for work, write books, and make TV shows. I'm also a new dad, which has taught me the art of one-handed cooking. Trust me, I know what a busy life feels like, and I know you do too.

However, a home-cooked meal is always worth the effort. Food simply tastes better—and is better for you—when you cook it yourself. Each day of the week presents its own set of challenges, and the right recipe is one that works at the right time. Whether you're looking for healthier fare, living on a budget, or having friends over for dinner on Saturday, this book can help you put a delicious meal on the table every night of the week.

Motivating Mondays
Healthy meals that start the week off right

Time-Saving Tuesdays
Dinner on the table in 15 to 40 minutes

One-Pot Wednesdays
Flavorful dishes made in just one pot, pan, or skillet— or on the grill—leaving you with less cleanup

Thrifty Thursdays
Feeding your family on a budget and getting more for less

Five-Ingredient Fridays
Simple recipes that are fun and help kick off the weekend

Dinner Party Saturdays
Extraordinary dinners to bring out your inner chef

Family Supper Sundays
Comforting family favorites made with lots of love

I've also included a chapter of luscious desserts, because sweet things deserve their own time to shine. In addition, I serve up some refreshing cocktails (and mocktails) and scores of tips and techniques to save time, money, and effort. I hope you find these recipes so easy to make and full of flavor that they become the best thing your family has ever eaten.

So call everyone to the table. Dinner is ready.

WHAT'S FOR DINNER?

MOTIVATING MONDAYS

Grilled Chicken with Arugula and Zucchini Salad
with Lemon-Caper Vinaigrette   6

Chicken Masala with Cucumber Raita   8

Fennel-Roasted Chicken and Winter Squash with
Endive-Apple Salad   11

Turkey Meatballs with Marinara Sauce   12

Grilled Pork Satay and Peaches with Carrot-Cilantro Salad   15

Grilled Fish Tacos with Pico de Gallo   16

Poached Salmon with Green and Yellow Bean Salad   19

Grilled Salmon with Orzo, Feta, and Red Wine Vinaigrette   20

Grilled Shrimp and Rice Noodle Salad   23

Angel Hair Pasta with Clams, Radishes, and Spinach   24

Cauliflower and Spinach Dal   27

Salt-Baked Russets with Ratatouille   28

Quinoa Salad with Chickpeas and Tomatoes   31

Mango-Pineapple Smoothie   32

THE WEEKEND IS ALL ABOUT ENJOYMENT. That means second helpings, extra glasses of wine, and the gooiest chocolate desserts. Well, the weekend has ended, and it's time to turn over a new leaf. I'm a huge believer in the idea that when you start the week off right, you're more likely to end it better as well. My work with contestants on *The Biggest Loser* taught me many things, but none more important than the power of positive temptation. We crave what we see, whether it's a pan of brownies or a bowl of fresh raspberries. So start by washing some fruit and putting it out on the counter, your desk, or anywhere in your line of sight. Then cut up your favorite veggies and keep them in a container nearby. When you're itching for a snack, the fruit and vegetables will be as easy to grab as a bag of chips.

One of the rewards of cooking dinner is putting together a beautiful plate of food. And while I love family-style dining, where everyone serves themselves from platters and bowls, plating each person's meal is a great way to ensure portion control. If I see a bowl of mashed potatoes on the table, I guarantee you I'm going back for seconds.

Just remember that healthy eating is about balance, not deprivation. You don't need to skimp on flavor to eat food that's good for you. Let this chapter be your positive temptation. Cook with seasonal ingredients, which pack extra zest, and use fresh herbs. That vibrant touch of green brings food to life. In addition to herbs, the recipes in this chapter rely on lean proteins, whole grains, and tons of vegetables—even some you may have never tried—to make satisfying Monday meals that'll help you put your best foot forward.

A main-course salad brimming with lots of vegetables and lean meat is one of my favorite ways to put a healthy meal on the dinner table. This one is zesty, with arugula and peperoncini (pickled Italian peppers) in the citrusy vinaigrette. The zucchini ribbons, which look like wide pappardelle pasta, have an appetizing, fresh texture and look beautiful on the plate. When weather permits, cook the chicken breasts on an outdoor grill.

GRILLED CHICKEN WITH ARUGULA AND ZUCCHINI SALAD WITH LEMON-CAPER VINAIGRETTE

serves
4

PREP TIME: 15 minutes

COOKING TIME: 10 minutes

Lemon-Caper Vinaigrette

2 tablespoons finely chopped shallots

Finely grated zest of 1 lemon

3 tablespoons fresh lemon juice

1 tablespoon coarsely chopped drained nonpareil capers

1 tablespoon finely chopped peperoncini

1 tablespoon finely chopped fresh flat-leaf parsley

2 teaspoons champagne vinegar or white wine vinegar

¼ cup extra-virgin olive oil

Kosher salt and freshly ground black pepper

Chicken

4 skinless, boneless chicken breast halves (about 6 ounces each)

1 tablespoon olive oil

Kosher salt and freshly ground black pepper

Salad

5 ounces baby arugula (about 8 cups not packed)

1 cup halved cherry tomatoes

2 small, thin zucchini

Kosher salt and freshly ground black pepper

1 To make the vinaigrette: In a medium bowl, whisk the shallots, lemon zest, lemon juice, capers, peperoncini, parsley, and vinegar together. Gradually whisk in the olive oil. Season to taste with salt and pepper.

2 To cook the chicken: Heat a grill pan over medium-high heat. Coat the chicken with the olive oil and season with salt and pepper. Grill the chicken for about 4 minutes per side, or until it is seared with grill marks and shows no sign of pink when pierced in the thickest part with the tip of a small sharp knife. Transfer to a cutting board.

3 To assemble the salad: In a large bowl, combine the arugula and tomatoes. Trim the ends of the zucchini. One at a time, lay the zucchini flat on a work surface and, using a vegetable peeler and working from the stem end to the blossom end, shave off long, thin ribbons until you reach the seedy center. Turn the zucchini around and repeat on the second side, then repeat on the third and fourth sides. Add the ribbons to the bowl and discard the seedy centers of the zucchini.

4 Using your hands to avoid breaking the ribbons, gently toss the salad with enough vinaigrette to coat. Season with salt and pepper.

5 Cut each chicken breast crosswise into thirds. Transfer a cut chicken breast to each dinner plate and heap some of the salad alongside. Drizzle the chicken and salad with the remaining vinaigrette and serve immediately.

This dish is a far cry from the common diet dinner of broiled chicken breasts and steamed broccoli. It starts with chicken and continues with lots of spinach, cucumber, and onion, along with aromatics such as ginger, garlic, and curry powder. It adds up to a highly flavorful meal with a generous amount of sauce, to leave you feeling totally fulfilled.

CHICKEN MASALA WITH CUCUMBER RAITA

serves
4

PREP TIME: 10 minutes
COOKING TIME: 45 minutes

Chicken

4 skinless, boneless chicken breast halves (about 6 ounces each)

Kosher salt and freshly ground black pepper

¼ cup curry powder, such as Madras

3 tablespoons olive oil, or as needed

1 large yellow onion, thinly sliced

3 tablespoons finely chopped peeled fresh ginger

5 garlic cloves, finely chopped

One 28-ounce can whole tomatoes with juices, squeezed to coarsely crush

1 cup reduced-sodium chicken broth

One 6-ounce package fresh baby spinach

¼ cup coarsely chopped fresh cilantro

Raita

¾ cup plain low-fat Greek yogurt

1 tablespoon finely chopped fresh cilantro

Finely grated zest of 1 lemon

1 teaspoon fresh lemon juice

½ teaspoon ground cumin

1 cucumber, peeled, halved lengthwise, and seeded

Kosher salt and freshly ground black pepper

Perfect Basmati Rice (page 9), for serving

1 To cook the chicken: Season the chicken with salt and pepper, then rub 2 tablespoons of the curry powder all over it. Heat a large heavy skillet over medium-high heat. Add the 3 tablespoons olive oil, then add the chicken and cook for 2 to 3 minutes per side, or until browned on both sides. Transfer to a plate and set aside. Reduce the heat to medium.

2 Add the onions to the pan and sauté for about 3 minutes, or until they begin to soften. Stir in the ginger, garlic, and the remaining 2 tablespoons curry powder and cook, stirring often, for about 2 minutes, being careful not to burn the mixture. If the pan is dry, add another teaspoon of olive oil. Add the tomatoes and their juices and season with salt. Cook, stirring occasionally, for about 5 minutes, or until the onions are tender.

3 Stir in the broth and bring to a simmer. Reduce the heat to medium-low and simmer gently, stirring occasionally, for about 10 minutes to thicken the sauce slightly and blend the flavors. Nestle the chicken into the sauce and simmer gently, turning it once, for about 5 minutes per side, or until the chicken is opaque when pierced in the thickest part with the tip of a small sharp knife. Season to taste with salt and pepper.

4 Meanwhile, make the raita: In a medium bowl, whisk the yogurt, cilantro, lemon zest, lemon juice, and cumin to blend. Using the fine holes of a box grater, grate the cucumber into the yogurt mixture. Stir to blend and season to taste with salt and pepper.

5 Transfer each chicken breast half to a dinner plate. Stir the spinach into the sauce and cook for about 2 minutes, or until it wilts. Stir in the cilantro.

6 Spoon the sauce over the chicken and serve with the rice and raita.

Perfect Rice

Rice is the perfect canvas for many dishes, ready to soak up a delicious sauce. There are many different kinds of rice sold in the market today. Aromatic rice, such as basmati or jasmine, has a more interesting flavor and texture than standard long-grain white rice, although the latter makes a reliable side dish for simply cooked chops and fish fillets. If your rice has boiled over in the past, it was probably because the pan was too small. Choose a saucepan that easily holds the rice and water with enough room for the rice to triple in size. Use a heavy-bottomed pan to keep the rice from sticking, and be sure the lid fits tightly.

serves 4

PREP TIME: 5 minutes

COOKING TIME: 15 to 20 minutes, plus 5 minutes standing time

1 cup long-grain white rice

1½ cups water

¾ teaspoon kosher salt

1 In a small heavy saucepan, bring the rice, water, and salt to a boil over high heat. Reduce the heat to low, cover the saucepan, and simmer gently for about 15 minutes, or until the water has been absorbed and the rice is tender. Don't stir the rice during cooking, as this can release starches that will lead to sticking.

2 Fluff the rice with a fork and let stand, covered, for 5 minutes before serving.

VARIATION: **PERFECT JASMINE OR BASMATI RICE**
Substitute jasmine or basmati rice for the white rice. These imported rices are often coated with a fine powder to protect them through long periods of storage during transport. The powder should be rinsed off before cooking the rice. Put the rice in a sieve and rinse under cold running water, stirring the rice with your hand, until the water runs relatively clear. Drain well and proceed. There's no need to rinse domestic long-grain white rice.

The aromas from this dish—roasting chicken, with sweetness from the squash—evoke autumn. It just *smells* like a comforting and indulgent family dinner from my childhood. With those memories in mind, I created this main-course salad with its pleasing mix of bitter, crunchy, and sweet by pairing roasted kabocha with endives and apples. Part of eating well is experimenting with new choices to expand your horizons.

FENNEL-ROASTED CHICKEN AND WINTER SQUASH WITH ENDIVE-APPLE SALAD

serves
4

PREP TIME: 15 minutes
COOKING TIME: 35 minutes

Chicken and Squash

8 chicken thighs (with skin and bones)

2 tablespoons fennel seeds, coarsely crushed (use a mortar and pestle or crush under a heavy skillet)

Kosher salt and freshly ground black pepper

1 small or ½ large kabocha or acorn squash (about 2¼ pounds), halved if whole, seeded, and cut into 1-inch-wide wedges

2 tablespoons olive oil

Tarragon-Dijon Vinaigrette

3 tablespoons cider vinegar

3 tablespoons minced shallots

2 tablespoons honey

1 tablespoon Dijon mustard

1 tablespoon finely chopped fresh tarragon

¼ cup extra-virgin olive oil

Kosher salt and freshly ground black pepper

Salad

6 ounces Belgian endive (about 2 heads)

5 ounces baby arugula (about 8 cups not packed)

1 Fuji or Gala apple, cored and very thinly sliced

¾ cup walnuts, toasted (see Kitchen Note, page 113), and very coarsely chopped

¾ cup coarsely crumbled blue cheese

1. To roast the chicken and squash: Preheat the oven to 450°F.

2. On a large heavy baking sheet, toss the chicken with 1 tablespoon of the fennel seeds to coat. Season with salt and pepper. Arrange the chicken pieces well apart on the baking sheet. Roast the chicken on the bottom shelf of the oven for 10 minutes.

3. Meanwhile, on another large heavy baking sheet, toss the squash with the olive oil and the remaining 1 tablespoon fennel seeds to coat. Season with salt and pepper. Arrange the squash in a single layer on the baking sheet.

4. Move the chicken to the top shelf of the oven and place the squash on the bottom shelf. Roast for about 25 minutes, or until the squash is tender and the undersides are deep golden brown and the chicken shows no sign of pink when pierced at the bone with the tip of a small sharp knife.

5. Meanwhile, make the vinaigrette: In a medium bowl, whisk the vinegar, shallots, honey, mustard, and tarragon until blended. Whisk in the olive oil. Season to taste with salt and pepper.

6. To assemble the salad and serve: Remove hard cores from the endive. Cut the small leaves in half lengthwise, and quarter the large leaves lengthwise. In a large bowl, toss the endive, arugula, and apple slices with about half of the vinaigrette. Divide the salad among four dinner plates. Top each with 2 chicken thighs and some squash, and sprinkle with the walnuts and blue cheese. Drizzle the remaining vinaigrette over and around the salads and serve immediately.

Who doesn't love meatballs in basil-scented tomato sauce? But who would have thought that they could still be on the family table when you are trying to eat healthfully? These are so juicy and satisfying that you won't need the pasta. The recipe makes fairly large meatballs with a generous amount of sauce, allowing for a single ball per serving. Trust me, one will be plenty and you'll have extra for tomorrow.

TURKEY MEATBALLS WITH MARINARA SAUCE

serves
8

PREP TIME: 15 minutes

COOKING TIME: 40 minutes

Marinara Sauce

3 tablespoons olive oil

½ cup finely chopped shallots

6 large garlic cloves, finely chopped

4 large sprigs of fresh thyme

1 bay leaf

½ cup dry white wine

Two 28-ounce cans whole tomatoes, undrained

½ cup loosely packed torn fresh basil leaves

Kosher salt and freshly ground black pepper

Meatballs

1½ cups cubed (¾-inch) crustless Italian or French bread (about 2 ounces)

⅔ cup reduced-fat (2%) milk

½ cup finely chopped shallots

5 large garlic cloves, finely chopped

⅓ cup finely chopped fresh flat-leaf parsley

1 tablespoon chopped fresh thyme

2 tablespoons Dijon mustard

2 teaspoons kosher salt

1½ teaspoons sweet paprika

1 large egg

2 pounds ground turkey

¼ cup olive oil

Freshly grated Parmesan cheese, for serving

1 To make the marinara sauce: Heat a wide heavy pot over medium heat. Add the olive oil, then add the shallots and garlic and cook, stirring often, for about 2 minutes, or until tender but not browned. Add the thyme, bay leaf, and wine, then add the tomatoes. Crush them with a potato masher to break them up.

2 Bring to a simmer, then reduce the heat to medium-low and simmer, uncovered, stirring occasionally, for about 25 minutes, or until the liquid has reduced slightly and the flavors are well blended. Discard the thyme stems and bay leaf. Stir in the basil. Season to taste with salt and pepper.

3 Meanwhile, make the meatballs: In a large bowl, combine the bread cubes and milk. Set aside for about 5 minutes, or until the bread is soggy. Using your hands, mash the bread mixture. Add the shallots, garlic, parsley, thyme, mustard, salt, paprika, and egg and mix until blended. Add the turkey and, using your hands, gently mix until blended. The mixture will be soft, which will ensure tender meatballs. Form the mixture into 8 large meatballs.

4 Heat a large heavy skillet over medium heat. Add the olive oil. Working in batches, add the meatballs and cook, turning occasionally, for about 12 minutes per batch, or until browned all over. Using a slotted spoon, transfer to a plate.

5 When the sauce is ready, add the meatballs and simmer for about 5 minutes more, or until the meatballs are cooked through, with no sign of pink.

6 Spoon the meatballs and tomato sauce into serving bowls. Sprinkle with Parmesan cheese and serve hot.

ROUNDING OUT THE MEAL **BABY ROMAINE LETTUCE SALAD WITH SHAVED PARMESAN** The cheese and lemon in this salad make it a perfect match for Italian dishes, such as these meatballs. In a medium bowl, toss baby romaine lettuce leaves with enough Lemon-Caper Vinaigrette (page 6) to coat. Season to taste with salt and pepper. Divide the salad among plates. Using a vegetable peeler, shave Parmesan cheese over the salads and serve.

atay is the Indonesian word for kebab, and it does not always need to be served with peanut sauce. In these Southeast Asian kebabs, peaches are grilled alongside pork to get fruit onto your dinner plate. The sweet and salty marinade does double duty as a dipping sauce, saving time. I love the light, smoky char the grill gives the pork and peaches, but they can also be cooked indoors under a hot broiler for about the same amount of time. Serve this with Perfect Jasmine Rice (page 9).

GRILLED PORK SATAY AND PEACHES WITH CARROT-CILANTRO SALAD

serves
4

PREP TIME: 15 minutes
COOKING TIME: 10 minutes

¾ cup packed fresh cilantro leaves

½ cup honey

¼ cup Thai or Vietnamese fish sauce (nam pla or nuoc mam; see Kitchen Note)

3 garlic cloves, smashed and peeled

2 tablespoons coarsely chopped peeled fresh ginger

Finely grated zest of 2 limes

3 tablespoons fresh lime juice

¼ cup canola oil

2 teaspoons toasted sesame oil

1 large shallot, finely chopped

One 1½-pound pork tenderloin, trimmed of fat and sinew

Kosher salt

4 large peaches, rinsed, fuzz wiped away with a wet towel, cut in half, and pitted

1 large carrot, cut into thin matchstick-size strips (see Kitchen Note, page 23)

1 Thai or other small hot chili, sliced into paper-thin rounds

4 flat metal or bamboo skewers

1. In a blender, pulse ½ cup of the cilantro with the honey, fish sauce, garlic, ginger, lime zest, and lime juice a few times, just to finely chop the solids. Transfer to a bowl and whisk in the canola oil, sesame oil, and shallots.

2. Cut the pork tenderloin lengthwise in half, then cut each half crosswise into ⅓-inch-thick slices, for a total of 24 pieces. In a large bowl, toss the pork with half of the marinade. Set aside.

3. Prepare an outdoor grill for medium-high cooking over direct heat.

4. Remove the pork from the marinade (discard the used marinade) and thread the pork onto the skewers. Season with salt. Lightly brush the peaches with some of the reserved marinade; reserve the remaining marinade.

5. Grill the pork and peaches, turning occasionally, for about 4 minutes, or until the pork is just barely pink when pierced to the skewer with the tip of a small, sharp knife and the peaches are tinged brown and heated through. Arrange the pork on the skewers, and peaches on four dinner plates.

6. In a medium bowl, toss the carrot strips with the remaining ¼ cup cilantro. Mound alongside the pork and peaches. Stir the chili into the reserved marinade and drizzle about a tablespoon over each serving. Serve immediately with the remaining marinade as a dipping sauce.

FISH SAUCE is essential to Southeast Asian cuisine and you can it at Asian grocers and many supermarkets. Buy Thai (*nam pla*) or Vietnamese (*nuoc mam*) fish sauce for the best flavor. My favorite brand is Viet Huong Three Crabs from Vietnam, easily identified by the trio of crustaceans on the label, but there are many good ones out there. Keep in mind that fish sauce is very salty, so don't overdo it.

I was in Hawaii when I tasted my first fish taco. I had been surfing all morning, and I was waterlogged, sun-kissed, and seriously starving when I spotted a woman at a beachside cart tucking grilled mahi mahi into tortillas. While this recipe is simple, there are a couple of things that will ensure success. Use super fresh fish, and don't leave out the cabbage—it adds a nice crunch that accentuates the tenderness of the fish. To relive the outdoor experience, I prefer to grill these, but you can also cook the fish under a hot broiler for about the same amount of time and heat the tortillas over a gas burner.

GRILLED FISH TACOS WITH PICO DE GALLO

serves
4

PREP TIME: 15 minutes

COOKING TIME: 10 minutes

Pico de Gallo

4 ripe plum tomatoes (about 1 pound total), cut into ½-inch pieces

1 small white onion, finely chopped

2 red jalapeño peppers, seeded and finely chopped

¼ cup finely chopped fresh cilantro

3 tablespoons fresh lemon juice

1 teaspoon kosher salt

Tacos

2 tablespoons olive oil

1 tablespoon finely chopped fresh cilantro

1 garlic clove, finely chopped

1¼ pounds fresh mahi mahi fillet, cut into 8 pieces

Kosher salt and freshly ground black pepper

2 limes, halved

Eight 6-inch corn tortillas

2 cups very thinly sliced green cabbage

¼ cup Mexican crema or sour cream

Fresh cilantro leaves, for garnish

1 To make the pico de gallo: In a medium bowl, toss the tomatoes, onions, jalapeños, cilantro, lemon juice, and salt together. Set aside at room temperature.

2 To make the tacos: Prepare an outdoor grill for medium-high cooking over direct heat.

3 In a wide shallow bowl, whisk the olive oil, cilantro, and garlic to blend. Lightly coat the fish with the oil mixture and season with salt and pepper. Oil the cooking grate. Add the fish and grill for 2 to 3 minutes per side, or until barely opaque when flaked in the thickest part with the tip of a small knife. Using a spatula, transfer the fish to a cutting board and let stand for 2 minutes.

4 Meanwhile, grill the limes cut side down for about 3 minutes, or until they begin to char on the bottom. Remove from the grill. Add the tortillas to the grill and cook, turning halfway through, for about 1 minute, until warmed.

5 Coarsely break or cut the fish into large flaky chunks and divide it among the tortillas. Top with the cabbage, pico de gallo, crema, and a sprinkle of cilantro leaves. Serve hot with the grilled limes.

ROUNDING OUT THE MEAL **ROMAINE WITH CHERRY TOMATOES, RED ONION, AND LIME-CILANTRO VINAIGRETTE** This refreshing salad is an easy accompaniment for tacos, quesadillas, and other Latin-inspired recipes, such as my Southwestern Chili (page 223). In a small bowl, whisk fresh lime juice, chopped fresh cilantro, and finely chopped garlic together. Whisk in extra-virgin olive oil to blend. In a medium bowl, combine torn romaine lettuce, halved cherry tomatoes, and very thinly sliced red onion. Toss with enough of the lime vinaigrette to coat. Season to taste with salt and pepper. Sprinkle with crumbled queso fresco or feta cheese and serve.

When you have gorgeous fresh food in the house, it begs to be cooked. This dish grew out of a trip to a summer farmers' market, where I couldn't resist the yellow wax beans and red radishes. (You can make it with just green beans when yellow beans aren't around.) Poaching is a wonderful way to cook salmon without any added fat. I buy wild salmon whenever I can, as I prefer its flavor to the farm-raised kind. This is another meal that I like to serve when entertaining, because you can make the components ahead of time. Steamed baby potatoes would be a good accompaniment.

POACHED SALMON WITH
GREEN AND YELLOW BEAN SALAD

serves
4

PREP TIME: 15 minutes

COOKING TIME: 10 minutes, plus 45 minutes chilling time

4 sprigs of fresh tarragon

2 lemons

10 white pearl onions, peeled and thinly sliced

Four 5-ounce skinless salmon fillets

Kosher salt and freshly ground black pepper

12 ounces thin green beans, trimmed

12 ounces thin yellow wax beans, trimmed

6 radishes, sliced into paper-thin rounds

¼ cup extra-virgin olive oil

1 Remove the leaves from the tarragon; reserve the stems. Coarsely chop enough leaves to make 2 teaspoons.

2 Slice 1 lemon into thin rounds. In a large skillet, combine the lemon rounds, tarragon stems, and one-third of the onions and add enough cold water to come two-thirds of the way up the sides. Cover and bring the water to a simmer over medium-high heat.

3 Season the salmon with salt and pepper. Lay the fillets in the skillet and add hot water if needed to submerge them completely. Cover, reduce the heat to low, and cook the salmon, without simmering, for about 7 minutes, or until opaque with a rosy center when flaked in the thickest part with the tip of a small knife. Using a slotted spatula, transfer the salmon fillets to a baking sheet. Refrigerate, uncovered, until cold, about 45 minutes.

4 Meanwhile, bring a large pot of salted water to a boil. Add the green and yellow beans and cook for about 3 minutes, or until crisp-tender. Drain well, then plunge the beans into a large bowl of ice water to cool. Drain well and pat dry with paper towels.

5 In a large bowl, toss the beans, radishes, and the remaining onions with the chopped tarragon. Grate the zest from the remaining lemon over the vegetables. Squeeze the juice from the lemon and add to the bowl. Drizzle with the olive oil and toss to coat. Season with salt and pepper and toss again.

6 Place a salmon fillet on each of four dinner plates. Divide the salad among the plates and serve at once.

almon is rich in omega-3 fatty acids, which are known to lower cholesterol, and it is about as healthy as fish can get. But that is really a side benefit to this great-tasting main-course salad. It fits into the Motivating Mondays scenario, but I would happily serve it any day of the week and for any occasion. The warm orzo salad, with crunchy pine nuts, fresh basil, tender spinach, and tangy feta, is also good on its own. The salmon can also be cooked in a ridged grill pan.

GRILLED SALMON WITH ORZO, FETA, AND RED WINE VINAIGRETTE

serves
4

PREP TIME: 15 minutes
COOKING TIME: 20 minutes

Orzo

1½ cups orzo

3 tablespoons red wine vinegar

3 tablespoons finely chopped shallots

2 garlic cloves, finely chopped

⅓ cup extra-virgin olive oil

Kosher salt and freshly ground black pepper

2 ounces fresh baby spinach (about 3 cups not packed)

1½ cups grape tomatoes, cut in half

½ cup pine nuts, toasted (see Kitchen Note)

¼ cup thinly sliced fresh basil leaves

1 cup crumbled feta cheese (4 ounces)

2 tablespoons chopped fresh chives, for garnish

Salmon

Four 5-ounce skinless salmon fillets

Olive oil, for coating the fish

Kosher salt and freshly ground black pepper

1 Prepare an outdoor grill for medium-high cooking over direct heat.

2 Meanwhile, make the orzo salad: Bring a large saucepan of salted water to a boil over high heat. Add the orzo and cook, stirring often, for about 8 minutes, or until just tender. Drain the orzo in a sieve and set aside.

3 In a medium bowl, whisk the vinegar, shallots, and garlic together. Gradually whisk in the olive oil. Season to taste with salt and pepper.

4 In a large bowl, toss the warm orzo, spinach, tomatoes, pine nuts, and basil with the vinaigrette. Season to taste with salt and pepper. Set aside at room temperature.

5 To cook the salmon: Coat the salmon with olive oil and season with salt and pepper. Oil the cooking grate. Place the salmon on the grill with the top right corner of each fillet facing the 2-o'clock position and cook for 4 minutes, without moving the salmon. (This will help give the salmon a good sear of nice grill marks and help it release from the grate.) Using a thin metal spatula, starting at the corner of each fillet nearest you, flip the fillets over. Grill for about 2 minutes, or until the fish is opaque with a slightly rosy center when flaked in the thickest part with the tip of a small knife. Remove from the grill.

6 Mound the salad in the center of a large serving platter or four dinner plates. Sprinkle with the feta cheese. Top with the salmon, sprinkle with the chives, and serve.

TOASTING PINE NUTS To toast pine nuts, heat a dry medium skillet over medium heat. Add the nuts and cook, stirring often, for 2 to 3 minutes, or until lightly browned. Transfer to a plate and let cool.

I live in Los Angeles, where it can get pretty hot in the summer, so I like to have some cool, refreshing main-course salads in my repertoire. This one uses *mai fun,* the thin rice noodles that you'll find in Southeast Asian cuisine. It has all of the flavor attributes that make me love this kind of cooking—sweet, sour, salty, and spicy—and tender and crunchy textures. Just writing about it makes my mouth water.

GRILLED SHRIMP AND RICE NOODLE SALAD

serves
4

PREP TIME: 15 minutes
COOKING TIME: 10 minutes

6 ounces rice vermicelli (mai fun noodles) or angel hair pasta

⅓ cup fresh lime juice

⅓ cup packed dark brown sugar

⅓ cup Thai or Vietnamese fish sauce (nam pla or nuoc mam; see Kitchen Note, page 15)

1 teaspoon toasted sesame oil

1¼ pounds extra-large shrimp (16 to 20 count), peeled and deveined

1 tablespoon olive oil

Kosher salt and freshly ground black pepper

2 carrots, cut into thin matchstick-size strips (about 1½ cups; see Kitchen Note)

1 ripe mango, peeled, pitted, and thinly sliced

3 scallions (white and green parts), thinly sliced

¼ cup thinly sliced fresh mint leaves, plus ¼ cup small leaves

1 red jalapeño pepper, sliced into thin rounds (seeded if desired)

⅓ cup roasted peanuts

1. Bring a large pot of salted water to a boil over high heat. Stir in the vermicelli and cook, stirring often, for about 3 minutes, or until barely tender. Drain in a colander and rinse under cold water until cooled. Drain well and transfer to a large serving bowl.

2. In a medium bowl, whisk the lime juice, brown sugar, fish sauce, and sesame oil together. Pour about half of this dressing over the vermicelli and toss. Refrigerate while you grill the shrimp. Reserve the remaining dressing.

3. Heat a large grill pan over high heat. In a large bowl, toss the shrimp with the olive oil to coat. Season with salt and pepper. Add the shrimp to the pan and cook for about 2 minutes per side, or until opaque throughout. Remove from the pan.

4. Add the carrots, mango, half of the scallions, the sliced mint, and jalapeños to the noodles and toss with the remaining dressing. Top with the shrimp. Sprinkle with the peanuts, mint leaves, and the remaining scallions and serve.

JULIENNED CARROTS Uniformly cut vegetables not only make a dish look attractive, they also soak up dressing more evenly. Carrots in particular should be cut into the thin matchstick shapes known as julienne. Shredding carrots on the large holes of a box grater is no substitute. It cuts them into fluffy flakes that are just too thin for some recipes.

The classic way to cut julienne is with a chef's knife, but there are other ways, including the metal mandoline and its cousins, the inexpensive plastic V-slicer and Benriner.

ere's my healthy version of spaghetti with clams (*spaghetti alle vongole*). Whole wheat pasta provides a lot of beneficial dietary fiber, antioxidants, vitamins, and minerals, and limiting the amount of pasta and increasing the vegetables means the dish not only tastes great, but looks great too. With fresh spinach and the unexpected crunch and peppery flavor of radishes, this isn't your run-of-the-mill pasta with clam sauce. For a salad, serve the Baby Spinach and Arugula with Roasted Tomato Vinaigrette on page 38.

ANGEL HAIR PASTA WITH CLAMS, RADISHES, AND SPINACH

serves
4

PREP TIME: 10 minutes
COOKING TIME: 10 minutes

8 ounces whole wheat angel hair pasta

¼ cup extra-virgin olive oil, plus more for serving

2 pounds Manila or littleneck clams, scrubbed

⅓ cup finely chopped shallots

6 garlic cloves, finely chopped

Zest of 1 lemon, removed in wide strips with a vegetable peeler

1 fresh or dried bay leaf (see Kitchen Note)

½ teaspoon red pepper flakes

1 cup dry white wine

Kosher salt and freshly ground black pepper

3 ounces fresh baby spinach (about 4 cups loosely packed)

4 large radishes, cut into small matchstick-size strips (about ½ cup)

2 scallions (white and green parts), thinly sliced on the diagonal

1. Bring a large pot of salted water to a boil over high heat. Stir the pasta into the boiling water and cook, stirring often to keep the strands separated, for about 2 minutes, or until tender but still firm to the bite. Scoop out and reserve ½ cup of the pasta cooking water. Drain the pasta.

2. Meanwhile, heat a large heavy skillet over high heat. Add 1 tablespoon of the olive oil, then add the clams and cook for 1 minute. Stir in the shallots, garlic, lemon zest, bay leaf, and red pepper flakes. Add the wine, cover, and cook for about 2 minutes, or until the clams open. Using tongs, transfer the clams to a large bowl, then cover to keep warm.

3. Simmer the clam-wine broth until it is reduced by about one-fourth, about 2 minutes (the pasta will absorb a lot of liquid, so don't reduce the liquid too much). Stir in the remaining 3 tablespoons olive oil and season with salt and pepper. Reduce the heat to low.

4. Add the pasta to the skillet and toss to coat with the liquid. Add the clams and any accumulated juices in the bowl to the pasta. Add the spinach and half of the radishes and toss, adding enough of the reserved pasta water to make a light sauce.

5. Using tongs, divide the pasta and clams among four wide pasta bowls or place them in one large shallow serving bowl. Pour in the broth. Drizzle olive oil over each serving and sprinkle with the scallions and the remaining radishes. Discard the lemon zest and bay leaf and serve immediately.

BAY LEAVES Fresh bay leaves are more aromatic and flavorful than dried leaves. Their flavor quickly infuses into a sauce, while dried bay leaves need to be in contact with liquid for a long time to coax out the flavor. (Both kinds have their uses, so it isn't a question of one being better than the other.) If you buy fresh bay leaves for this dish, the leftover leaves can be frozen in a Ziploc plastic bag for up to a few months.

*D*al is both the Indian word for dried split legumes (such as lentils and peas) and the name of a stew made with these foods. This vegetarian dish takes humble yellow split peas, which are low in calories and high in protein and, with a few spices and vegetables, turns them into something extraordinary. While it's thoroughly satisfying on its own, it is especially good served with Perfect Basmati Rice (page 9) or warm naan.

CAULIFLOWER AND SPINACH DAL

serves
4 to **6**

PREP TIME: 10 minutes
COOKING TIME: 1 hour 30 minutes

2 tablespoons olive oil

1 yellow onion, finely chopped

3 tablespoons finely chopped peeled fresh ginger

4 large garlic cloves, finely chopped

1 red jalapeño pepper, seeded and finely chopped

2½ teaspoons ground coriander

2½ teaspoons ground cumin

½ teaspoon cayenne pepper

½ teaspoon ground turmeric

10 fresh curry leaves (optional)

1 pound (about 2 cups) yellow split peas, rinsed

Kosher salt and freshly ground black pepper

1 head cauliflower, cored and cut into bite-size florets

One 6-ounce package fresh baby spinach

½ cup fresh cilantro leaves

Perfect Basmati Rice (page 9) or 4 to 6 naan, warmed, for serving

1. Heat a large heavy pot over medium heat. Add the olive oil, then add the onions and cook, stirring often, for about 5 minutes, or until tender. Add the ginger, garlic, and jalapeños and cook for about 1 minute, or until fragrant. Add the coriander, cumin, cayenne pepper, turmeric, and curry leaves, if using, and stir constantly for 2 minutes to toast the spices.

2. Stir in the split peas and enough water to cover, about 8 cups. Season with salt and pepper. Bring to a boil over high heat, then reduce the heat to medium-low, partially cover the pot, and simmer, stirring occasionally, for about 45 minutes, or until the split peas are tender.

3. Add the cauliflower, partially cover again, and cook, stirring occasionally, and adding more water as needed to adjust the thickness to your desired consistency, for about 35 minutes, or until the cauliflower is falling apart and the mixture has thickened slightly. Season to taste again with salt and pepper. Remove from the heat, add the spinach, and stir until wilted.

4. Spoon the dal into bowls and sprinkle with the cilantro. Serve hot with the rice or naan.

A baked potato can be a healthy dinner, as long as you pay attention to what you put on top (or, in this case, inside). Baking the spuds on a bed of coarse salt may seem odd, but it is my favorite method, as the salt wicks out extra moisture, resulting in fluffy potato flesh. (By the way, the salt doesn't transfer to the potatoes, so don't be concerned about the amount.) While the potatoes are baking, make ratatouille, a vegetarian classic with sunny Mediterranean flavors, to use as a stuffing.

SALT-BAKED RUSSETS WITH RATATOUILLE

serves
4

PREP TIME: 10 minutes
COOKING TIME: 45 minutes

1 cup kosher salt

4 large baking potatoes, such as russets

Ratatouille

2 tablespoons olive oil

2 large shallots, cut into ½-inch pieces

3 garlic cloves, finely chopped

1 small eggplant, unpeeled, cut into ½-inch pieces

1 zucchini, cut into ½-inch pieces

½ cup diced (½-inch) red and/or yellow bell peppers (preferably a combination)

¼ cup dry red wine

3 ripe plum tomatoes, cut into ½-inch pieces

Kosher salt and freshly ground black pepper

1 tablespoon thinly sliced fresh basil leaves

Topping

½ cup plain low-fat yogurt

3 tablespoons chopped fresh chives

¼ cup shaved or freshly grated Parmesan cheese (see Kitchen Note, page 103)

1 Preheat the oven to 400°F.

2 Spread the salt in a thin layer on a small, rimmed baking sheet. Pierce the potatoes with a fork, then nestle them in the salt and sprinkle a small amount of the salt over them. Bake the potatoes for about 45 minutes, or until tender when pierced with a small sharp knife. Remove from the oven and let cool for 5 minutes (discard the salt).

3 Meanwhile, make the ratatouille: Heat a medium saucepan over medium heat. Add the olive oil, then add the shallots and garlic and cook, stirring often, for about 2 minutes, or until tender. Add the eggplant, zucchini, and bell peppers and cook for about 5 minutes, stirring occasionally, or until the eggplant is softened. Add the wine and tomatoes and cook, stirring occasionally, for about 8 minutes, or until the tomatoes have broken down into a coarse sauce. Season generously with salt and pepper to taste. Stir in the basil and remove from the heat.

4 Wipe off any excess salt on the outside of the potatoes. Cut each potato one at a time, lengthwise and then crosswise in half, almost but not quite all the way through, and squeeze the ends to open it up. Divide the ratatouille among the potatoes.

5 Transfer the potatoes to a plate, then top with the yogurt, chives, and Parmesan cheese, and serve hot.

ROUNDING OUT THE MEAL **BUTTER LETTUCE WEDGES WITH HARD-BOILED EGGS, RADISHES, AND DIJON VINAIGRETTE** You might expect to find a salad like this at a French bistro, and I like it with these French-inspired baked potatoes. For each serving, place 2 wedges of butter lettuce (cut from ½ head) on a plate. Sprinkle thinly sliced radishes and chopped hard-boiled eggs over the lettuce. Drizzle with Dijon Vinaigrette (page 125) and serve.

The beauty of quinoa is that it is a complete protein—other grains are usually combined with legumes to achieve the same nutritional content. (Quinoa is really a grass, though it is categorized as a grain.) I like the flavorful and earthy combination of chickpeas and quinoa, brightened up with lots of vegetables. You can add grilled skinless, boneless chicken breasts for a heartier dish.

QUINOA SALAD WITH CHICKPEAS AND TOMATOES

serves
4

PREP TIME: 10 minutes

COOKING TIME: 25 minutes, plus cooling time

Quinoa

2 cups quinoa

1 tablespoon extra-virgin olive oil

2 tablespoons finely chopped shallots

1 garlic clove, finely chopped

3 cups reduced-sodium chicken or vegetable broth

Shallot–Red Wine Vinaigrette

2 tablespoons finely chopped shallots

2 tablespoons red wine vinegar

¼ cup extra-virgin olive oil

2 tablespoons thinly sliced fresh flat-leaf parsley leaves

Kosher salt and freshly ground black pepper

Salad

One 15-ounce can chickpeas (garbanzo beans), drained and rinsed

2 cups not packed baby arugula

½ cup halved cherry tomatoes

½ English cucumber, peeled, halved lengthwise, seeded, and diced

¼ cup diced red bell peppers

Kosher salt and freshly ground black pepper

1 To make the quinoa: Put the quinoa in a fine-mesh sieve and rinse under cold running water. Set aside to drain well.

2 Heat a medium saucepan over medium-high heat. Add the olive oil, then add the shallots and cook for about 2 minutes, or until softened. Add the garlic and cook for about 1 minute, or until fragrant. Add the quinoa and stir well. Add the broth and bring to a simmer, then reduce the heat to medium-low and simmer gently for 15 to 20 minutes, or until the quinoa is tender but not mushy and the broth has been absorbed.

3 Spread the quinoa on a baking sheet and let it cool, then fluff with a fork.

4 To make the vinaigrette: In a medium bowl, whisk the shallots and vinegar together. Gradually whisk in the olive oil. Add the parsley and season to taste with salt and pepper.

5 To make the salad: In a large bowl, combine the cooled quinoa, chickpeas, arugula, tomatoes, cucumbers, and bell peppers. Toss with the vinaigrette and season to taste with salt and pepper. Divide among four plates and serve immediately.

ubstitute your usual evening cocktail with this fruity mocktail. Or submit to temptation and blend ½ cup golden rum into the smoothie mixture.

MANGO-PINEAPPLE SMOOTHIE

serves
6

PREP TIME: 10 minutes

1 ripe mango, peeled, pitted, and coarsely cubed

¼ fresh pineapple, peeled, cored, and coarsely cubed

1 cup fresh orange juice

3 cups ice cubes

Lime slices for garnish

1 In a blender, combine the mangoes, pineapples, orange juice, and ice cubes and blend until smooth and frothy. (If your blender is not large enough to hold all the ingredients, blend in two batches.)

2 Pour the smoothie into six glasses. Garnish with lime slices and serve immediately.

TIME-SAVING TUESDAYS

I THINK WE SHOULD CONSIDER RENAMING Tuesday "to-do day." After all, this is the day when our week seems to kick into high gear. There are meetings to schedule and phone calls to make. We have doctors' appointments and deadlines, playdates and parent-teacher conferences. Everyone's to-do list is different, but by the time dinner rolls around, most of us would rather not add cooking to it. Don't ditch your apron for take-out Chinese just yet. Good food doesn't need to take hours to make. **In fact, all of the recipes in this chapter can be made in 15 to 40 minutes.** None of them requires fancy kitchen gadgets, hard-to-find foods, or complicated culinary techniques. All you need are good-quality ingredients, a sharp knife, and a little kitchen choreography to help you move more efficiently through the recipes.

For starters, be prepared. It's one of the easiest things you can do to shorten your cooking time. Read through the entire recipe before you start cooking to make sure you have everything you need and know the steps. Then prep your ingredients. You can even enlist your kids to give you a hand peeling cucumbers or grating cheese, and, of course, any stirring or mixing. Place each prepped ingredient in a separate bowl and pull out any other ingredients from the cupboard or fridge. Chefs call this mise en place, a fancy way of describing measuring, chopping, and slicing everything for the recipe before you start cooking. With it all at arm's reach, the cooking time will fly by. You've accomplished great things today. You deserve a wonderful meal.

esto has gone from a simple, uncooked pasta sauce in the Italian province of Liguria to a worldwide phenomenon. It is so easy to make—just whiz it in a food processor or grind it up with a mortar and pestle. Here it is a topping for chicken breasts. I love the way the pesto gets a bit toasty in the oven, and how the pesto and juices from the chicken mix into the spaghetti.

PESTO-GLAZED CHICKEN BREASTS WITH SPAGHETTI

serves
4

PREP TIME: 10 minutes
COOKING TIME: 20 minutes

Chicken

4 skinless, boneless chicken breast halves (about 6 ounces each)

Kosher salt and freshly ground black pepper

1 tablespoon olive oil

Pesto (page 40)

Spaghetti

12 ounces spaghetti

2 tablespoons extra-virgin olive oil, plus more for drizzling

2 tablespoons coarsely chopped fresh flat-leaf parsley

¼ cup pine nuts, toasted (see Kitchen Note, page 20)

2 tablespoons torn fresh basil leaves, for garnish

⅓ cup shaved or freshly grated Parmesan cheese, for garnish

1 Preheat the oven to 400°F. Bring a large pot of salted water to a boil over high heat.

2 To make the chicken: Season the chicken breast halves with salt and pepper. Heat a large ovenproof skillet over high heat. Add the olive oil, then add the chicken and cook for about 4 minutes per side, or until golden brown. Remove the pan from the heat.

3 Spread the pesto generously over the chicken. Transfer the pan to the oven and bake the chicken for about 8 minutes, or until it shows no sign of pink when pierced in the thickest part with the tip of a small sharp knife. Transfer the chicken to a cutting board and let stand for 3 minutes.

4 Meanwhile, add the spaghetti to the boiling water and cook, stirring often to keep the strands from sticking together, for about 8 minutes, or until it is tender but still firm to the bite. Scoop out and reserve ⅔ cup of the cooking water. Drain the spaghetti.

5 Pour the reserved cooking water back into the pot and whisk in the olive oil. Add the spaghetti and parsley and stir well to coat the spaghetti. Cover with the lid ajar to keep warm, if necessary.

6 Arrange each chicken breast half on one side of a dinner plate and place the spaghetti alongside. Sprinkle with the pine nuts and torn basil and drizzle with olive oil. Sprinkle Parmesan cheese over the pasta and serve.

ROUNDING OUT THE MEAL **BABY SPINACH AND ARUGULA WITH ROASTED TOMATO VINAIGRETTE** This salad pairs beautifully with pasta dishes, especially those without tomatoes, such as this spaghetti with pesto-glazed chicken. In a medium bowl, toss baby spinach and baby arugula with Roasted Tomato Vinaigrette (page 172) to coat. Season with salt to taste and serve.

Pesto

The classic way to make pesto is with a mortar and pestle, which I like to call a "bump and grind." I still like to make it that way—the texture just feels more rustic and homemade.

makes about 1¼ cups

PREP TIME: 10 minutes

MAKE-AHEAD: The pesto can be made up to 2 weeks ahead, covered and refrigerated.

2 garlic cloves

¼ teaspoon kosher salt

¼ teaspoon red pepper flakes

1½ cups lightly packed fresh basil leaves

¼ cup pine nuts, toasted (see Kitchen Note, page 20)

½ cup freshly grated Parmesan cheese (about 2 ounces)

⅓ cup extra-virgin olive oil, plus more to cover the pesto

1 *To make the pesto with a mortar and pestle:* Mash the garlic, salt, and red pepper flakes into a coarse paste. Add 1 cup of the basil and pound until it is coarsely ground. Add the remaining ½ cup basil and pound until a coarse puree forms. Add the pine nuts and pound just to break them up. Add the Parmesan cheese and olive oil and mash until the nuts are coarsely ground and the mixture is well blended.

To make the pesto in a food processor: Pulse the pine nuts, garlic, salt, and red pepper flakes together until the nuts and garlic are finely chopped. Add the basil and Parmesan cheese and pulse about 10 times to chop the basil. With the machine running, gradually pour in the olive oil.

2 Transfer the pesto to a container and float a thin layer of olive oil on top. Cover and keep refrigerated, but bring to room temperature before using.

oreans celebrate the first one hundred days of life, so for my son, Hudson's, hundredth-day party, we had a bash with lots of Korean food. The next day, with my taste buds toned and thinking of the great Korean tacos I've devoured at food trucks in Los Angeles, I created this version. The marinade for the steak is to die for. I guarantee you'll want to try it with Korean-style short ribs, pork tenderloin, and grilled chicken.

A little planning and prep a day ahead is a great way to save time on hurried weeknights. This steak gets even better with an overnight marinade, so you could marinate it on Monday, and it's ready to grill on Tuesday night. If you're doing it all on the same night, use the marinating time to multitask—prep your vegetables and whip up the guacamole. You'll be surprised how quickly it comes together.

KOREAN STEAK TACOS

serves
6

PREP TIME: 10 minutes, plus at least 20 minutes marinating time
COOKING TIME: 10 minutes

Steak

½ cup finely chopped fresh cilantro

¼ cup packed dark brown sugar

3 tablespoons canola oil

3 tablespoons soy sauce

1 tablespoon toasted sesame oil

2 large garlic cloves, minced

1 jalapeño pepper, seeded and finely chopped

1 teaspoon freshly ground black pepper

1 teaspoon ground coriander

One 2-pound flank steak (about 1½ inches thick), fat trimmed

Tacos

½ head napa cabbage, halved lengthwise and shredded crosswise (about 3 cups)

1 large carrot, cut into 2-inch-long matchstick-size strips

8 scallions (white and green parts), thinly sliced on a sharp diagonal

½ cup lightly packed fresh cilantro sprigs

Twelve 6-inch corn tortillas

Guacamole for Lindsay (recipe follows)

1 To marinate the steak: In a large baking dish, whisk the cilantro, brown sugar, canola oil, soy sauce, sesame oil, garlic, jalapeños, black pepper, and coriander to blend well. Reserve ¼ cup of the mixture in a small bowl for serving. Place the steak in the remaining marinade and turn to coat. Marinate for at least 20 minutes at room temperature, or cover and refrigerate for up to 1 day, turning occasionally. Cover and refrigerate the reserved marinade.

2 Prepare an outdoor grill for medium-high cooking over direct heat.

3 Remove the steak from the marinade (discard the marinade) and grill, turning halfway through cooking, for a total of about 10 minutes, until the meat feels only slightly resilient when pressed with a fingertip for medium-rare (see Kitchen Note, page 140). Transfer the steak to a cutting board and let stand for 5 to 10 minutes.

4 Meanwhile, prepare the tacos: In a large bowl, toss the cabbage, carrots, scallions, and cilantro together.

5 Heat the tortillas on the grill, turning occasionally, for about 1 minute, or until hot. Transfer to a serving bowl and cover to keep warm.

6 Cut the steak across the grain into ¼-inch-thick slices. Transfer the steak slices and any carving juices to a platter. Serve the steak with the reserved marinade, tortillas, cabbage mixture, and guacamole. Let each guest fill two tortillas with some steak and cabbage mixture and top with some of the marinade and guacamole.

Guacamole for Lindsay

I had my chance to perfect this guacamole recipe when my wife, Lindsay, was pregnant and it was all she wanted to eat. My first piece of advice is to use properly ripened avocados—they should just "give" when you squeeze them. Be generous with the lime juice and salt and, above all, keep it chunky.

serves 4

PREP TIME: 10 minutes

3 firm but ripe Hass avocados, halved, pitted, peeled, and cut into ½-inch pieces

3 tablespoons finely chopped fresh cilantro

2 tablespoons fresh lime juice

½ jalapeño pepper, seeded and finely chopped

1 garlic clove, finely chopped

¼ teaspoon ground cumin

Kosher salt

In a large bowl, gently fold the avocados, cilantro, lime juice, jalapeños, garlic, and cumin together. Season to taste with salt.

KEEPING IT GREEN Guacamole can be made up to 6 hours ahead. To keep it from browning, lay a sheet of plastic wrap directly on the surface of the guacamole and refrigerate until ready to serve.

If you have the grill going to cook the main course, why not put it into service for the vegetables too? Here broccolini, tossed with a heady mix of oil, garlic, lemon zest, and red pepper flakes, is grilled to perfection alongside steak and cheese-topped tomatoes. Using heirloom tomatoes can steal the show, I like Yellow Valencia, but any tomato that is in season and ripe would work.

GRILLED STEAK AND BROCCOLINI WITH PARMESAN TOMATOES

serves
4

PREP TIME: 10 minutes
COOKING TIME: 20 minutes

Steak

One 1½-pound flank or top sirloin steak

1 tablespoon olive oil

Kosher salt

2 teaspoons coarsely cracked black peppercorns (use a mortar and pestle or crush under a heavy skillet)

Parmesan Tomatoes

¾ cup freshly grated Parmesan cheese (about 3 ounces)

3 tablespoons panko (Japanese bread crumbs)

3 tablespoons finely chopped fresh basil

4 medium tomatoes (about 6 ounces each), cut crosswise in half

2 tablespoons olive oil

Kosher salt and freshly ground black pepper

Broccolini

1¼ pounds broccolini, tough bottoms trimmed and discarded

1 tablespoon olive oil

2 garlic cloves, finely chopped

Finely grated zest of ½ lemon

¼ teaspoon red pepper flakes

Kosher salt and freshly ground black pepper

Balsamic vinegar, preferably aged, for drizzling

1 Heat an outdoor grill for high heat. Remove the steak from the refrigerator and let stand at room temperature while you prepare the tomatoes.

2 To prepare the tomatoes: In a medium bowl, mix the Parmesan cheese, panko, and basil. Place the tomatoes on a small rimmed baking sheet and coat them all over with 1 tablespoon of the olive oil. Turn the tomatoes cut side up and then season them all over with salt and pepper and pat a generous topping of the Parmesan mixture onto the top of each one. Drizzle with the remaining 1 tablespoon olive oil.

3 Turn off one burner if using a gas grill, or heap the coals on one side of a charcoal grill, to create areas of both direct and indirect heat. Put the baking sheet of tomatoes on the cooler area of the grill. Cook with the lid closed for 5 minutes.

4 Meanwhile, to prepare the broccolini and steak: In a large bowl, toss the broccolini with the olive oil, garlic, lemon zest, and red pepper flakes to coat. Season with salt and pepper. Coat the steak with the tablespoon of olive oil and season with salt and pepper.

5 After the tomatoes have cooked for 5 minutes, place the steak and broccolini on the grill over the lighted burner(s) or the coals. Cook, with the lid closed, turning the broccolini occasionally and turning the steak halfway through cooking, for a total of about 6 minutes, or until the meat feels only slightly resilient when pressed with a fingertip and an instant-read thermometer inserted into the center of the steak registers 120°F for medium-rare (see Kitchen Note, page 140). Transfer the steak to a platter and let rest for 5 minutes. Meanwhile, continue cooking until the broccolini is tender and beginning to char and the topping on the tomatoes is golden brown, about 2 minutes more. Add the broccolini and tomatoes to the platter.

6 Transfer the steak to a cutting board and cut it across the grain into ¼-inch-thick slices. Divide the sliced steak, tomatoes, and broccolini among four dinner plates. Drizzle with balsamic vinegar, sprinkle with salt, and serve.

This stir-fry is Cantonese comfort food, with familiar flavors and ingredients put together in a delicious way that takes just a few minutes to cook. I usually call everyone to the table as I'm heating the pan, and by the time they all sit down, I'm ready to dish up dinner. Serve it over Perfect Rice (page 9).

STEAK AND GREEN BEAN STIR-FRY WITH GINGER AND GARLIC

serves
4

PREP TIME: 10 minutes
COOKING TIME: 10 minutes

3 tablespoons oyster sauce

2 tablespoons Chinese rice wine or dry white wine

2 tablespoons soy sauce

2 tablespoons canola oil

1 pound flank steak, excess fat trimmed and cut across the grain into ¼-inch-thick slices

1 large red bell pepper, cored, seeded, and cut into ¼-inch-wide strips

8 ounces green beans, trimmed and cut in half on the diagonal

½ cup thinly sliced shallots

2 large garlic cloves, finely chopped

2 tablespoons finely chopped peeled fresh ginger

3 large scallions (white and green parts), thinly sliced on the diagonal

1 teaspoon toasted sesame oil

Fresh cilantro leaves, for garnish

2 teaspoons toasted sesame seeds (see Kitchen Note, page 68), for sprinkling

Perfect Rice (page 9), for serving

1 In a small bowl, mix ¼ cup water with the oyster sauce, rice wine, and soy sauce; set aside. Heat a wok or large skillet over high heat. Add 1 tablespoon of the canola oil and swirl it to coat the cooking surface. Add the beef, spreading it out in a single layer, and cook, without stirring, for about 2 minutes, or until well browned on the bottom. Transfer the beef to a rimmed baking sheet.

2 Add the remaining 1 tablespoon canola oil to the wok, then add the bell peppers and green beans and cook, stirring often, for about 2 minutes, or until the vegetables soften slightly. Stir in the shallots, garlic, and ginger, then stir the oyster sauce mixture, add to the wok, and cook, stirring often, for about 2 minutes, or until the vegetables are crisp-tender and the sauce has reduced slightly. Return the beef and its accumulated juices to the wok, add the scallions, and stir for about 1 minute, or just until the beef is heated through. Stir in the sesame oil and remove from the heat.

3 Divide the stir-fry among four dinner plates. Sprinkle with the cilantro leaves and sesame seeds and serve immediately, with the rice.

MEASURE AND PREP all of the ingredients, including the seasoning sauce, before you heat the pan. Have your dinner plates ready, too. If you are serving rice with the stir-fry, put it on to cook before you begin any other prep so it is done when you are ready to serve.

I n California, long-stemmed rosemary grows everywhere, ready to cut and use to skewer meat and seafood for grilling. The scent of the rosemary on the grill is intoxicating. If you can't find long sturdy rosemary branches at the market, simply shape the kebabs on metal skewers, and toss a handful of fresh rosemary sprigs onto the grill's heat source during cooking to make rosemary-scented smoke.

GRILLED MOROCCAN GROUND BEEF SKEWERS WITH COUSCOUS AND YOGURT SAUCE

serves
4

PREP TIME: 15 minutes
COOKING TIME: 10 minutes

Yogurt Sauce

½ English cucumber, peeled, halved lengthwise, and seeded

1 cup plain low-fat or whole milk yogurt

2 tablespoons fresh lemon juice

1 tablespoon chopped fresh dill

Kosher salt and freshly ground black pepper

Beef Skewers

Eight 12-inch branches of fresh rosemary

1¼ pounds lean ground beef or ground lamb

⅓ cup plain dry bread crumbs

¼ cup finely chopped fresh cilantro

1 tablespoon finely chopped fresh flat-leaf parsley

4 garlic cloves, finely chopped

2 teaspoons ground cumin

¼ teaspoon ground allspice

2 teaspoons kosher salt

1½ teaspoons freshly ground black pepper

1 large egg, lightly beaten

1 tablespoon olive oil

Cumin-Cilantro Couscous (recipe follows)

1. To make the yogurt sauce: Using the large holes of a box grater, grate the cucumber into a small bowl. Squeeze the grated cucumber to extract as much liquid as possible, then return the cucumber to the bowl. Mix in the yogurt, lemon juice, and dill. Season to taste with salt and pepper.

2. To make the beef skewers: Prepare an outdoor grill for medium-high cooking over direct heat.

3. Remove most of the leaves from the rosemary branches, leaving about 2 inches of leaves at the tip of each one. Soak the stems in cold water to cover while you prepare the meat.

4. In a large bowl, mix the ground beef, bread crumbs, cilantro, parsley, garlic, cumin, allspice, salt, and pepper thoroughly with your hands. Mix in the egg. Divide the meat mixture evenly into 8 balls. Place a meatball on the bottom end of each rosemary skewer and gently mold it into a sausage shape along the stem, packing it tightly. The meat mixture on each stem should be about 4 inches long, 1½ inches wide, and 1 inch thick. Rub the olive oil over the meat.

5. Arrange the skewers on the grill, with the leafy ends positioned away from the heat source to prevent burning (don't worry if the rosemary chars a bit). Grill the skewers, turning occasionally, for about 8 minutes, or until the beef is thoroughly browned and crusty on the outside and the center shows no sign of pink when pierced with the tip of a knife. Transfer the skewers to a plate and let rest for 3 minutes.

6. Spoon the couscous onto four dinner plates. Top each serving with two skewers, add the sauce, and serve immediately.

Cumin-Cilantro Couscous

This all-purpose couscous is so much more tasty than plain couscous and very easy to make. It's perfect for any Moroccan-inspired dish, and it goes with many main courses in this book, such as the Curried Lamb Shanks with Carrots, Chickpeas, and Potatoes (page 239), Moroccan Braised Lamb Shoulder with Golden Raisin–Lemon Puree (page 177), and Grilled Harissa Rack of Lamb with Summer Succotash (page 143).

serves 4

PREP TIME: 5 minutes

COOKING TIME: 5 minutes, plus 5 minutes standing time

1½ cups reduced-sodium chicken broth

1 teaspoon ground cumin

1 teaspoon kosher salt

1½ cups plain couscous

2 tablespoons chopped fresh cilantro

2 tablespoons olive oil

Finely grated zest of 1 lemon

Freshly ground black pepper

1 In a medium saucepan, bring the broth, cumin, and salt to a boil over high heat. Remove the pan from the heat and stir in the couscous. Cover the pan tightly and let stand for about 5 minutes, or until the liquid is absorbed and the couscous is tender.

2 Fluff the couscous with a fork, then mix in the cilantro, olive oil, and lemon zest. Season to taste with pepper. Cover to keep warm until ready to serve.

ROUNDING OUT THE MEAL **BULGUR PILAF WITH LEMON AND PISTACHIOS** Bulgur (precooked cracked wheat) is as versatile as rice and deserves to be used as often. For something different, try this bulgur with the beef skewers instead of the couscous. In a medium heavy saucepan, sauté chopped yellow onions in olive oil over medium heat until tender. Add equal parts fine bulgur and boiling water. Remove the pan from the heat and let stand, covered, for about 25 minutes, or until the bulgur softens and the liquid has been absorbed. Fluff with a fork, then mix in chopped fresh parsley, grated lemon zest, and chopped toasted pistachios. Season to taste with salt and pepper.

This gratin was a specialty of my gran, who used to make it to serve with her pork chops. I've revved it up with a caper vinaigrette. Note that the caper brine acts as the vinegar here, so taste the dressing to be sure that it is sharp enough and add more brine if needed.

GRILLED PORK CHOPS AND VEGETABLE GRATIN WITH CAPER-PARSLEY VINAIGRETTE

serves
4

PREP TIME: 10 minutes
COOKING TIME: 20 minutes

Caper-Parsley Vinaigrette

¼ cup nonpareil capers, with their brine

¼ cup extra-virgin olive oil

2 tablespoons coarsely chopped fresh flat-leaf parsley

Kosher salt and freshly ground black pepper

Gratin and Pork

1 yellow onion, cut into ⅓-inch-thick rounds

3 zucchini, halved lengthwise

3 tablespoons olive oil

Kosher salt and freshly ground black pepper

8 ounces cherry tomatoes, halved

4 center-cut pork loin chops (each about 8 ounces and ¾ inch thick, frenched if desired; see Kitchen Note)

1 cup freshly grated Parmesan cheese (about 4 ounces)

1. Prepare an outdoor grill for direct cooking over high heat. Position the broiler rack about 6 inches from the heat source and preheat the broiler.

2. To make the vinaigrette: In a small bowl, mix the capers, their brine, olive oil, and parsley with a fork to combine. Season to taste with salt and pepper.

3. To prepare the gratin: Coat the onions and zucchini with 2 tablespoons of the olive oil and season with salt and pepper. Grill the onions and zucchini for about 2 to 3 minutes per side, or until seared with grill marks and just tender. Remove from the grill and transfer to a cutting board.

4. Cut the zucchini diagonally in half. Very coarsely chop the onions. Toss the zucchini and onions with the cherry tomatoes in a 1½- to 2-quart flameproof baking dish. Set aside at room temperature.

5. To cook the pork: Pat the pork dry with paper towels. Coat with the remaining 1 tablespoon oil and season with salt and pepper. Grill the pork for about 3 minutes per side, or until seared golden brown and barely pink when pierced at the bone with the tip of a small sharp knife. Transfer to a platter and cover loosely with aluminum foil.

6. Sprinkle the Parmesan cheese generously over the vegetables. Broil, watching closely, for about 5 minutes, or until the Parmesan cheese has melted and is pale golden.

7. Divide the vegetables among four dinner plates and top each with a pork chop. Stir the vinaigrette, drizzle over the chops, and serve.

FRENCHED PORK CHOPS Frenching the pork chop exposes more of the bone for restaurant-style presentation. The butcher can do this for you. Or use a paring knife to cut the meat from the bone, stopping at the eye of each chop, and scrape the bone clean.

Sautéing is another fast way to make a meal, especially when the pan juices are turned into a sweet and savory sauce, as they are here. This comforting dish features an array of autumn ingredients—apples, fennel, and sweet potatoes—roasted in the oven to caramelize lightly and bring their sugars to the forefront. The sauce, which mingles apple cider with the meaty browned bits in the skillet, is sharpened with a bit of Dijon mustard to balance the sweetness.

CIDER-DIJON PORK CHOPS WITH ROASTED SWEET POTATOES AND APPLES

serves
4

PREP TIME: 10 minutes

COOKING TIME: 15 minutes

Pork

4 boneless pork loin chops (each about 7 ounces and 1 inch thick)

Kosher salt and freshly ground black pepper

2 tablespoons olive oil

1 cup apple cider or apple juice

1 tablespoon Dijon mustard

2 tablespoons unsalted butter, cut into 2 pieces

Vegetables and Apples

1 pound red-skinned sweet potatoes (yams), peeled and cut lengthwise in half, then cut crosswise into 2-inch pieces

2 Pink Lady or Fuji apples, cored and cut lengthwise into eighths

1 large fennel bulb, trimmed and cut lengthwise into eighths

2 sprigs of fresh rosemary, cut into 1-inch pieces

2 tablespoons olive oil

Kosher salt and freshly ground black pepper

1. Remove the pork from the refrigerator and let stand at room temperature while the oven preheats. Preheat the oven to 450°F. Place a large rimmed baking sheet in the oven and heat until very hot.

2. To cook the vegetables and apples: In a large bowl, toss the sweet potatoes, apples, fennel, and rosemary with the olive oil to coat. Season with salt and pepper. Carefully remove the baking sheet from the oven and spread the vegetables and apples on it. Roast, turning the ingredients over halfway through, for about 15 minutes, or until the potatoes are nicely browned and tender.

3. Meanwhile, cook the pork: Season the pork with salt and pepper. Heat a large heavy skillet over medium-high heat. Add the olive oil, then add the chops to the skillet and cook for about 5 minutes per side, or until golden brown and barely pink when pierced in the center with the tip of a small sharp knife. Transfer to a platter (reserving the oil in the skillet) and let stand for 5 minutes.

4. Pour off all but 1 teaspoon of the oil from the skillet, leaving the brown bits in the pan. Return the pan to medium-low heat, add the apple cider, and bring to a simmer, scraping up the brown bits with a wooden spoon. Whisk in the mustard and simmer for about 2 minutes to reduce the liquid slightly. Remove from the heat and whisk in the butter to lightly thicken the sauce. Season to taste with salt and pepper.

5. Divide the sweet potato mixture among four dinner plates. Place a pork chop alongside the vegetables on each plate. Drizzle with the pan sauce and serve.

ROUNDING OUT THE MEAL **SHAVED RADICCHIO AND ESCAROLE SALAD WITH GOAT CHEESE AND WALNUTS** A refreshing salad is always a good pairing with hearty main courses, like this pork with its rich, delicious pan sauce. In a medium bowl, toss thinly sliced radicchio and escarole with toasted walnuts and Tarragon-Dijon Vinaigrette (page 11) to coat. Season with salt. Crumble goat cheese over and serve.

Bangers and mash (sausages with mashed potatoes and gravy) is classic British comfort food, and I ate more than my share when I lived in London. Bangers got their name because during the lean years in the UK, they were made with more filler and water than meat and would explode loudly when cooked! Use your favorite pork (or chicken or turkey) sausage. Any will work, because when all is said and done, it's the onion gravy that really makes the dish. Follow my lead, make a double batch of it, and freeze some for another meal. You might want to pour a cold glass of beer or hard cider to go with this, and serve a mixed green salad tossed with your favorite vinaigrette alongside.

SAUSAGE AND MASH WITH CARAMELIZED ONION GRAVY

serves
4

PREP TIME: 10 minutes
COOKING TIME: 25 minutes

Mash

2½ pounds large baking potatoes, such as russets, peeled and quartered

3 tablespoons unsalted butter

½ cup whole milk

Kosher salt and freshly ground black pepper

Gravy and Sausage

1 tablespoon olive oil

1 large yellow onion, halved and cut into ½-inch-thick half-moons

2 teaspoons unsalted butter

2 teaspoons all-purpose flour

1 tablespoon white wine vinegar

¾ cup reduced-sodium beef broth

Kosher salt and freshly ground black pepper

1 pound pork sausages, pricked with a fork

¼ cup 1-inch lengths fresh chives, for serving (optional)

1. To make the mash: Put the potatoes in a large saucepan, cover completely with salted water, and bring the water to a boil over high heat. Reduce the heat to medium-low and simmer for about 15 minutes, or until the potatoes are tender. Drain.

2. Return the potatoes to the saucepan and cook over medium-low heat, stirring occasionally, for about 2 minutes to evaporate the excess liquid. Reduce the heat to low, add the butter, and mash the potatoes with a potato masher or ricer until nearly smooth. Whisk in the milk. Season to taste with salt and pepper. Keep warm over very low heat.

3. Meanwhile, prepare the gravy and sausage: Heat a large heavy skillet over medium-high heat. Add the olive oil, then add the onion and cook, stirring occasionally, for about 8 minutes, or until golden and caramelized. Reduce the heat and stir in the butter. Stir in the flour and cook, stirring often, for about 4 minutes, or until the flour is lightly browned. Stir in the vinegar and cook for 1 minute. Stir in the broth, bring to a simmer, and cook until the sauce has thickened slightly and has no raw flour taste, about 2 minutes. Season to taste with salt and pepper. Cover and keep warm.

4. Heat another large heavy skillet over medium-high heat. Add the sausages and cook, turning occasionally, for about 10 minutes, or until they are browned and show no sign of pink when pierced to the center with the tip of a small sharp knife.

5. Mound the mash on four dinner plates. Top with the sausages and spoon the gravy over all. Sprinkle with the chives, if using, and serve.

When making vinaigrette, think outside of the salad bowl: It is also a great sauce for fish and other light proteins. There's no cooking involved, and the variations are practically endless. And there is no law that says lemon is the only citrus to serve with fish—orange makes a guest appearance here to great effect. The halibut and spinach cook in just a few minutes, so you'll have dinner ready in about the time it takes to set the table.

HALIBUT AND SPINACH WITH ORANGE–PINE NUT VINAIGRETTE

serves
4

PREP TIME: 10 minutes
COOKING TIME: 10 minutes

Orange–Pine Nut Vinaigrette

⅓ cup extra-virgin olive oil

¼ cup champagne vinegar or white wine vinegar

3 tablespoons very finely chopped shallots

2 tablespoons honey

1 tablespoon chopped fresh tarragon

Finely grated zest of 1 orange

¼ cup pine nuts, toasted (see Kitchen Note, page 20) and coarsely crushed

Kosher salt and freshly ground black pepper

Fish and Spinach

Four 5- to 6-ounce skinless halibut fillets

Kosher salt and freshly ground black pepper

2 tablespoons olive oil

2 shallots, thinly sliced into rings

Two 6-ounce bags fresh baby spinach

1 To make the vinaigrette: In a small bowl, mix the olive oil, vinegar, shallots, honey, tarragon, and orange zest with a fork to combine (but not emulsify). Stir in the pine nuts. Season to taste with salt and pepper. Set aside.

2 To cook the fish: Season the halibut with salt and pepper. Heat a large non-stick skillet over high heat. Add 1 tablespoon of the oil, then add the halibut and cook, without moving it, for about 3 minutes, or until deep golden brown on the underside. Turn the halibut over and cook for about 3 minutes more, or just until it is barely opaque in the center when flaked with the tip of a small knife. Transfer to a plate.

3 To cook the spinach: Wipe out the skillet and return it to medium-high heat. Add the remaining 1 tablespoon olive oil, then add the shallots and cook, stirring occasionally, for about 2 minutes, or until they just begin to soften. Add the spinach in batches and stir for about 1 minute, or just until it begins to wilt. Season to taste with salt and pepper.

4 Divide the spinach among four dinner plates. Top each with a fillet. Spoon the vinaigrette over the fillets and spinach mixture. Serve immediately.

OLIVE OIL There are two basic kinds of olive oil, and they have different uses in the kitchen, which is why I sometimes call for both in the same recipe.

Regular olive oil is golden yellow and moderately priced. It's made from crushed and refined olives, and its light body and flavor make it perfect for sautéing.

Extra-virgin olive oil is also made from crushed olives, but the resulting oil isn't refined and so retains its green color. Like wine, the flavor of extra-virgin olive oil varies according to its origin. Some are spicy, some are floral, and some are thicker than others. Extra-virgin olive oil is mainly used to make vinaigrettes and to season a finished dish.

epending on the country, Mexico or Italy, salsa verde means different things. Both are green sauces, but Mexican cooks make theirs from tomatillos and cilantro, like in my Roasted Butterflied Chicken and Tomatillos on page 83. This Italian version is made with herbs, capers, shallots, olive oil, and lemon. When you want to put something more than a squeeze of lemon on your fish, make this truly great uncooked sauce that can also be served with chicken or pork.

PAN-FRIED SNAPPER WITH FENNEL AND SALSA VERDE

serves
4

PREP TIME: 10 minutes
COOKING TIME: 20 minutes

Salsa Verde

½ cup extra-virgin olive oil

3 tablespoons finely chopped scallions (white and green parts)

2 tablespoons chopped fresh basil

2 tablespoons chopped fresh flat-leaf parsley

1 teaspoon chopped fresh rosemary

2 tablespoons chopped drained nonpareil capers

1 tablespoon minced shallots

Finely grated zest of 1 lemon

Kosher salt and freshly ground black pepper

Vegetables and Fish

5 tablespoons olive oil

3 small fennel bulbs (about 1 pound total), trimmed and cut from tip to core into ¼-inch-thick slices

1 small yellow onion, thinly sliced

4 small lemons, cut in half crosswise

Four 6-ounce red snapper fillets with skin

Kosher salt and freshly ground black pepper

1 To make the salsa verde: In a medium bowl, whisk the olive oil, scallions, basil, parsley, rosemary, capers, shallots, and lemon zest together. Set aside at room temperature.

2 To cook the vegetables and fish: Heat a large skillet over medium-high heat. Add 2 tablespoons of the olive oil, then lay half of the fennel and onion slices in the pan. Cook for about 3 minutes on each side, or until tender and golden brown (don't worry if the slices fall apart). Transfer to a plate and cover to keep warm. Repeat with 1 tablespoon of the remaining olive oil and the remaining fennel and onions. This time, place the lemon halves cut side down in the skillet alongside the vegetables and cook for about 1 minute, or until they begin to brown on the cut sides. Remove the lemons from the skillet and squeeze ¼ cup of juice from about 4 of the lemon halves. Stir the juice into the salsa verde. Season the salsa to taste with salt and pepper. Reserve the remaining lemons for serving.

3 Meanwhile, using a sharp knife, lightly score the skin side of each fillet. Season the fillets with salt and pepper. Heat a large nonstick skillet over medium-high heat. Add the remaining 2 tablespoons olive oil, then lay the snapper fillets skin side down in the skillet and cook for about 3 minutes, or until the skin is golden brown and crisp. Turn the fish over and cook for about 1 minute more, or until the fish is barely opaque when pierced in the thickest part with the tip of a small knife.

4 Divide the fennel mixture evenly among four dinner plates and place the fish alongside. Drizzle with the salsa verde and serve with the reserved caramelized lemons.

GRILLED LEMON HALVES One way to improve your cooking is to find quick techniques that bring extra flavor without much effort. French chefs call these *trucs*, which mean tricks. Grilling lemon halves is one that you can use over and over. Searing grill marks onto the lemon halves is more than just visually appealing: The browning caramelizes the sugars in the lemon juice and the heat slightly, but noticeably, intensifies the lemon flavor. When you are cooking fish indoors, you can try this trick in a ridged grill pan or skillet.

This down-home New Orleans classic of shell-on shrimp in a spicy garlic sauce is quick and delectable. The dish has always been referred to as "barbecued" even though it's made on the stovetop in a skillet. Cooking the shrimp in the shell helps prevent overcooking and gives extra flavor to the sauce. You get down and dirty devouring these, so provide lemon wedges and paper towels for easy at-table cleanup. Have crusty bread on hand to sop up the buttery sauce. The Shaved Radicchio and Escarole Salad with Goat Cheese and Walnuts on page 55 is a great match for this.

NEW ORLEANS "BARBECUED" SHRIMP WITH AMBER ALE

serves
4

PREP TIME: 10 minutes
COOKING TIME: 5 minutes

2 pounds extra-large (16 to 20 count) shrimp in the shell

1 tablespoon olive oil

5 tablespoons unsalted butter

8 garlic cloves, finely chopped

¼ teaspoon cayenne pepper

Kosher salt and freshly ground black pepper

½ cup amber ale

2 tablespoons fresh lemon juice

1 tablespoon hot pepper sauce, such as Crystal or Tabasco

1 tablespoon Worcestershire sauce

3 tablespoons finely chopped fresh flat-leaf parsley

1 teaspoon chopped fresh oregano

1 teaspoon chopped fresh thyme

½ teaspoon chopped fresh rosemary

Sliced French bread, warmed or lightly toasted

1 Using a small sharp knife or small sharp kitchen shears, cut down the back of each shrimp just deep enough to expose the dark vein. Devein the shrimp under cold running water, leaving the shells intact.

2 Heat a large heavy skillet over medium-high heat. Add the olive oil, then add 2 tablespoons of the butter and swirl to melt it. Add the garlic, sprinkle with the cayenne pepper, and season with 1 teaspoon salt and ½ teaspoon pepper. Cook for about 1 minute, or just until the garlic is tender. Add the shrimp and toss to coat well with the butter mixture. Add the ale, lemon juice, hot sauce, and Worcestershire sauce and simmer for about 2 minutes, or until the shrimp are almost cooked through, turning the shrimp after 1 minute.

3 Add the remaining 3 tablespoons butter, the parsley, oregano, thyme, and rosemary and simmer gently for about 1 minute, or until the butter melts and the shrimp are just cooked through. Season to taste with salt and pepper.

4 Transfer the shrimp and sauce to four wide shallow bowls. Serve with the bread to sop up the sauce.

USING FRESH HERBS brings your food to life with vibrant flavors. If you have leftover herbs (and most likely you will), chop them and stir into softened butter (say, 2 tablespoons herbs to 8 tablespoons butter), roll it up into a log in a piece of wax paper, and freeze for up to 3 months. Cut off a pat to stir into steamed vegetables or boiled pasta, or use as a quick topping for grilled steaks or chops.

Shrimp is a great time-saver because it cooks so quickly. For this fast pasta dinner, the vegetables for the tomato sauce are briefly cooked, so they retain their fresh flavor, and while it is the opposite of a long-simmered ragù, it is just as great in its own uncomplicated way. Fresh jalapeños give the dish a pleasant spiciness. Look for red jalapeños, which are riper and a bit sweeter than the green ones, or red Fresno peppers. If you can't find either, green jalapeños make a fine substitute.

FETTUCCINE WITH SHRIMP AND FRESH TOMATO SAUCE

serves
4

PREP TIME: 10 minutes
COOKING TIME: 10 minutes

1 pound dried fettuccine

¼ cup olive oil

1 pound large (21 to 30 count) shrimp, peeled, tails left on, and deveined

Kosher salt and freshly ground black pepper

⅔ cup finely chopped shallots

5 large garlic cloves, finely chopped

2 red chili peppers, such as Fresno or jalapeños, seeded and finely chopped

⅔ cup dry white wine

5 large ripe tomatoes (about 2½ pounds total), cut into ½-inch pieces

3 tablespoons coarsely chopped fresh flat-leaf parsley

2 tablespoons fresh lemon juice

3 tablespoons unsalted butter

1. Bring a large pot of salted water to a boil over high heat. Add the fettuccine and cook, stirring often to keep the strands from sticking together, for about 8 minutes, or until tender but still firm to the bite.

2. Meanwhile, heat a large heavy skillet over medium-high heat. Add 2 tablespoons of the oil, then add the shrimp and cook, stirring often, for about 2 minutes, or until opaque around the edges. Season with salt and pepper. Add the shallots, garlic, and jalapeños and cook, stirring occasionally, for about 2 minutes, or until the shallots soften. Add the wine and simmer for about 2 minutes, or until reduced slightly.

3. Drain the pasta well, add it to the shrimp mixture, and toss gently to coat with the sauce. Add the tomatoes, parsley, lemon juice, butter, and the remaining 2 tablespoons olive oil and toss again to melt the butter and coat the pasta. Season to taste with salt and pepper and toss well.

4. Divide the pasta and shrimp among four pasta bowls and serve.

SHRIMP The sizes given for shrimp that you see at the fish market are established by the seafood industry, not set by the USDA, so one store's extra-large shrimp may be another purveyor's jumbo. But shrimp are graded by count, and the number indicates how many you will find per pound. For example, 21- to 30-count shrimp (often designated as large) averages 25 shrimp per pound.

It is very economical to stash a bag of IQF (Individually Quick Frozen) shrimp, bought in bulk, in the freezer and have it ready to defrost quickly for a last-minute meal.

The first time I ate a lobster roll, at a waterfront shack on Cape Cod, I knew that it was one of the world's great sandwiches. This shrimp version, with a creamy herb dressing and a little heat from fresh chili, is the way I like to make the Yankee classic more economical. Boil up some corn on the cob to serve on the side.

SHRIMP ROLLS WITH HERB AÏOLI

serves
4

PREP TIME: 10 minutes

COOKING TIME: 5 minutes, plus 20 minutes chilling time

1¼ pounds medium shrimp (31 to 35 count), peeled and deveined

Aïoli

½ cup mayonnaise

3 tablespoons finely chopped fresh chives

3 tablespoons finely chopped scallions (white and green parts)

2 teaspoons finely chopped fresh tarragon

Finely grated zest of 1 lemon

1½ tablespoons fresh lemon juice

1 garlic clove, finely chopped

⅛ teaspoon cayenne pepper

Sandwich

Kosher salt and freshly ground black pepper

4 good-quality hot dog buns, preferably top-split

2 tablespoons unsalted butter, or as needed, at room temperature

1½ cups very thinly sliced iceberg lettuce

1 red chili pepper, such as Fresno or jalapeño, seeded and finely chopped, for garnish

1 To prepare the shrimp: Bring a large saucepan of salted water to a boil over high heat. Add the shrimp and cook for about 1 minute, or just until opaque. Drain, spread the shrimp on a rimmed baking sheet, and refrigerate until cold, about 20 minutes.

2 To make the aïoli: In a medium bowl, whisk the mayonnaise, chives, scallions, tarragon, lemon zest, lemon juice, garlic, and cayenne pepper together.

3 To make the sandwich: Toss the chilled shrimp with the aïoli to coat. Season to taste with salt and pepper. Cover and refrigerate until ready to use. (The shrimp salad can be made up to 8 hours ahead.)

4 Heat a large griddle or heavy flat nonstick skillet over medium-high heat. Open the buns (or cut the rolls in half) and spread lightly, inside and out, with the butter. Grill the buns on all the buttered sides, turning occasionally, for about 2 minutes, or until toasted and golden brown.

5 Fill the buns with the lettuce and top with the shrimp salad. Sprinkle with the chopped chili and serve.

 portobello mushrooms have a meaty quality that makes them a healthy stand-in for the steak that you might expect to find in this kind of Chinese-style stir-fry. (But you can add some sliced steak, if you wish.) Broccolini is great for stir-frying because its thin stalks cook quickly. Don't confuse it with broccoli rabe, which it resembles—broccolini is much milder. This stir-fry also gets a non-Asian seasoning of thyme, which works beautifully with the other flavors.

PORTOBELLO MUSHROOM, GREEN ONION, AND BROCCOLINI STIR-FRY

serves
4

PREP TIME: 10 minutes
COOKING TIME: 10 minutes

¼ cup finely chopped shallots

¼ cup unseasoned rice vinegar

2 tablespoons oyster sauce

2 teaspoons finely chopped fresh thyme

3 tablespoons olive oil

10 ounces broccolini, thick bottoms trimmed, large stalks halved lengthwise

2 large portobello mushroom caps, dark gills scraped out with a spoon, cut into ½-inch-thick slices

6 scallions (white and green parts), cut into 1½-inch lengths

1 tablespoon finely chopped peeled fresh ginger

3 garlic cloves, finely chopped

1½ teaspoons sesame seeds, toasted (see Kitchen Note)

Perfect Rice (page 9), for serving

1. In a small bowl, whisk the shallots, vinegar, oyster sauce, thyme, and 2 tablespoons of the olive oil together.

2. Heat a wok or large skillet over high heat until very hot. Add the remaining 1 tablespoon olive oil and swirl it to coat the cooking surface with olive oil. Add the broccolini and cook, stirring often, for about 2 minutes, or until it is bright green and beginning to char in spots. Stir in the mushrooms and cook, stirring often, for about 1 minute, or until they just begin to soften. Stir in the scallions, ginger, and garlic, add the shallot mixture, and stir for about 3 minutes, or until the broccolini is tender. Stir in half of the sesame seeds.

3. Transfer to a large platter and sprinkle with the remaining sesame seeds. Serve immediately, with the rice.

TOASTING SEEDS It only takes a minute or two to toast seeds, and this easy step brings their oils to the surface and really pumps up their flavor. Heat a dry small skillet or wok over medium-high heat. Add the seeds and cook, stirring almost constantly, for about 1 minute (a little longer for pumpkin seeds), or until lightly toasted and fragrant. Transfer to a plate to cool.

My friend Steven came up with the idea to spike an Arnold Palmer (iced tea and lemonade), but it took a detour somewhere, and we ended up with this libation. It was fun experimenting, even though we suffered the consequences the next day.

TIPSY PALMER

serves
4

PREP TIME: 10 minutes

1 cup good-quality ginger ale

1 cup lemonade, preferably homemade

½ cup bourbon

1 small lemon, thinly sliced

½ English cucumber, thinly sliced

½ cup loosely packed fresh mint leaves

One 3-inch piece of fresh ginger

About 2 cups ice cubes

1. In a large pitcher, combine the ginger ale, lemonade, bourbon, lemon, cucumbers, and mint. Peel the ginger; then, using the vegetable peeler, shave the ginger lengthwise into paper-thin ribbons. Add them to the lemonade mixture and stir well to muddle the ingredients and blend all the flavors.

2. Fill four large glasses with ice cubes and pour in the lemonade mixture, including the lemon, mint, cucumbers, and ginger. Serve immediately.

ONE-POT WEDNESDAYS

IN MY HOUSE, WE GET ALL OF OUR HOUSE-
work done on Wednesdays. By the end of the day, the kitchen is spot-
less: The counters are uncluttered, the stovetop shines, and there's
not a dish in the sink, drying rack, or dishwasher. There's nothing
worse than mucking up that nice clean kitchen, so Wednesday dinners have to be no mess, no fuss. **Enter one-pot cooking, which
makes cleanup a breeze and a midweek meal a snap.**

There are a few types of pans that work beautifully when making
one-pot meals. Heavy cast-iron skillets and Dutch ovens can easily
go from stovetop to oven. What's more, they distribute heat evenly
and brown meats and vegetables perfectly. My stockpot and roasting
pan also get a workout on Wednesdays. Big enough to hold an entire
meal, these "slow-cookers" allow the flavors of the ingredients to
mingle and deepen as they cook. But my favorite way of cooking
one-pot meals doesn't require a pot at all: Grilling is a quick way to
prepare meat and vegetables together. And nothing beats that smoky
charred flavor. During cool-weather months, try a stovetop grill pan
to bring a touch of summer indoors. Whichever pot you choose, relax
and enjoy your dinner. After all, the dishes are almost done.

have a friend who doesn't eat dairy products, so I was interested in creating a dinner entrée that we would all enjoy together. I started with Thai flavors, knowing that it is a cuisine that doesn't use much (if any) dairy, getting its richness from coconut milk, fish sauce, ginger, garlic, and basil. I ended up with a variation of *tom kha gai*, one of my favorite soups, but with enough vegetables to put it in the stew category. Chicken legs make succulent braises, because their extra fat allows them to withstand longer cooking times than lean chicken breasts. I've replaced most of the coconut milk with a lighter, but just as creamy, almond milk. Perfect Jasmine Rice (page 9) would be great with this.

SLOW-COOKED THAI CHICKEN WITH CORN AND ASPARAGUS

serves
4

PREP TIME: 10 minutes
COOKING TIME: 1 hour

4 whole chicken legs (thighs and drumsticks; about 11 ounces each)

Kosher salt

2 tablespoons olive oil

1 yellow onion, thinly sliced

1 cup fresh corn kernels (from about 2 ears of corn)

1 tablespoon finely chopped peeled fresh ginger

3 garlic cloves, finely chopped

2½ cups unsweetened almond milk

Zest of 1 lime, removed in wide strips with a vegetable peeler

2 tablespoons Thai or Vietnamese fish sauce (nam pla or nuoc mam)

8 ounces asparagus, woody stems trimmed, cut diagonally in half

¼ cup packed torn fresh basil leaves

½ cup unsweetened coconut milk

1 lime, cut into wedges, for serving

1 Season the chicken with salt. Heat a large deep heavy skillet over medium-high heat. Add the olive oil, then place the chicken skin side down in the skillet and cook for about 3 minutes, or until the skin side is browned. Turn and brown the other side, about 3 minutes more. Transfer the chicken to a plate.

2 Drain all but 1 tablespoon of fat from the skillet and return the pan to medium-high heat. Add the onions and cook, stirring often, for about 3 minutes, or until softened. Stir in the corn kernels, ginger, and garlic and cook, stirring often, for about 3 minutes, or until fragrant. Stir in the almond milk, lime zest, and fish sauce, return the chicken to the skillet, and bring the liquid to a simmer. Reduce the heat to medium-low, cover, and simmer gently for about 45 minutes, or until the chicken shows no sign of pink when pierced at the bone with the tip of a small sharp knife and the liquid has reduced slightly.

3 Add the asparagus and basil leaves to the chicken and cook for about 2 minutes, or until the asparagus is crisp-tender. Stir in the coconut milk and season to taste with salt.

4 Divide the stew among four deep soup bowls and serve hot with lime wedges.

Paella is the national dish of Spain and a classic one-pan meal. It is traditionally made on an outdoor grill, but I first learned to make paella in the oven, and I have stuck with the foolproof, utterly delicious version. Use a starchy medium-grain rice so the paella sticks together when it's being spooned up—this is one dish where you do not want fluffy individual grains. Drink White Sangría (page 104), and serve with the Frisée, Shaved Fennel, and Celery Salad with Caper-Parsley Vinaigrette (page 110).

CHICKEN AND CHORIZO PAELLA

serves
4

PREP TIME: 10 minutes
COOKING TIME: 50 minutes

4 to 6 chicken drumsticks

Kosher salt and freshly ground black pepper

2 tablespoons olive oil

8 ounces smoked Spanish chorizo links, casings removed and cut into ⅛-inch-thick rounds or wedges

1 yellow onion, finely chopped

1 red bell pepper, cored, seeded, and diced

5 garlic cloves, finely chopped

¾ teaspoon sweet smoked paprika

Large pinch of saffron threads

2 cups medium-grain white rice, such as Spanish Calasparra or Italian Arborio, or a domestic brand, such as Goya

3½ cups reduced-sodium chicken broth

1 medium tomato, halved, seeded, and finely diced

2 tablespoons chopped fresh flat-leaf parsley

1 Preheat the oven to 400°F.

2 Season the chicken with salt and pepper. Heat a paella pan or 12-inch heavy ovenproof skillet over medium-high heat. Add the olive oil, then add the chicken and cook, turning occasionally, for about 5 minutes, or until browned on all sides. Transfer to a plate.

3 Reduce the heat to medium, add the chorizo to the pan, and cook, stirring occasionally, for about 2 minutes, or until browned. Add the onions, bell peppers, garlic, paprika, and saffron and cook, stirring often, for about 3 minutes, or until the vegetables soften. Add the rice and cook, stirring often, for about 2 minutes, or until the rice is coated with olive oil and the mixture looks dry.

4 Stir in the broth, 1 teaspoon salt, and ¼ teaspoon pepper. Return the chicken to the pan, arranging it in a single layer and evenly spaced. Increase the heat to high and bring to a simmer.

5 Transfer the pan to the oven and bake, uncovered, for about 30 minutes, or until the rice is tender and the chicken shows no sign of pink when pierced at the bone with the tip of a small sharp knife. A sign of a good baked paella is crisp rice around the sides of the pan. Let stand at room temperature to allow the rice to settle for 5 minutes.

6 Sprinkle the paella with the diced tomato and parsley and serve hot.

You can put just about anything in a pot pie. But I have found that root vegetables hold up well during baking, and they add a layer of sweet, comforting flavor. To save time and effort, use a rotisserie chicken from the supermarket or leftover cooked chicken. When serving to company, I bake pot pies in individual casseroles for a nice presentation.

CHICKEN POT PIE WITH WINTER ROOT VEGETABLES

serves
6

PREP TIME: 10 minutes
COOKING TIME: 50 minutes

2 tablespoons unsalted butter

1 yellow onion, finely chopped

1 celery rib, thinly sliced

2 carrots, sliced into ¼-inch-thick rounds

2 parsnips (about the same size as the carrots), peeled and sliced into ¼-inch-thick rounds

1 turnip (about 8 ounces), peeled and cut into ½-inch pieces

2 garlic cloves, finely chopped

3 tablespoons all-purpose flour

1¾ cups reduced-sodium chicken broth

¾ cup plus 1 tablespoon whole milk

¾ cup heavy cream

3 large sprigs of fresh thyme

1 pound roasted chicken, torn into large bite-size pieces (about 3½ cups)

Kosher salt and freshly ground black pepper

1 large egg

1 sheet frozen all-butter puff pastry (about 8 ounces), thawed but still well chilled (see Kitchen Note)

1   Preheat the oven to 400°F.

2   Melt the butter in a 12-inch cast-iron or other heavy ovenproof skillet over medium heat. Add the onions, celery, carrots, parsnips, turnips, and garlic and cook, stirring occasionally, for about 10 minutes, or until the root vegetables are almost tender. Sprinkle in the flour and stir well for about 1 minute to cook the flour, without browning. Raise the heat to medium-high and stir in the broth, followed by ¾ cup of the milk, the cream, and the thyme. Bring to a simmer, reduce the heat to medium-low, and simmer gently, stirring occasionally, for about 5 minutes, or until the vegetables are tender. Remove from the heat and stir in the chicken. Season to taste with salt and pepper. Cool slightly, then remove and discard the thyme stems.

3   In a small bowl, mix the egg and the remaining 1 tablespoon milk with a fork to combine. On a lightly floured work surface, roll out the pastry into a 13-inch square.

4   Brush some of the egg mixture over the edges of the skillet. Lay the pastry over the pan and gently press the overhanging edges of pastry so they adhere to the sides of the pan. Lightly brush more of the egg mixture over the pastry and sprinkle with salt. Transfer to the oven and bake for about 30 minutes, or until the pastry is deep golden brown and puffed. Cool slightly and serve.

FROZEN PUFF PASTRY Flaky puff pastry takes practice to make properly, but don't fret if you aren't a master pâtissier. Frozen puff pastry will do the trick. For the best flavor, use all-butter puff pastry, available at specialty grocers and many supermarkets.

Butterflying a chicken before roasting it makes for easy carving and serving. But the true beauty of this one-pot wonder is how the flavors mix and mingle during cooking. As the tomatillos roast, they soften into a mouthwatering chunky salsa verde, seasoned with the chicken juices. The dish calls out for warm tortillas, but you can spoon it over rice, grits, or polenta.

ROASTED BUTTERFLIED CHICKEN AND TOMATILLOS

serves
4

PREP TIME: 15 minutes

COOKING TIME: 50 minutes, plus 10 minutes resting time

One 4-pound chicken

¼ cup olive oil

2 teaspoons sweet paprika

1 teaspoon ground cumin

Kosher salt and freshly ground black pepper

1½ pounds tomatillos, husked, rinsed, and cut in half

1 white onion, halved and cut into ½-inch-thick wedges

3 garlic cloves, finely chopped

1 jalapeño pepper, seeded and finely chopped (for a hotter sauce, keep the seeds)

¼ cup coarsely chopped fresh cilantro

1 lime, cut into wedges, for serving

8 whole wheat flour or corn tortillas, warmed, for serving

1 Preheat the oven to 400°F.

2 Using poultry shears, split the chicken open by cutting down one side of the backbone, then cut out and remove the backbone. Place the chicken skin side up on a chopping board. Put your hand on the breastbone and press hard to flatten the chicken.

3 Heat a very large cast-iron or other heavy ovenproof skillet over medium-high heat. Meanwhile, in a small bowl, mix 2 tablespoons of the olive oil with the paprika, cumin, 1 teaspoon salt, and 1 teaspoon pepper. Rub the mixture all over the chicken. Place the chicken skin side down in the hot skillet and cook for about 4 minutes, or just until the skin side is golden brown. Transfer the chicken to a large plate. Set the skillet aside.

4 In a large bowl, toss the tomatillos, onions, garlic, and jalapeños with the remaining 2 tablespoons olive oil. Season with salt and pepper. Arrange half of the tomatillo mixture in the skillet and nestle the chicken on top, skin side up. Scatter the remaining tomatillo mixture around the chicken.

5 Roast for about 45 minutes, or until the chicken shows no sign of pink when pierced in the thickest part with the tip of a small sharp knife and the tomatillos are falling apart into the sauce. Remove from the oven and let stand for 10 minutes.

6 Season the tomatillo salsa to taste with salt. Sprinkle the cilantro over the chicken and salsa and serve with the lime wedges and tortillas.

Tri-tip steak, a triangular cut from the bottom sirloin that looks more like a small roast than a steak, originated with California butchers, but it has become widely available. Like flank, it is a flavorful cut, and it should be cooked to medium-rare and cut across the grain, which makes it more tender. To get full use out of your grill, cook the green beans there too, to give them a sweet charred flavor.

GRILLED TRI-TIP WITH GREEN BEAN AND RED ONION SALAD

serves
4

PREP TIME: 10 minutes
COOKING TIME: 15 minutes

One 2-pound tri-tip steak (about 2 inches thick)

2 tablespoons balsamic vinegar, preferably aged

1 tablespoon finely chopped shallots

1 garlic clove, finely chopped

¼ teaspoon red pepper flakes

¼ cup extra-virgin olive oil

Kosher salt and freshly ground black pepper

1 large red onion, sliced into ¼-inch-thick rounds

1 pound green beans, trimmed

3 ounces soft fresh goat cheese

1 Remove the tri-tip from the refrigerator and let stand at room temperature while the grill is heating. Prepare an outdoor grill for medium-high cooking over direct heat.

2 In a medium bowl, whisk the vinegar, shallots, garlic, and red pepper flakes together. Gradually whisk in 2 tablespoons of the olive oil. Season the vinaigrette to taste with salt and pepper. Set aside.

3 Coat the tri-tip with 1 tablespoon of the remaining olive oil and season with salt and pepper. Grill the tri-tip, turning halfway through cooking, for about 12 minutes, or until an instant-read thermometer inserted in the thickest part of the beef reads 120°F for medium-rare (the tri-tip will continue to cook as it rests). Transfer to a cutting board and let stand while you grill the onions and green beans.

4 Coat the onion rounds and green beans with 1 tablespoon of the remaining olive oil. Transfer the beans and onions to the grill and cook for about 3 minutes, or until lightly charred and crisp-tender. Transfer to the bowl with the vinaigrette and toss to coat. Season to taste with salt and pepper.

5 Divide the green bean mixture among four dinner plates and coarsely crumble the goat cheese over the vegetables. Thinly slice the tri-tip across the grain. Divide the slices among the dinner plates, drizzle with the carving juices, and serve.

ROUNDING OUT THE MEAL · **CORN WITH SAGE BROWN BUTTER** This one-pan side dish only has three ingredients, but it is so tasty. In a large skillet over medium heat, stir butter and fresh sage leaves until the butter takes on a nice brown color and nutty aroma. Add fresh corn kernels and sauté until heated through. Season to taste with salt and pepper. If you wish, substitute cilantro leaves and ground cumin for the sage, and add a squeeze of lime juice.

ring the vibrant flavors of Greek cooking to your weeknight dinner with this main-course salad. You can marinate the lamb for 10 minutes or 10 hours. Of course, the more time you give it, the more flavorful it will be. So stick the chops in the marinade before you go to work, but don't worry if you forget to do so—you'll still have a delicious meal.

GRILLED LEMON-OREGANO LAMB CHOPS WITH RUSTIC BREAD SALAD

serves
4

PREP TIME: 15 minutes, plus at least 10 minutes marinating time
COOKING TIME: 10 minutes

Lamb

3 tablespoons olive oil

Finely grated zest of 2 lemons

2 tablespoons fresh lemon juice

2 tablespoons coarsely chopped fresh oregano

1 tablespoon finely chopped fresh rosemary

8 lamb loin chops (about 1¾ pounds total)

Kosher salt and freshly ground black pepper

Oregano–Red Wine Vinaigrette

3 tablespoons red wine vinegar

2 teaspoons Dijon mustard

¼ cup finely chopped shallots

1 garlic clove, finely chopped

½ teaspoon dried oregano

½ cup extra-virgin olive oil

Kosher salt and freshly ground black pepper

Salad

4 slices crusty rustic bread

Olive oil, for brushing the bread

Kosher salt

4 ounces fresh baby spinach (about 6 cups not packed)

1 cup halved cherry tomatoes

½ small red onion, very thinly sliced

4 ounces feta cheese, crumbled

1. To marinate the lamb: In a medium bowl, whisk the olive oil, lemon zest, lemon juice, oregano, and rosemary together. Add the lamb and turn to coat with the marinade. Cover with plastic wrap and marinate at room temperature for at least 10 minutes or in the refrigerator for up to 10 hours.

2. About 30 minutes before grilling, remove the marinated lamb from the refrigerator (if it's been chilled) and let stand at room temperature.

3. Meanwhile, make the vinaigrette: In a small bowl, whisk the vinegar, mustard, shallots, garlic, and oregano together. Gradually whisk in the olive oil. Season to taste with salt and pepper. Set aside.

4. Prepare an outdoor grill for medium-high cooking over direct heat.

5. To make the salad: Lightly brush both sides of the bread with olive oil and sprinkle lightly with salt. Grill the bread, turning halfway through cooking, for about 2 minutes, or until lightly toasted. Remove the bread from the grill, tear it into bite-size pieces, and put it into a large bowl.

6. Season the lamb with salt and pepper. Grill the lamb chops, turning them over halfway through cooking, for about 7 minutes for medium-rare, or until the meat feels resilient when pressed with a finger (see Kitchen Note, page 140). Transfer to a platter, tent with aluminum foil, and let rest while you finish the salad.

7. Add the spinach, tomatoes, and onions to the bowl with the grilled bread. Toss with enough of the vinaigrette to lightly coat.

8. Mound equal amounts of the salad on four dinner plates and sprinkle with the feta cheese. Arrange two lamb chops on top of each salad, drizzle with some of the remaining vinaigrette, and serve.

A proper pork roast, cooked in a pan full of vegetables, gives off a tantalizing, old-fashioned aroma. The combination of meat juices and roasted vegetables is heaven on a plate. As for the rosemary salt, it is a great trick that you can use with other cuts of meat and other herbs. Try a thyme salt on your next roast beef. For extra flavor, order a roast with a ¼-inch layer of fat on top.

ROASTED PORK LOIN WITH ROSEMARY SALT, SHALLOTS, POTATOES, CARROTS, AND PARSNIPS

serves
6

PREP TIME: 15 minutes
COOKING TIME: 55 minutes

2 pounds medium Yukon Gold potatoes, scrubbed and quartered

1 pound shallots, cut in half

3 carrots, cut crosswise on the diagonal into 2-inch pieces

3 parsnips (the same size as the carrots), peeled and cut diagonally into 2-inch pieces

4 garlic cloves, finely chopped

1 teaspoon smoked paprika (hot or sweet)

¼ cup olive oil

Kosher salt and freshly ground black pepper

4 sprigs of fresh rosemary

One 2½-pound boneless pork loin roast, preferably with the top layer of fat still intact

⅔ cup reduced-sodium chicken broth

1. Preheat the oven to 450°F.

2. Put the potatoes, shallots, carrots, parsnips, and garlic in a large heavy roasting pan, sprinkle with the smoked paprika, and toss with 3 tablespoons of the olive oil to coat. Season with salt and pepper. Spread the vegetables evenly over the bottom of the pan. Place 2 of the rosemary sprigs on top.

3. Finely chop enough of the remaining 2 rosemary sprigs to equal 2 teaspoons. In a small bowl, combine 1 tablespoon salt and the chopped rosemary. Rub the mixture together with your fingertips for about 1 minute, or until fragrant.

4. Using a sharp knife, score the fat that covers the top of the pork by cutting shallow slashes (about ¼ inch deep) at 1-inch intervals, cutting into the fat but not the flesh. Rub the pork all over with the remaining 1 tablespoon olive oil. Rub the rosemary salt all over the pork, working it into the score marks. If desired, tie the pork crosswise with kitchen twine in three or four places to help maintain its shape while roasting.

5. Place the pork fat side up on top of the bed of vegetables. Roast for about 40 minutes, or until the pork is golden brown and an instant-read thermometer inserted into the center reads 125°F. Transfer the pork to a serving platter. Tent with aluminum foil and let rest for 10 minutes before slicing (the pork will continue to cook as it rests).

6. Meanwhile, stir the vegetables in the pan and continue roasting them for about 10 minutes, or until tender and golden brown. Transfer the vegetables to the platter with the pork.

7. Add the broth to the hot roasting pan and bring to a boil over medium-high heat, stirring with a wooden spoon to scrape up the browned bits in the bottom of the pan. Season with salt and pepper. Pour the pan juices into a sauceboat.

8. Untie the pork if necessary. Slice the pork and serve it with the roasted vegetables and pan juices.

This dish of greens and fork-tender pork is home cooking at its best, and the kind of food that gave Southern hospitality its fine reputation. I have provided instructions for one of my favorite kitchen tools, the pressure cooker, which enables you to trim the long original cooking time by at least half. However, directions for cooking it in a traditional pot follow the recipe.

SUCCULENT PORK AND GREENS

serves
6

PREP TIME: 15 minutes

COOKING TIME: 1 hour

3 tablespoons olive oil

3 pounds boneless pork shoulder, well trimmed of excess fat and cut into 2- to 3-inch chunks

1 large yellow onion, thinly sliced

2 garlic cloves, finely chopped

1 teaspoon red pepper flakes

5 cups reduced-sodium chicken broth

3 tablespoons cider vinegar

1 tablespoon dark brown sugar

1 teaspoon kosher salt

2 bay leaves

2 pounds kale (about 4 bunches), well rinsed, tough stems removed, and leaves very coarsely chopped

One 12-ounce smoked ham hock

1 Heat an 8-quart pressure cooker over medium-high heat. Add the olive oil and then, working in batches, add the pork and cook, turning occasionally, for about 5 minutes, or until browned. Transfer the pork to a bowl.

2 Stir the onions, garlic, and red pepper flakes into the fat remaining in the pot. Add the broth, vinegar, brown sugar, salt, and bay leaves and bring to a boil. Working in batches, stir in the kale, letting each batch wilt before adding more. Nestle the ham hock into the kale. Return the pork and its juices to the pressure cooker.

3 Lock the pressure cooker lid in place. Bring to high pressure over high heat, then reduce the heat to medium to stabilize the pressure and cook at high pressure for 30 minutes. Remove from the heat and allow the pressure to subside for 10 minutes.

4 Unlock the pressure cooker and remove the lid, tilting it away from you to allow the steam to escape. The greens, pork, and ham hock meat will be very tender.

5 Transfer the ham hock to a carving board. Flake the meat into bite-size pieces and discard the rind and bone. Stir into the greens. Spoon the pork and greens into wide shallow bowls and serve hot.

VARIATION: LONG-COOKED PORK AND GREENS
If you don't have a pressure cooker, this can be cooked in a heavy pot in the traditional manner. Heat a large Dutch oven over medium-high heat. Add the olive oil and heat until very hot but not smoking. Add the pork in batches and cook, turning occasionally, until browned, about 5 minutes. Transfer the pork to a plate. Add the onions, garlic, and red pepper flakes to the Dutch oven, reduce the heat to medium, and cook, stirring often, until the onions soften, about 5 minutes. Return the pork to the pot, add the broth, vinegar, brown sugar, salt, and bay leaves, and bring to a simmer. Add the ham hock. Reduce the heat to medium-low, cover, and simmer for 1 hour. Working in batches, add the kale, letting each addition wilt before adding the next. Partially cover and simmer until the pork is very tender, about 1 hour longer. Continue as directed in step 5.

This rustic soup is brimming with fresh veggies, including fennel, one of my absolute favorites for soup. When I make this soup, I always make a double batch. It's true, some soups are better the next day.

WHITE BEAN AND CHORIZO SOUP WITH CROSTINI

serves
4 to **6**

PREP TIME: 10 minutes
COOKING TIME: 50 minutes

3 tablespoons olive oil

6 ounces smoked Spanish chorizo links, casings removed, halved lengthwise and cut into ¼-inch-thick half-moons

1 yellow onion, finely chopped

2 carrots, cut into ½-inch-thick rounds

2 celery ribs, cut into ½-inch-thick slices

2 small fennel bulbs, trimmed and cut into ½-inch pieces (about 2 cups)

4 garlic cloves, finely chopped

2 large sprigs of fresh thyme

1 sprig of fresh rosemary

¾ cup dry white wine

6 cups reduced-sodium chicken broth

Kosher salt and freshly ground black pepper

Two 15-ounce cans small white beans, drained and rinsed (about 3 cups)

½ demi-baguette, cut on a diagonal into ½-inch-thick slices

Extra-virgin olive oil, for serving

1. Heat a large heavy pot over medium heat. Add 1 tablespoon of the olive oil, then add the chorizo and cook, stirring occasionally, for about 5 minutes, or until browned. Add the onions and cook, stirring occasionally, for about 5 minutes, or until tender. Add the carrots, celery, fennel, garlic, thyme, and rosemary and cook, stirring occasionally, for about 5 minutes, or until the vegetables begin to soften. Add the wine and bring to a simmer. Stir in the broth and season to taste with salt and pepper. Bring to a simmer, then reduce the heat to medium-low and simmer, uncovered, for about 20 minutes, or until the vegetables are tender.

2. Stir in the beans and simmer gently for about 10 minutes to blend the flavors. Remove and discard the thyme and rosemary stems.

3. Meanwhile, brush the baguette slices with the remaining 2 tablespoons olive oil and sprinkle with salt. Toast in a toaster oven until golden brown, about 5 minutes.

4. Ladle the soup into four soup bowls. Drizzle with extra-virgin olive oil and serve with the crostini.

COOKING WINE Cook with a wine that isn't expensive but you would happily drink.

Good wine for cooking, whether it is red or white, is dry (not fruity or sweet) with some body (by that, I mean not thin on your palate). Although most wines with friendly prices aren't aged in oak barrels, think twice before you use an oaked Cabernet or Chardonnay, as the wood flavor can transfer to the food.

Shiraz, or a Cabernet/Shiraz blend, is a nice choice for a red cooking wine, and Pinot Grigio is a reliable white. It just so happens that there are some excellent, reasonably priced Australian wines that make good cooking companions.

I always think of corn as soaking up the sun, so by the end of summer, the kernels are bursting with sweetness. My nan used to make a soup similar to this, and now I make it in her honor. You could add peeled and deveined shrimp to this soup during the last few minutes, cooking just until they turn opaque.

BACON, CORN, AND POTATO CHOWDER

serves
6 to **8**

PREP TIME: 10 minutes
COOKING TIME: 25 minutes

4 slices bacon, coarsely chopped

2 yellow onions, finely chopped

4 garlic cloves, finely chopped

4 large sprigs of fresh thyme

¼ teaspoon cayenne pepper

4 celery ribs, cut into ½-inch pieces

1½ pounds Yukon Gold potatoes, scrubbed and cut into ½-inch pieces

2 tablespoons all-purpose flour

2 cups reduced-sodium chicken broth

2 cups heavy cream

2 cups whole milk

7 ears corn, husked and kernels cut off

Kosher salt and freshly ground black pepper

¼ cup coarsely chopped fresh flat-leaf parsley

1 Heat a large heavy pot over medium-high heat. Add the bacon and cook, stirring occasionally, for about 5 minutes, or until crisp and golden. Add the onions, garlic, thyme, and cayenne and cook, stirring often, for about 4 minutes, or until the onions are tender but not browned.

2 Add the celery and cook, stirring often and being careful not to brown the vegetables, for about 4 minutes. Reduce the heat if the vegetables begin to brown. Add the potatoes, sprinkle in the flour, and stir for about 2 minutes to cook the flour; do not allow to brown. Stir in the broth, cover, and bring to a simmer, stirring occasionally. Stir in the cream and milk and bring just to a simmer, stirring constantly. Reduce the heat to medium-low and simmer gently for about 3 minutes, or until the potatoes are tender but not falling apart.

3 Stir the corn kernels into the chowder and simmer for about 4 minutes, or just until the corn is heated through and the chowder thickens slightly. Remove and discard the thyme stems. Season to taste with salt and pepper.

4 Stir in half of the parsley. Ladle the chowder into bowls, sprinkle with the remaining parsley, and serve.

WHOLE SPRIGS I often toss whole herb sprigs into braises, soups, and stews, as I like the fuller flavor that the stems provide. The leaves will fall off during cooking, and then you can remove and discard the stems before serving. You can tie the herbs together with a piece of kitchen twine to make removal easier, if you wish. For a stronger flavor, choose large, full sprigs; for a gentler herb note, use just a single stem.

The aromas of bacon, onion, and red pepper for this frittata make my mouth water. It reminds me of my mum's tradition of occasionally serving breakfast for dinner. I serve it often for brunch or, cooled and cut into bite-size pieces, as a tapas-style nibble.

POTATO AND BACON FRITTATA

serves
4

PREP TIME: 10 minutes
COOKING TIME: 40 minutes

5 ounces sliced bacon, cut into ⅓-inch pieces

1 small yellow onion, finely chopped

1 red bell pepper, cored, seeded, and cut into ½-inch pieces

2 scallions (white and green parts), sliced into ⅓-inch-wide pieces

2 garlic cloves, finely chopped

1 teaspoon chopped fresh thyme

2 medium baking potatoes, such as russets (7 ounces each), peeled

12 large eggs

1½ teaspoons kosher salt

¾ teaspoon sweet smoked paprika

1 Preheat the oven to 400°F.

2 Heat a 12-inch cast-iron skillet or ovenproof nonstick pan over medium heat. Add the bacon and cook, stirring occasionally, for about 5 minutes, or until crisp and golden. Using a slotted spoon, transfer the bacon to a medium bowl. Add the onions, bell peppers, scallions, garlic, and thyme to the drippings in the skillet and cook, stirring often, for about 3 minutes, or until the onions are tender. Using a slotted spoon, transfer the vegetable mixture to the bowl with the bacon, leaving the pan drippings in the skillet.

3 Meanwhile, grate the potatoes on the large holes of a box grater.

4 Increase the heat under the pan to medium-high, add the potatoes, and stir to coat with the drippings. Press down the potatoes with a metal spatula and cook, without stirring, for about 5 minutes, or until the bottom is lightly browned. Scatter the bacon-vegetable mixture over the potatoes.

5 In a large bowl, whisk the eggs, salt, and paprika together just until combined. Pour over the vegetables and bacon. Transfer the pan to the oven and bake for about 25 minutes, or until the frittata is puffed and golden.

6 Loosen the edges of the frittata with a silicone spatula and gently slide it onto a large serving plate. Cut into 4 wedges and serve.

CURTIS'S KITCHEN NOTE **SMOKED PAPRIKA** Paprika is ground from dried sweet peppers. The best comes from Spain or Hungary, and it is most commonly sold as sweet (mild) or hot (spicy). When you want to add even more smoky flavor to your food, look for Spanish smoked paprika, such as my favorite, pimentón de la Vera; the peppers are dried over oak to impart a wonderful flavor.

ere's a light and tasty dinner for when it's so warm that you can't bear to turn on the stove. It takes no time to prep and cook, and if you want to linger over a predinner glass of wine, it tastes just as good when not piping hot.

GRILLED TUNA AND VEGETABLES WITH GARLIC OIL

serves
4

PREP TIME: 10 minutes
COOKING TIME: 15 minutes

7 tablespoons extra-virgin olive oil

4 garlic cloves, minced

2 tablespoons chopped fresh flat-leaf parsley

Kosher salt and freshly ground black pepper

4 small Japanese eggplants (about 1 pound total), halved lengthwise

4 small zucchini (about 1 pound total), halved lengthwise

1 large yellow onion, cut into ½-inch-thick rounds

Four 5-ounce tuna steaks (about 1 inch thick)

2 lemons, cut in half and seeds removed

1 Prepare an outdoor grill for medium-high cooking over direct heat.

2 In a small bowl, mix the olive oil, garlic, and parsley together. Season to taste with salt and pepper. Put the eggplant, zucchini, and onions on a large, rimmed baking sheet and coat with 2 tablespoons of the garlic oil.

3 Arrange the vegetables on the grill and cook, turning occasionally, for about 6 minutes, or until the zucchini and onion are barely tender. Transfer the zucchini and onions to a plate. Grill the eggplant for about 4 minutes more, or until tender and lightly charred. Transfer to the plate. Brush the vegetables with 2 tablespoons of the remaining garlic oil and tent with aluminum foil to keep warm.

4 Coat the tuna with 1 tablespoon of the remaining garlic oil and season with salt and pepper. Grill the tuna for about 1½ minutes, or until the bottom is opaque and seared with grill marks. Starting at the corner nearest to you, slide a metal spatula under each tuna steak and turn over. Add the lemon halves, cut side down, to the grill. Cook the tuna for about 1½ minutes longer, or until the tuna is just seared and opaque on the outside but still red in the center. Cook the lemons for about 2 minutes total, or until seared with grill marks, and remove from the grill.

5 Transfer the vegetables and tuna to plates and drizzle with the remaining garlic oil. Serve with the grilled lemons so guests can squeeze the juice over the tuna and vegetables.

 **ACINI WITH PARMESAN AND PEPPER**
Acini pasta (sometimes called acini de pepe) is named for its peppercorn shape, and I love its ability to soak up sauces, such as the garlic oil and juices from the tuna and vegetables in this recipe. In a large pot of boiling salted water, cook the acini until al dente. Drain. Return the hot acini to the pot and toss with a bit of extra-virgin olive oil, pepper, and grated Parmesan cheese. Season to taste with salt.

To me, Korean cuisine is better at home than in restaurants. I was lucky enough to learn how to cook it from the best. My Korean mother-in-law, Diane, makes an incredible kimchi, and I now know that if you have a jar of kimchi and leftover steamed rice in the fridge, you always have a delicious meal on hand. We eat this fried rice most often as a main course for dinner, but it can also be served as a side dish to Korean Steak Tacos (page 41).

KIMCHI FRIED RICE

serves
4

PREP TIME: 10 minutes
COOKING TIME: 10 minutes

10 scallions

6 tablespoons canola oil

4 large eggs, beaten

4 cups cold Perfect Rice (see page 9)

3 carrots, cut into ¼-inch pieces

1½ cups napa cabbage kimchi, drained and very coarsely chopped

¼ cup soy sauce

2 teaspoons toasted sesame oil

Kosher salt

1½ teaspoons black or white sesame seeds, toasted (see Kitchen Note, page 68)

Sriracha or other hot sauce, for serving

1. Cut the dark green tops of the scallions on the diagonal into 1-inch pieces. Finely chop the white and pale green parts. Reserve one-fourth of the dark green scallion tops for garnish.

2. Heat a wok or large skillet over medium-high heat. Add 2 tablespoons of the canola oil and tilt to coat the cooking surface. Add the eggs and quickly stir for about 30 seconds, or until just cooked but still wet. Transfer to a plate.

3. Add the remaining ¼ cup canola oil to the pan. Once the oil is hot, add the rice and cook, allowing the rice to become slightly crisp on the bottom of the wok before stirring, for about 4 minutes, or until heated through. Add the carrots and stir for about 1 minute, or until beginning to soften. Stir in the kimchi, followed by the scallions (both tops and bottoms), and stir for about 2 minutes, or until heated through. Add the soy sauce and sesame oil and stir for about 1 minute. Stir in the eggs and season to taste with salt.

4. Transfer the rice to a large serving bowl. Sprinkle with the sesame seeds and the reserved scallions. Serve hot, with the hot sauce.

isotto was one of the first dishes I had to master while cooking in fine-dining restaurants. I wanted to share this recipe because once you find a good risotto, you'll come back to it time and time again. This version uses a combination of mushrooms to give loads of earthy flavor. I found the selection suggested below at my local Asian market, but feel free to swap them for any mushrooms you like. Most risotto recipes call for constant stirring, but you can actually leave the stove occasionally to chop some herbs or do another quick job.

MUSHROOM RISOTTO WITH FRESH HERBS

serves
4

PREP TIME: 10 minutes
COOKING TIME: 40 minutes

4 tablespoons (½ stick) unsalted butter

2 large portobello mushroom caps (about 10 ounces total), dark gills scraped out with a spoon, cut into ½-inch-thick slices

1¼ pounds assorted mushrooms, such as oyster, maitake, and bunashimeji, trimmed

2 large sprigs of fresh thyme

Kosher salt and freshly ground black pepper

2 tablespoons extra-virgin olive oil

½ cup thinly sliced shallots

3 garlic cloves, finely chopped

2 cups Arborio rice

1 cup dry white wine

6 cups reduced-sodium chicken broth, or as needed

⅔ cup freshly grated Parmesan cheese, plus grated or shaved cheese (see Kitchen Note), for serving

3 tablespoons chopped fresh chives

2 tablespoons chopped fresh basil

1 Heat a large heavy pot over medium-high heat. Add 2 tablespoons of the butter and swirl the pan to melt the butter. Add the mushrooms and thyme and cook, stirring occasionally, for about 12 minutes, or until the mushrooms are tender and beginning to brown. (It may look like a lot of mushrooms when you first add them to the pan, but they cook down considerably.) Season the mushrooms to taste with salt and pepper. Transfer the mushrooms to a medium bowl, cover to keep warm, and set aside.

2 Return the saucepan to medium heat. Add the olive oil, then add the shallots and cook, stirring often, for about 2 minutes, or until tender but not brown. Stir in the garlic and cook for about 1 minute, or until fragrant. Add the rice and stir for about 1 minute, or until it is well coated. Add the wine and stir constantly for about 2 minutes, or until most of the wine has evaporated. Raise the heat to medium-high, add 1 cup of the broth, and cook, stirring almost constantly and keeping the mixture at a steady simmer, until it is absorbed. Continuing to add the broth 1 cup at a time, stirring until each addition is almost completely absorbed before adding more, cook for 20 to 25 minutes, or until the rice is al dente (the center of a grain of rice should be slightly firm when bitten into) and has formed a creamy sauce.

3 Remove from the heat and remove and discard the thyme stems. Stir in the ⅔ cup grated Parmesan cheese, the reserved mushrooms, and the remaining 2 tablespoons butter. Season to taste with salt.

4 Immediately spoon the risotto into four warm serving bowls. Sprinkle with the chives and basil. Sprinkle grated or shaved Parmesan cheese over the top and serve at once.

PARMESAN CHEESE The ultimate grating cheese, true Parmesan cheese is imported from Italy and can be identified by the words *Parmigiano-Reggiano* stamped all over the rind. Our domestic Parmesan cheese (sold refrigerated, not the canned stuff) is good too, and it is certainly a budget-saver. For the best, freshest flavor, buy Parmesan cheese in a wedge and grate it just before using.

For a change of pace and to add a bit of visual flair to your food, Parmesan shavings are a nice alternative to grated cheese. You'll need a wedge of cheese and a vegetable peeler. Working over the food, shave curls of cheese from the wedge. That's it! Just as with shredded Parmesan cheese, use as much or as little as you wish.

This festive cocktail is the perfect thing to serve on a beautiful summer day. It's a delicate balance of light, crisp Sauvignon Blanc and St-Germain, an elderflower liqueur. I've added a bunch of summer fruits that not only taste amazing but look stunning too.

WHITE SANGRÍA

serves
4

PREP TIME: 5 minutes, plus at least 2 hours chilling time

One 750-ml bottle Sauvignon Blanc

½ cup St-Germain elderflower liqueur

½ cup sugar, preferably superfine

10 ounces fresh strawberries, hulled, halved if large

2 ripe plums, preferably yellow, pitted and cut into thin wedges

2 nectarines, preferably white, pitted and cut into thin wedges

1 cup green or red seedless grapes, halved if large

1 lemon

Ice cubes

1 In a large pitcher, combine the wine, elderflower liqueur, and sugar and stir to dissolve the sugar. Add the strawberries, plums, nectarines, and grapes.

2 Using a vegetable peeler, remove the zest from the lemon, trying to avoid the white pith that lies beneath the yellow skin. Add the zest to the pitcher. Squeeze and strain the lemon juice and add to the pitcher. Cover and refrigerate for at least 2 hours, or, preferably, overnight.

3 Pour the sangría into ice-filled glasses, making sure that each serving includes some fruit. Serve immediately.

THRIFTY THURSDAYS

Chicken Cassoulet with Fennel and Bacon   110

Grilled Ginger-Sesame Chicken Salad   113

Sliders with Red Onion Marmalade and Blue Cheese   114

Asian Beef and Vegetable Lettuce Cups   117

Hearty Split Pea Soup with Cheesy Croutons   118

Winter Vegetable and Italian Sausage Soup   121

Conchiglie Pasta with Chorizo, Red Bell Peppers, and Spinach   122

Grilled Vegetable and Arugula Salad with Goat Cheese Crostini   125

Roasted Cauliflower, Broccoli, and Pasta Bake with White Cheddar   126

Bow-Tie Pasta with Corn, Thyme, and Parmesan   129

Cinnamon Rice Milk (Horchata)   130

THURSDAY BUZZES ALONG IN TYPICAL WORK- week fashion, but you can almost taste the weekend. While you're cooking up plans for date-night dinners and barbecues with friends, save up for the fun ahead by serving an inexpensive dinner tonight.

Let me let you in on a little culinary secret: Less expensive cuts of meat aren't necessarily of lower quality. Often they're just less popular. It's funny, because these cheaper cuts can be the most flavorful. Just compare economical chicken thighs to higher-priced chicken breasts, and you'll see what I mean. All around the world, from Italy to Mexico, people use these less desirable cuts to create mouthwatering "peasant" dishes. Slow-cooked with an emphasis on flavor, these humble recipes have become culinary classics of a culture for good reason.

There are a few tricks to cutting down on food costs, any day of the week: Grow your own veggies or buy what's in season. When produce is at its peak, the market will have a surplus and prices will be lower. Excite your palate with unexpected proteins, such as lentils, split peas, and beans. Simmer them with a touch of bacon or sausage to give their flavors a meaty edge. (To save even more, replace canned beans with dried ones and cook them yourself.) When you do splurge for more costly proteins, stretch them farther. They'll shine just as brightly when accompanied by loads of irresistible veggies or pasta. And, maybe most important, when you find a recipe you love, make extra. Leftovers become the best money-saving lunches.

There are few recipes that are better suited for warming you up on a cold night than cassoulet, a slow-cooked casserole from southwestern France traditionally made with beans, duck, and pork. My version is much lighter but just as satisfying. Fresh herbs, bacon, and a Parmesan bread crumb topping lend loads of flavor.

CHICKEN CASSOULET WITH FENNEL AND BACON

serves
4

PREP TIME: 10 minutes

COOKING TIME: 1 hour 20 minutes, plus 15 minutes resting time

4 whole chicken legs (thighs and drumsticks; about 10 ounces each), excess fat removed

2 teaspoons olive oil

Kosher salt and freshly ground black pepper

4 slices bacon, coarsely chopped

1 yellow onion, finely chopped

1 fennel bulb, trimmed and cut into ½-inch pieces

1 carrot, cut into ½-inch pieces

1 tablespoon finely chopped fresh rosemary

1 tablespoon finely chopped fresh thyme

4 garlic cloves, finely chopped

2 teaspoons fennel seeds, ground with a mortar and pestle or spice grinder

1 cup reduced-sodium chicken broth

One 15-ounce can cannellini beans, drained and rinsed

½ cup panko (Japanese bread crumbs)

⅓ cup freshly grated Parmesan cheese

1 Preheat the oven to 375°F.

2 Coat the chicken legs with the olive oil and season with salt and pepper. Place the legs on a large heavy rimmed baking sheet and roast for about 40 minutes, or until they are golden brown and barely pink at the bone when pierced with the tip of a small sharp knife and much of their fat has been rendered. Remove from the oven; leave the oven on.

3 Meanwhile, heat a large heavy skillet over medium heat. Add the bacon and cook, stirring occasionally, for about 8 minutes, or until crisp. Add the onions and cook, stirring occasionally, for about 5 minutes, or until tender. Add the fennel and carrots and cook, stirring occasionally, for about 5 minutes, or until tender. Stir in the rosemary, thyme, garlic, and ground fennel seeds and cook for about 2 minutes, or until fragrant. Stir in the broth and beans.

4 Transfer the bean mixture to a 13 × 9 × 2-inch baking dish. Nestle the chicken legs in the beans. In a small bowl, mix the panko and Parmesan cheese to blend. Sprinkle most of the panko mixture over the beans (don't worry if the juices are soaked up by some of the crumbs) and the remainder over the chicken.

5 Bake for about 40 minutes, or until the bean mixture is bubbling all over and the panko topping is crisp and golden brown. Let stand for about 15 minutes before serving.

ROUNDING OUT THE MEAL FRISÉE, SHAVED FENNEL, AND CELERY SALAD WITH CAPER-PARSLEY VINAIGRETTE With its classic French flavors, this salad is great with a cassoulet, but it is also delicious with the Chicken and Chorizo Paella (page 79). Using a mandolin, V-slicer, or chef's knife, cut fennel bulbs and celery ribs into very thin slices. In a medium bowl, toss the frisée with the sliced fennel and celery and enough Caper-Parsley Vinaigrette (page 52) to coat. Season to taste with salt and pepper and serve.

I had never had a Chinese chicken salad until I came to the States. I'm just going to say it out loud—I love it. The secret to this dish is the dressing: sweet hoisin, spicy Sriracha, salty soy, rich sesame oil, with the fresh flavor of ginger punching through it all. It's so good that I use it as the chicken marinade as well.

GRILLED GINGER-SESAME CHICKEN SALAD

serves
4

PREP TIME: 15 minutes, plus at least 30 minutes marinating time
COOKING TIME: 10 minutes, plus 15 minutes cooling time

Ginger-Sesame Marinade/ Dressing

¼ cup reduced-sodium soy sauce

3 tablespoons very finely chopped peeled fresh ginger

3 tablespoons canola oil

2 tablespoons hoisin sauce

1 tablespoon toasted sesame oil

1 teaspoon Sriracha sauce

1 teaspoon kosher salt

2 boneless, skinless chicken breast halves (about 9 ounces each)

¼ cup red wine vinegar

¼ cup minced scallions (white and green parts)

Salad

1 pound napa cabbage, halved lengthwise and very thinly sliced crosswise

2 carrots, cut into matchstick-size strips

3 scallions (white and green parts), thinly sliced on a sharp diagonal

⅔ cup lightly packed fresh cilantro leaves

½ cup slivered almonds, toasted (see Kitchen Note)

1 teaspoon white sesame seeds, toasted (see Kitchen Note, page 68)

1 teaspoon black sesame seeds (optional)

1 To make the marinade: In a medium bowl, whisk the soy sauce, ginger, canola oil, hoisin sauce, sesame oil, Sriracha, and salt to blend. Transfer 3 tablespoons of the mixture to a baking dish, then add the chicken and turn to coat it. Cover and refrigerate for 30 minutes, turning after 15 minutes, or up to 1 day, turning occasionally.

2 To make the dressing: Whisk the vinegar and scallions into the remaining marinade. Set aside.

3 Heat a grill pan over medium-high heat. Remove the chicken from the marinade, add to the grill pan, and cook for about 4 minutes per side, or until the chicken shows no sign of pink when pierced in the thickest part with the tip of a small sharp knife. Transfer to a cutting board and let cool for 15 minutes.

4 Cut the chicken crosswise into ¼-inch-thick slices.

5 To assemble the salad: In a large bowl, toss the chicken, cabbage, carrots, scallions, and cilantro with enough dressing to coat lightly.

6 Mound the salad in the center of four plates. Rewhisk the dressing and drizzle a little over and around the salad. Sprinkle the almonds and sesame seeds over and serve.

TOASTING NUTS To toast walnuts, pecans, or almonds, spread them on a large, rimmed baking sheet. Bake in a 350°F oven, stirring occasionally, until lightly toasted and fragrant, about 10 minutes. Transfer to a plate and let cool before using.

ere's how to take something as familiar as a burger and make it special. The red onion marmalade has become a staple at my house; I put it on sausages and pork chops as well as on these miniature burgers. Spicy arugula and sharp blue cheese pair perfectly with the rich beef and sweet marmalade. The creamy but crunchy "Fireworks" Coleslaw on page 231 goes great with the sliders.

SLIDERS WITH RED ONION MARMALADE AND BLUE CHEESE

serves
4

PREP TIME: 10 minutes
COOKING TIME: 40 minutes

Red Onion Marmalade

3 tablespoons unsalted butter

3 medium red onions, halved and cut into ¼-inch-thick half-moons

½ cup sugar

1 cup dry red wine

¼ cup red wine vinegar

Kosher salt and freshly ground black pepper

Quick Aïoli

½ cup mayonnaise

1½ teaspoons fresh lemon juice

1 teaspoon Dijon mustard

2 garlic cloves, finely chopped

Kosher salt and freshly ground black pepper

Sliders

1½ pounds lean ground beef

Olive oil, for coating

Kosher salt and freshly ground black pepper

8 slider buns or whole wheat dinner rolls, split in half

1 cup crumbled blue cheese (4 ounces)

2 ounces baby arugula (about 3 cups)

1   To make the marmalade: Heat a large heavy skillet over medium-high heat. Add the butter and swirl the pan to melt the butter. Add the onions and cook, stirring occasionally, for about 5 minutes, or until they begin to soften. Reduce the heat to low and cook for about 12 minutes, or until the onions are tender.

2   Sprinkle in the sugar and stir well. Add the wine and vinegar and cook, stirring often, for about 15 minutes, or until the liquid is reduced and syrupy. Season to taste with salt and pepper. Reduce the heat to very low and keep warm, stirring occasionally.

3   Meanwhile, make the aïoli: In a small bowl, whisk the mayonnaise, lemon juice, mustard, and garlic together. Season to taste with salt and pepper. Set aside until ready to serve.

4   To make the sliders: Prepare an outdoor grill for medium-high cooking over direct heat.

5   Shape the ground beef into 8 patties slightly wider than the diameter of the buns. Set the patties on a baking sheet, coat them with a little olive oil, and season with salt and pepper. Brush the cut sides of the buns lightly with olive oil.

6   Transfer the patties to the grill and cook for about 3 minutes, or until the bottoms are browned. Turn the patties over and top with the blue cheese. Grill, covered, for about 2 minutes longer, or until an edge of a patty (not covered with cheese), pressed lightly with a forefinger, feels slightly resilient, for medium-rare. Remove the patties from the grill.

7   Add the buns to the grill, oiled side down, and grill for about 1 minute, or until lightly toasted, with grill marks. Remove from the grill.

8   Spread the buns with the aïoli and mound the arugula on the bottom halves. Top each bottom half with a patty, followed by a generous amount of the marmalade and the upper half of the bun. Serve hot.

nytime you get to eat food with your hands, the fun factor goes up . . . and it somehow tastes better for having to lick your fingers clean. This is a variation on Chinese *san choy bow*, where budget-friendly ground meat and lots of fresh vegetables (including bean sprouts, carrots, and cabbage) are spooned into lettuce leaves and eaten like a taco. The Perfect Jasmine Rice on page 9 complements these well.

ASIAN BEEF AND VEGETABLE LETTUCE CUPS

serves
4

PREP TIME: 10 minutes
COOKING TIME: 10 minutes

1 tablespoon olive oil

1 pound lean ground beef

1 yellow onion, finely chopped

¼ teaspoon cayenne pepper

2 garlic cloves, finely chopped

1 celery rib, finely chopped

1¼ cups finely shredded green cabbage

⅓ cup hoisin sauce, plus more for serving

1½ cups fresh bean sprouts

1 large carrot, coarsely shredded on the large holes of a box grater

3 scallions (white and green parts), thinly sliced on the diagonal

Kosher salt and freshly ground black pepper

1½ heads iceberg lettuce (12 to 20 leaves)

2 tablespoons coarsely chopped fresh cilantro

Lime wedges, for serving

1. Heat a large heavy skillet over medium-high heat. Add 2 teaspoons of the olive oil, then add the beef and cook, stirring occasionally and breaking up the meat with a wooden spoon, for about 4 minutes, or until it loses its raw look. Using a slotted spoon, transfer the beef to a bowl.

2. Return the pan to medium-high heat and add the remaining 1 teaspoon olive oil. Add the onions and cayenne and cook, stirring occasionally, for about 1 minute, or until the onions begin to soften. Stir in the garlic, followed by the celery and cabbage, and cook, stirring often, for about 3 minutes, or until the vegetables are slightly tender.

3. Stir in the hoisin sauce. Return the meat to the pan and cook for about 30 seconds to blend the flavors. Stir in 1 cup of the bean sprouts, the carrots, and one-third of the scallions and season to taste with salt and pepper. Remove the pan from the heat.

4. Arrange the lettuce leaves on four plates. Spoon some of the beef mixture into each of the leaves and garnish with the cilantro, remaining bean sprouts, and scallions. Serve immediately, with lime wedges and hoisin sauce on the side.

ROUNDING OUT THE MEAL BROCCOLI AND CARROT SLAW WITH PEANUTS AND SESAME-GINGER VINAIGRETTE Serve this with Asian-flavored dishes, such as these lettuce cups or Korean Steak Tacos (page 41). Save the broccoli florets to use at another meal. Fit a processor with the large-hole grating disk. Working with a few pieces at a time, push broccoli stems and peeled carrots through the feed tube to grate them. Transfer the vegetables to a medium bowl. Add coarsely chopped roasted peanuts and toss with Ginger-Sesame Dressing (page 113) to coat. Season with salt and serve.

humble peasant dish, this split pea soup costs next to nothing to make. While most soups rely on chicken broth, this one gets its flavorful base mainly from simmering a ham hock in no-cost water. What's more, the hock adds morsels of meat to the soup.

HEARTY SPLIT PEA SOUP WITH CHEESY CROUTONS

serves
6

PREP TIME: 10 minutes
COOKING TIME: 2 hours, plus 10 minutes cooling time

¼ cup olive oil

1 large yellow onion, coarsely chopped

2 carrots, cut into ½-inch pieces

2 celery ribs, cut into ½-inch pieces

3 garlic cloves, finely chopped

3 large sprigs of fresh thyme

Kosher salt and freshly ground black pepper

1 pound green split peas

4 cups reduced-sodium chicken broth

One 14-ounce smoked ham hock

One baguette, crust removed

⅓ cup freshly grated Parmesan cheese

1 Preheat the oven to 425°F.

2 Heat a large heavy pot over medium heat. Add 2 tablespoons of the olive oil, then add the onions, carrots, celery, garlic, and thyme and cook, stirring occasionally, for about 5 minutes, or until the onions are tender. Season with salt and pepper. Stir in the split peas, 8 cups water, and the broth. Add the ham hock, cover the pot, and bring to a simmer. Reduce the heat to medium-low and simmer gently, stirring occasionally, for about 1 hour and 45 minutes, or until the ham hock meat is tender.

3 Meanwhile, tear the baguette into bite-size pieces. On a large, rimmed baking sheet, toss the bread pieces with the remaining 2 tablespoons oil. Season with salt and pepper. Arrange the bread pieces close together in a single layer on the baking sheet and sprinkle with the Parmesan cheese. Bake for about 10 minutes, or until golden brown. Set the croutons aside at room temperature.

4 Reduce the heat under the pot to very low. Using a slotted spoon or tongs, transfer the ham hock to a cutting board. Let stand for about 10 minutes, or until cool enough to handle, then remove the meat, discarding the skin and bone, and chop into bite-size pieces. Stir the ham into the soup. Remove the thyme stems and season the soup to taste with salt and pepper.

5 Ladle the soup into six soup bowls, top with the croutons, and serve.

Throughout the year, Italian cooks will change their minestrone according to what is on hand. During the summer, the soup might include tomatoes and zucchini. This heartier cold-weather version, with root vegetables and chunks of sausage, is perfect with a glass of Chianti and crusty bread. I've purposely given a recipe for a big pot of soup, all the better for creating leftovers for another meal.

WINTER VEGETABLE AND ITALIAN SAUSAGE SOUP

serves
8

PREP TIME: 10 minutes
COOKING TIME: 30 minutes

2 pounds Italian pork sausage, casings removed

2 tablespoons olive oil

2 large yellow onions, finely chopped

10 garlic cloves, finely chopped

2 teaspoons fennel seeds, lightly crushed (use a mortar and pestle or crush under a heavy skillet)

4 sprigs of fresh rosemary

4 carrots, cut into ⅓-inch pieces

4 parsnips, peeled and cut into ⅓-inch pieces

Kosher salt and freshly ground black pepper

8 cups reduced-sodium chicken broth

2 cups shell-shaped pasta

Two 15-ounce cans white kidney (cannellini) beans, rinsed and drained

One 6-ounce bag baby spinach

½ cup shredded Parmesan cheese

1 Heat a large heavy pot over medium-high heat. Add the sausage and cook, stirring and breaking up the meat into bite-size pieces with a wooden spoon, for about 5 minutes, or until browned. Using a slotted spoon, transfer the sausage to a bowl. Pour off the fat from the pot.

2 Add the olive oil to the pot, then add the onions and cook, stirring occasionally, for about 4 minutes, or until softened slightly. Stir in the garlic, fennel seeds, and rosemary and cook for about 1 minute, or until fragrant. Reduce the heat to medium, add the carrots and parsnips, and cook for about 5 minutes, or until almost tender. Season with salt and pepper.

3 Return the sausage to the pot. Stir in the broth and 2 cups water, raise the heat to high, cover, and bring to a boil. Skim any fat or foam that rises to the top of the soup.

4 Add the pasta to the boiling soup and cook, stirring often, for about 8 minutes, or until tender but still firm to the bite. Remove and discard the rosemary stems.

5 Gently stir in the beans and simmer for about 2 minutes, or until heated through. Remove from the heat and fold in the spinach. Season to taste with salt and pepper.

6 Ladle the soup into bowls, top with Parmesan cheese, and serve.

The spicy smoked chorizo sausage with sweet red bell peppers, onions, and garlic give this pasta dish a Spanish feel. The curves in conchiglie, shell pasta, catch the chopped ingredients so you get a little of everything in every bite, but any curly pasta you have on hand—such as fusilli, gemelli, campanelle, or radiatore—will do also.

CONCHIGLIE PASTA WITH CHORIZO, RED BELL PEPPERS, AND SPINACH

serves
4

PREP TIME: 10 minutes
COOKING TIME: 15 minutes

3 tablespoons olive oil

6 ounces smoked Spanish chorizo links, casings removed and cut into ¼-inch pieces

2 large red bell peppers, cored, seeded, and cut into ½-inch pieces

1 large yellow onion, finely chopped

4 garlic cloves, finely chopped

Finely grated zest of 1 lemon

1 tablespoon fresh lemon juice

1 pound conchiglie (pasta shells)

5 ounces fresh baby spinach (about 7 cups not packed)

Kosher salt and freshly ground black pepper

1. Heat a large heavy nonstick skillet over medium-high heat. Add the olive oil, then add the chorizo and cook, stirring occasionally, for about 3 minutes, or until beginning to brown. Add the bell peppers and onions and cook, stirring occasionally, for about 5 minutes, or until the onions are translucent and tender. Stir in the garlic and cook for about 2 minutes, or until tender. Stir in the lemon zest and lemon juice.

2. Meanwhile, bring a large pot of salted water to a boil over high heat. Add the pasta and cook, stirring often to prevent the pasta from sticking together, for about 8 minutes, or until tender but still firm to the bite. Scoop out and reserve ¾ cup of the pasta cooking water. Drain the pasta.

3. Add the pasta, reserved cooking water, and the spinach to the chorizo mixture and stir until the spinach wilts. Season to taste with salt and pepper.

4. Divide the pasta among four pasta bowls and serve.

The surprise in this salad is the grilled avocados. They are a great addition to the time-proven combination of tomatoes, zucchini, and asparagus. Warmed, the avocados become even more unctuous, and they help create a creamy dressing when tossed with the other ingredients.

GRILLED VEGETABLE AND ARUGULA SALAD WITH GOAT CHEESE CROSTINI

serves
4

PREP TIME: 10 minutes
COOKING TIME: 20 minutes

Dijon Vinaigrette

¼ cup extra-virgin olive oil

3 tablespoons white wine vinegar

2 tablespoons finely chopped shallots

1½ tablespoons coarse-grain Dijon mustard

Kosher salt and freshly ground black pepper

Salad and Crostini

5 ounces baby arugula (about 7 cups not packed)

2 firm but ripe Hass avocados, quartered and pitted but not peeled

2 medium tomatoes (preferably heirloom), halved lengthwise

2 plum tomatoes, halved lengthwise

2 zucchini, halved lengthwise

1 pound thin asparagus, woody stems trimmed

Olive oil, for brushing

Kosher salt and freshly ground black pepper

1 small baguette, cut on a very sharp diagonal into twelve ¼-inch-thick slices

4 ounces fresh goat cheese, at room temperature

1. Prepare an outdoor grill for medium-high cooking over direct heat.

2. To make the vinaigrette: In a small bowl, whisk the extra-virgin olive oil, vinegar, shallots, and mustard together to combine (but not emulsify). Season to taste with salt and pepper.

3. To make the salad and crostini: Place the arugula in a large wide shallow bowl or on a large platter and set aside.

4. Lightly coat the cut sides of the avocado quarters, tomatoes, zucchini, and the asparagus with olive oil and season with salt and pepper. Brush one side of the baguette slices with olive oil and season with salt and pepper.

5. Grill the baguette slices for about 2 minutes per side, or until they are toasted. Spread the goat cheese over the crostini. Set aside on a plate.

6. Next, grill the avocados, cut side down, for about 3 minutes, or until they are slightly charred and grill marks form. Using your fingers, remove the peel from the avocados and place the avocados on top of the arugula. Grill the remaining vegetables, turning them as needed, until they are slightly charred, about 5 minutes per side for the tomatoes, about 4 minutes per side for the zucchini, and about 5 minutes for the asparagus. As the vegetables come off the grill, arrange them on top of the arugula.

7. Drizzle the vinaigrette over the salad and the crostini. Season to taste with salt and pepper. Toss the salad at the table and serve with the crostini.

We didn't call it mac and cheese, but when I was a kid my mum would toss veggies and pasta in cheese sauce and bake it until it was bubbling and golden brown. Roasting the vegetables first deepens their flavor and keeps the sauce creamy. This one's for you, Lozza.

ROASTED CAULIFLOWER, BROCCOLI, AND PASTA BAKE WITH WHITE CHEDDAR

serves
4

PREP TIME: 10 minutes
COOKING TIME: 50 minutes

6 tablespoons olive oil, plus more for the baking dish

1 head cauliflower (about 2 pounds), cored and cut into large bite-size florets

Kosher salt and freshly ground black pepper

18 ounces (about 8 cups) broccoli florets

1½ cups (about 5 ounces) penne

4 ounces pancetta, coarsely chopped (about ¾ cup)

1 small yellow onion, finely chopped

1 tablespoon finely chopped fresh thyme

1 tablespoon all-purpose flour

2 cups whole milk

1 cup heavy cream

1¼ cups shredded white Cheddar cheese (5 ounces)

1 cup very coarse fresh multigrain bread crumbs (made in a food processor or blender from 2 slices bread)

1 Position racks in the top third and center of the oven and preheat the oven to 400°F. Lightly oil your quart baking dish or three individual crocks.

2 On a large baking sheet, toss the cauliflower with 2 tablespoons of the olive oil to coat. Season with salt and pepper. Spread evenly on the baking sheet. On a second baking sheet, repeat with the broccoli florets and 2 more tablespoons of the olive oil. Bake for 10 minutes. Stir each sheet of vegetables and switch the positions of the baking sheets from top to bottom. Bake for about 10 minutes more, or until the vegetables are tinged with brown. Set aside. (Leave the oven on.)

3 Meanwhile, bring a large pot of salted water to a boil over high heat. Add the penne and cook, stirring often to prevent the pasta from sticking together, for about 7 minutes, or until tender but still firm to the bite. Drain the penne.

4 Heat a large heavy pot over medium heat. Add 1 tablespoon of the olive oil and the pancetta and cook, stirring occasionally, for about 4 minutes, or until the pancetta is browned and crisp. Add the onions and thyme and cook, stirring occasionally, for about 2 minutes, or until the onions are tender and slightly browned. Sprinkle the flour over the onion mixture, then stir in the flour and cook for about 1 minute, or until it is very pale golden brown.

5 Gradually stir in the milk and cream. Increase the heat to medium-high, and bring to a simmer. Reduce the heat to medium-low and simmer, stirring often, for about 4 minutes, or until the sauce is lightly thickened and has no raw flour taste. Remove from the heat, add the Cheddar cheese, and stir until melted. Season to taste with salt and pepper.

6 Add the vegetables and penne to the cheese sauce and fold together. Spread evenly in the baking dish. In a small bowl, toss the bread crumbs and the remaining 1 tablespoon olive oil to coat, then sprinkle over the vegetable mixture. Bake for about 10 minutes, or until the crumbs are golden. Let stand at room temperature for 5 minutes before serving.

This super-simple pasta shines in late summer, when corn is in season and you can buy it at a good price. Think of it as a corn Alfredo that gets an extra burst of flavor from shallots, garlic, thyme, and white wine, which also balances the richness. If you'd like to add a bit of protein, stir in some shredded roasted chicken or sautéed shrimp.

BOW-TIE PASTA WITH CORN, THYME, AND PARMESAN

serves
4

PREP TIME: 10 minutes
COOKING TIME: 20 minutes

1 pound bow-tie pasta (farfalle)

2 tablespoons olive oil

½ cup thinly sliced shallots

6 garlic cloves, finely chopped

1 cup dry white wine

4 large sprigs of fresh thyme

2 cups fresh corn kernels (cut from about 4 ears)

1¼ cups heavy cream

Kosher salt and freshly ground black pepper

½ cup freshly grated Parmesan cheese

¼ cup chopped fresh chives

1 Bring a large pot of salted water to a boil over high heat. Add the pasta and cook, stirring often to prevent it from sticking together, for about 7 minutes, or until tender but still firm to the bite.

2 Meanwhile, heat a large heavy skillet over medium heat. Add the olive oil, then add the shallots and garlic and cook, stirring occasionally, for about 3 minutes, or until tender. Add the wine and thyme, raise the heat to medium-high, and cook for about 5 minutes, or until the liquid is reduced by three-quarters.

3 Add the corn and cream and bring to a simmer. Reduce the heat to medium-low and simmer gently, stirring occasionally, for about 2 minutes, or until the corn is hot. Keep the sauce warm over very low heat. (The sauce may seem thin at this point, but it will thicken up when combined with the pasta.)

4 Scoop out and reserve ½ cup of the pasta water and drain the pasta. Add the pasta to the corn sauce and toss to coat. Add enough of the reserved pasta water to adjust the sauce to the desired consistency. Season to taste with salt and pepper.

5 Divide the pasta among four pasta bowls. Sprinkle with the Parmesan cheese, chives, and pepper and serve.

CORN KERNELS Cutting the corn kernels off the cobs is easy, but if you do it on a cutting board without some foresight, the kernels may end up all over the kitchen counter. Instead, stand each ear up, on its stalk end, in a wide shallow bowl and, using a sharp knife, cut down the length of the ear where the kernels meet the cob. The kernels will fall neatly into the bowl. You can find a corn cutter, an odd-looking but very useful tool, at kitchenware shops and online. But you will still have to use the bowl trick to contain the kernels.

orchata is a cool and refreshing Mexican beverage, made easily and economically from pantry ingredients. It's the perfect drink to tame the heat of spicy foods, but I love it with just about anything, anytime. This makes a large amount, but it is a treat to have in the refrigerator. See the variation for a truly amazing coffee-flavored cocktail version.

CINNAMON RICE MILK (HORCHATA)

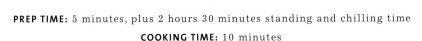

serves
8

PREP TIME: 5 minutes, plus 2 hours 30 minutes standing and chilling time
COOKING TIME: 10 minutes

2½ cups long-grain white rice

1 large cinnamon stick, broken in half

One 12-ounce can evaporated skim milk

One 14-ounce can sweetened condensed milk

½ teaspoon pure vanilla extract

Ice cubes

1. In a medium saucepan, bring 4 cups water to a boil over high heat, about 10 minutes. Remove from the heat and stir in the rice. Set aside for about 30 minutes, or until the rice softens slightly (it will still be crunchy). Drain the rice in a fine-mesh sieve.

2. In a blender, combine 1 cup of the soaked rice, a cinnamon stick half, and 4 cups cold water and blend until the water becomes milky and the rice has dissolved. Strain the rice mixture through a fine-mesh sieve into a large glass or stainless steel bowl. Repeat two times with the remaining rice, using 3 cups water for each batch and adding the remaining cinnamon stick to the second batch. Stir the evaporated milk, condensed milk, and vanilla into the rice mixture. Cover and refrigerate for about 2 hours, or until the mixture is cold and a thick rice sediment has settled on the bottom of the bowl.

3. Slowly pour the mixture into a pitcher, leaving the rice sediment behind. You should have about 8 cups (discard the rice sediment). To serve, pour into ice-filled tall glasses.

VARIATION: HORCHATA AND KAHLÚA COCKTAILS
For each cocktail, fill a cocktail shaker halfway with ice. Add ½ cup of the cinnamon rice milk and 2 tablespoons Kahlúa. Shake the mixture vigorously. Strain into an ice-filled old-fashioned glass. Grate a little orange zest on top and serve immediately, while the milk is still frothy.

FIVE-INGREDIENT FRIDAYS

CONGRATULATIONS! YOU'VE MADE IT TO THE weekend. Fridays are one of my favorite days, because after a hectic week, everyone is focused on having fun. Whether friends are stopping over for a bite or you're settling in for movie night with the kids, Friday dinners should be no fuss. **That's why I created the low-maintenance recipes in this chapter—all of them are made with just five ingredients, not including the staples oil, butter, flour, salt, and pepper.** They're fast, flavorful, and a fitting way to kick off two full days of free time.

I learned that Fridays are fun from my mum. When I was a kid, Lozza worked hard at a flower shop, and by the end of the week she needed a day off from cooking. Enter "Snack Fridays," the do-it-yourself dinners. Whether we were having eggs on toast or homemade pizza, we would all gather in the kitchen and cook up our own creations. It was my favorite meal of the week, and the recipes in this chapter remind me of those dinners.

Even when they're not DIY, all these recipes are easy to pull together and designed to share. Some don't even require forks and knives to eat, and many showcase boldly flavored ingredients such as chorizo, chipotle peppers, and curry paste, which means you won't have to fiddle with seasonings to get a tasty meal. And with just five ingredients, they're simple enough to invite the kids to help and delicious enough to enjoy with friends.

What a classic! Roast chicken is so easy, and this recipe makes it even easier by using chicken legs instead of a whole chicken. The smell of them roasting away really sets the atmosphere. Let the Brussels sprouts cook with the chicken to pick up some of its fabulous flavor, then add a shallot-flavored pilaf, and dinner is served.

ROASTED CHICKEN AND BRUSSELS SPROUTS WITH RICE PILAF

serves
4

PREP TIME: 10 minutes
COOKING TIME: 40 minutes

4 whole chicken legs (thigh and drumsticks; about 12 ounces each)

¼ cup olive oil

Kosher salt and freshly ground black pepper

1 pound Brussels sprouts, trimmed and halved lengthwise

6 shallots: 4 halved, 2 finely chopped

1¼ cups long-grain white rice

1¾ cups reduced-sodium chicken broth

1 Preheat the oven to 450°F.

2 Place the chicken legs on a large heavy rimmed baking sheet. Coat with 1 tablespoon of the olive oil and season with salt and pepper. Roast for about 20 minutes, or until beginning to brown.

3 In a medium bowl, toss the Brussels sprouts and halved shallots with 1 tablespoon of the olive oil and scatter them around the chicken. Continue roasting the chicken with the vegetables for about 20 minutes longer, or until the chicken shows no sign of pink when pierced at the bone with the tip of a small sharp knife and the Brussels sprouts are golden brown and tender but not mushy.

4 Meanwhile, heat a medium heavy saucepan over medium-high heat. Add the remaining 2 tablespoons olive oil, then add the chopped shallots and cook, stirring occasionally, for about 2 minutes, or until tender. Add the rice and stir to coat with the olive oil. Stir in the broth, ½ teaspoon salt, and ⅛ teaspoon pepper and bring to a simmer. Reduce the heat to low, cover the pan tightly, and simmer gently for about 18 minutes, or until the rice is tender and the liquid has been absorbed. Uncover the rice and fluff it with a fork. Cover and let stand off the heat for 5 minutes.

5 Divide the rice, chicken, and vegetables among four dinner plates. Drizzle with the pan juices and serve.

juicy steak is delicious seasoned with nothing more than salt and pepper. But beef can stand up to some serious spicing, like this Mexican-inspired blend of chili powder, cumin, and garlic. The spice rub does double duty as seasoning for the corn on the cob. The "Fireworks" Coleslaw (page 231) is a good choice for a side salad.

GRILLED CHILI-RUBBED T-BONE STEAKS AND CORN ON THE COB

serves
4

PREP TIME: 5 minutes, plus at least 1 hour marinating time
COOKING TIME: 15 minutes

1 tablespoon chili powder

2 teaspoons ground cumin

2 teaspoons garlic powder

Kosher salt and freshly ground black pepper

Two 1¾-pound T-bone steaks

4 ears corn, husked

2 tablespoons extra-virgin olive oil

1 In a small bowl, mix the chili powder, cumin, garlic powder, 1½ teaspoons salt, and 1 teaspoon pepper together. Put the steaks on a platter and generously sprinkle 4 teaspoons of the spice mixture among the steaks; reserve the remaining spice mixture. Cover the steaks with plastic wrap and refrigerate for at least 1 hour, and up to 1 day.

2 Let the steaks stand at room temperature while you preheat the grill. Prepare an outdoor grill for medium-high cooking over direct heat.

3 Place the corn and steaks on a baking sheet and coat with the olive oil. Season the corn with salt and pepper.

4 Transfer the steaks to the grill and cook for about 7 minutes, or until the underside is well browned. Turn the steaks over and add the corn to the grill. Continue grilling the steaks, turning the corn occasionally, for about 7 minutes more, or until the meat feels only slightly resilient when pressed with a fingertip for medium-rare (see Kitchen Note, page 140). Transfer the steaks to a carving board and let rest, uncovered, for about 5 minutes.

5 Meanwhile, continue grilling the corn, with the lid closed, for about 3 more minutes, or until hot and charred in spots. Transfer the corn to a platter and season with the remaining spice mixture.

6 Carve the steaks and transfer to a platter. Pour the carving juices over the steak and serve with the corn.

RESTING AND CARRY-OVER COOKING During cooking, the heat and juices move toward the center of the food. Resting the food at room temperature redistributes the juices throughout, so the meat stays juicy when carved.

Keep in mind that your food will continue to cook slightly while it rests. During the resting period, the food's temperature will rise by a few degrees before it begins to cool off. This phenomenon is called carry-over cooking. My rule of thumb is to let meat rest for about half the time it took to cook, with a maximum resting time of 30 minutes, regardless of the cooking time.

I love a great steak dinner, especially when it is prepared as quickly as this meal, and with only five fabulous ingredients (plus salt, pepper, and oil). The combination of beef and blue cheese is terrific, and that steak-house staple, creamed spinach, is a snap to make.

PEPPERED RIB-EYE STEAKS AND CREAMED SPINACH WITH BLUE CHEESE

serves
4

PREP TIME: 5 minutes
COOKING TIME: 25 minutes

Creamed Spinach

1½ tablespoons olive oil

1 cup finely chopped yellow onions

1 pound fresh baby spinach

¾ cup heavy cream

3 ounces blue cheese, such as Maytag

Kosher salt and freshly ground black pepper

Steaks

Four 12-ounce boneless rib-eye steaks (about 1 inch thick)

Kosher salt

2 tablespoons coarsely cracked black pepper (use a mortar and pestle or crush under a heavy skillet)

¼ cup olive oil

1 To make the creamed spinach: Heat a large saucepan over medium-high heat. Add the olive oil, then add the onions and cook, stirring often, for about 3 minutes, or until translucent. Add the spinach a handful at a time and sauté for 2 to 3 minutes, or just until it wilts. Transfer the spinach to a sieve and press firmly to remove as much liquid as possible.

2 Add the cream to the saucepan, bring to a simmer over high heat, and simmer for about 2 minutes, or until slightly thickened. Stir in the spinach. Coarsely crumble half of the blue cheese over the spinach and toss to coat. Season lightly to taste with salt and pepper. Keep warm over very low heat.

3 To cook the steaks: Place a wire rack on a rimmed baking sheet. Sprinkle the steaks with salt and the cracked pepper, pressing the seasonings into the meat. Heat two large heavy skillets over high heat. Add 2 tablespoons of olive oil to each skillet, then add 2 steaks to each skillet and cook for about 4 minutes per side, or until the meat feels only slightly resilient when touched with a fingertip for medium-rare (see Kitchen Note). Transfer to the wire rack and let rest for 3 minutes.

4 Place the steaks on four dinner plates and spoon the creamed spinach alongside. Sprinkle with the remaining blue cheese and serve.

THE TOUCH TEST An instant-read thermometer is a must-have kitchen tool, but its probe doesn't register the temperature of thin chops and steaks well. For those cuts, rely on the touch test.

As meat cooks, its liquid evaporates and the flesh becomes firmer, and the texture changes as well. Press the meat with the tip of your forefinger. If the meat is rare, it will yield quite a bit. Cooked to medium, it will feel more resistant. Well-done meat will be firm. Let the meat stand for about 3 minutes before serving so that the juices can redistribute themselves.

O n my first trip to Morocco, I was bowled over by the layers of flavor in the food. Harissa is a classic Moroccan spice mixture, often used to flavor lamb. In this dish, it combines with the lamb juices to season everything on the plate. You'll find it in tubes and jars at specialty markets and online.

GRILLED HARISSA RACK OF LAMB
WITH SUMMER SUCCOTASH

serves
4

PREP TIME: 10 minutes

COOKING TIME: 15 minutes, plus 10 minutes resting time

6 tablespoons extra-virgin olive oil

2 tablespoons harissa paste

2 frenched small 8-rib racks of lamb (about 1¼ pounds each), trimmed of all but a thin layer of fat

Kosher salt and freshly ground black pepper

3 ears corn, husked

2 small zucchini, quartered lengthwise

4 ounces green beans, trimmed

1. Prepare an outdoor grill for medium-high cooking over direct heat.

2. Meanwhile, in a small bowl, mix 3 tablespoons of the olive oil and the harissa paste together. Season the lamb racks with salt and pepper. Spread the harissa mixture all over the lamb.

3. Grill the lamb for about 15 minutes, turning occasionally, or until an instant-read thermometer inserted horizontally into the center of the lamb registers 125°F for medium-rare. Transfer the lamb to a carving board and let stand for about 10 minutes.

4. Meanwhile, coat the corn, zucchini, and green beans with 2 tablespoons of the olive oil and season with salt and pepper. Grill the vegetables, turning occasionally and removing them from the grill when they are lightly charred, about 2 minutes for the green beans, about 5 minutes for the zucchini, and about 10 minutes for the corn.

5. Cut the corn kernels off the cobs; transfer the kernels to a large bowl. Cut the zucchini into bite-size pieces and add to the bowl. Add the green beans and drizzle the remaining 1 tablespoon olive oil over the succotash and toss to coat. Season to taste with salt and pepper.

6. Mound the succotash on four dinner plates or a large platter. Cut the lamb racks into individual chops and place over the succotash. Drizzle with the carving juices and serve.

Tacos are always fun to make and eat. I love this recipe because it shows how a terrific meal can come together with just a few well-thought-out ingredients. The smoky, fiery flavor of chipotle brings zest to these tacos. Grilling adds a nice char to the pork, but the meat can also be roasted (see the variation below).

CHIPOTLE PORK TACOS

serves
6

PREP TIME: 10 minutes
COOKING TIME: 20 minutes

⅓ cup canned chipotle chilies in adobo sauce (see Kitchen Note)

1 large white onion, cut in half, half coarsely chopped, half finely chopped

1¼ cups coarsely chopped fresh cilantro

1½ pounds pork tenderloin, trimmed of fat and sinew

Kosher salt

Olive oil, for coating the pork

Twelve 6-inch corn tortillas

1 In a food processor, puree the chipotle chilies, coarsely chopped onions, and 1 cup of the cilantro. To make the salsa, transfer ½ cup of the chipotle puree to a small bowl and mix with 2 tablespoons water. Season with salt and set the salsa aside.

2 Put the pork tenderloin in a baking dish and coat with the remaining chipotle puree. Let stand at room temperature while you prepare the grill.

3 Prepare an outdoor grill for medium-high cooking over direct heat.

4 Remove the pork from the marinade. Season generously with salt and coat with olive oil. Grill the pork, turning and basting it lightly with olive oil as needed, for 12 to 18 minutes, depending on the size of the tenderloin(s), or until an instant-read thermometer inserted in the center of the pork reads 130°F. Transfer to a cutting board and let rest for 5 minutes.

5 Meanwhile, grill the tortillas, turning once or twice, for about 1 minute, or until heated through but still pliable. Transfer to a plate and cover with aluminum foil to keep warm.

6 In another small bowl, mix the finely chopped onions and the remaining ¼ cup cilantro.

7 Cut the pork crosswise into ¼-inch-thick slices and transfer to a small serving platter. Pour the carving juices over the pork and serve with the tortillas, salsa, and onion-cilantro mixture. Have each guest fill two tortillas with pork, adding salsa and the onion-cilantro mixture as desired.

VARIATION: OVEN-ROASTED CHIPOTLE PORK TACOS

Preheat the oven to 400°F. Marinate the pork in the chipotle mixture while the oven preheats. Remove the pork from the marinade and transfer to an oiled baking sheet. Roast until an instant-read thermometer inserted in the center of the roast registers 130°F, about 25 minutes. Let stand for 5 minutes before slicing. Serve with the accompaniments as above.

Quesadillas are Mexico's version of a grilled cheese sandwich. Anything goes when making them, but I like them with chorizo and chilies. You'll find fresh soft chorizo at Latin markets and many supermarkets. If you can't find it, use diced firm Spanish chorizo instead. Be sure to bring out the guacamole (page 43) and tortilla chips.

TWO-CHEESE QUESADILLAS WITH CHORIZO AND HATCH CHILIES

serves
4

PREP TIME: 10 minutes
COOKING TIME: 30 minutes

About 3 tablespoons canola oil

12 ounces fresh Mexican-style chorizo, casings removed

4 large fresh Hatch, Anaheim, or poblano chilies (about 10 ounces total), seeded and cut lengthwise into long thin strips (see Kitchen Note)

Kosher salt

2¾ cups shredded Monterey Jack cheese (about 11 ounces)

2 cups crumbled queso fresco (about 8 ounces)

Four 9-inch flour or whole wheat tortillas

1 Heat a large heavy skillet over medium-high heat. Add 1 tablespoon of the canola oil, then add the chorizo and cook, breaking it up into bite-size pieces with a wooden spoon, for about 8 minutes, or until lightly browned. Using a slotted spoon, transfer the chorizo to a bowl; set aside. Pour out all but 1 tablespoon of the fat from the skillet, or add canola oil if needed.

2 Add the chilies to the skillet, season with salt, and cook, stirring occasionally, for about 10 minutes, or until crisp-tender and slightly charred. Remove from the heat.

3 Meanwhile, heat a griddle or large skillet over medium-low heat. In a medium bowl, mix the Jack cheese and queso fresco together. Brush one side of each tortilla with canola oil. Turn the tortillas oil side down on the work surface.

4 For each quesadilla, sprinkle a heaping ½ cup of the cheese mixture over the bottom half of a tortilla and top with one-fourth each of the chorizo and chilies, then another heaping ½ cup of the cheese mixture. Fold the top half of the tortilla over the filling and press lightly to compact.

5 Working in batches, place the quesadillas on the griddle and cook, turning halfway through cooking, for a total of about about 6 minutes, or until golden brown and the cheese is melted. Transfer to a cutting board, cut into wedges, and serve hot.

HATCH CHILIES Large and shiny green, with a full flavor that sets them apart from other varieties, Hatch chilies, grown in Hatch, New Mexico, are worth waiting for. Markets throughout the region celebrate their late-summer arrival by roasting them outdoors in special rotating drums. Hatch chilies are becoming available outside the Southwest, so look for them at gourmet markets and well-stocked supermarkets. Anaheim or poblano (fresh ancho) chilies are good substitutes.

When I was growing up in Australia, my mum would often make what we called "eggs on toast" for dinner. It was quick and simple, and we always had the ingredients on hand. This is my take on her dish. Broiling the buttered bread gives one side a nice crunch while keeping the other side soft and moist, reminiscent of freshly baked bread. At the same time, the butter takes on a delicious nutty flavor.

SEARED HAM STEAK AND EGGS WITH SMASHED POTATOES AND SOURDOUGH TOAST

serves
4

PREP TIME: 10 minutes
COOKING TIME: 30 minutes

12 small red-skinned potatoes (about 1½ pounds total), scrubbed

6 tablespoons (¾ stick) salted butter, 3 tablespoons softened

One 1¼- to 1½-pound bone-in smoked ham steak (about ¾ inch thick), patted dry

Kosher salt

2 tablespoons plus 2 teaspoons olive oil

Four ¾-inch-thick slices sourdough bread

Nonstick cooking spray

8 large eggs

Freshly ground black pepper

1 Preheat the oven to 200°F.

2 Put the potatoes in a medium saucepan, add enough cold salted water to cover, and bring to a boil over high heat. Reduce the heat to medium and cook for about 12 minutes, or until the potatoes are tender when pierced with the tip of a small sharp knife. Drain and transfer to a cutting board. Gently press on the potatoes with a metal spatula or the bottom of a small pan to crack them open but keep them mostly intact. Let cool.

3 Heat a large heavy nonstick skillet over medium-high heat. Melt 1 tablespoon of the butter in the pan, then add the ham and cook for about 3 minutes per side, or until it is heated through and beginning to caramelize. Transfer the ham to a heatproof platter, tent with foil, and keep warm in the oven.

4 Return the skillet to medium-high heat. Add 2 tablespoons of the butter and the olive oil and swirl to coat the cooking surface. Add the potatoes, sprinkle with salt, and cook, turning halfway through cooking, for about 3 minutes per side, or until golden brown. Transfer the potatoes to the platter with the ham and return to the oven to keep warm.

5 Spread the remaining 3 tablespoons butter over one side of the bread slices. Place the bread buttered side up on a broiler pan in a hot toaster oven and broil for about 3 minutes, or until the tops are toasted golden. (If you don't have a toaster oven, use a broiler.)

6 Meanwhile, heat a large heavy nonstick skillet over medium heat. Spray the pan with nonstick cooking spray. Crack 4 eggs into the pan and season them with salt and pepper. Cover and cook for about 2 minutes, or until the whites are set and the yolks have thickened slightly. Transfer the eggs to a platter and repeat with the remaining eggs.

7 Serve the eggs hot, with the ham, potatoes, and toast.

Homemade pizza is a great way to kick off the weekend. This is my go-to recipe; I like to keep things simple. With too many toppings, the pizza just gets soggy. Use top-notch ingredients—such as artisan salami and heirloom tomatoes—because their flavors are going to be front and center. Green, yellow, striped, or red heirloom tomatoes will add vibrant color. I am providing you with a recipe for my homemade dough, but feel free to use purchased pizza dough. If you don't have a pizza stone and baking paddle, stretch out the dough on oiled baking sheets, then add the topping and bake the pizzas on the baking sheets in the lower part of the oven.

TOMATO-SALAMI PIZZA

serves
4

PREP TIME: 10 minutes
COOKING TIME: 25 minutes

Two 13-ounce balls purchased pizza dough or Homemade Pizza Dough (recipe follows)

Unbleached all-purpose flour, for dusting

¼ cup extra-virgin olive oil

4 teaspoons finely chopped garlic

3 ounces paper-thin slices salami

2 small tomatoes (about 7 ounces each), cut into ¼-inch-thick rounds

10 ounces fresh mozzarella cheese, torn into 2-inch pieces

Kosher salt and freshly ground black pepper

1. Position an oven rack in the bottom third of the oven. Place a pizza stone on the rack and preheat the oven to 500° to 550°F (as high as possible).

2. Stretch out 1 dough ball with floured hands, or roll it out on a floured work surface, until it is about 12 inches in diameter (the dough does not have to be round). Dust a pizza paddle with flour and place the dough on the paddle.

3. Working quickly, drizzle and rub 2 tablespoons of the olive oil over the dough. Sprinkle half of the garlic evenly over the dough and gently rub it into the olive oil. Arrange half of the salami and tomato slices in a single layer, overlapping slightly, on the dough, leaving a 1-inch-wide border around the circumference. Scatter half of the cheese on top. Season with salt and pepper.

4. Carefully slide the pizza off the paddle and onto the hot pizza stone in the oven. Bake for 8 to 12 minutes, or until the crust is crisp and golden brown on the bottom and the cheese has melted and begun to brown. Transfer the pizza to a cutting board. Repeat to make a second pizza.

5. Using a pizza cutter or a large knife, cut the pizzas into wedges and serve.

PIZZA TOPPINGS When making pizza, be creative. If you like things a bit salty, throw on some olives and capers. If you love barbecue, replace the marinara with barbecue sauce. Pizza is a great way to cater to your palate, and if you follow a few tips, it will come out nice and crispy every time.

Vegetables: There are lots of options here, from asparagus to zucchini, but most raw vegetables will give off juices during baking that can make the pizza crust soggy. To solve this problem, slice the vegetables thin and use them sparingly, or sauté them in a little olive oil before adding to the crust.

Meats: Thinly sliced cured meats, such as salami, prosciutto, and soppressata, are all great toppings. If using fresh sausage, cook and drain it first, as raw sausage may not be cooked through by the time the crust is done. Sliced meatballs (check out the Turkey Meatballs with Marinara Sauce on page 12) are another choice.

Cheeses: Mozzarella is the classic pizza cheese. Instead of slicing fresh mozzarella, I tear it into rough chunks for a more rustic feel. Fontina, Gruyère, and Gorgonzola are other great cheeses that melt well and deliver lots of flavor.

Homemade Pizza Dough

Pizza dough is fun to make at home, especially with kids, who love to check on the progress of the magically rising dough. The dough is easily made in a food processor, but I also give instructions for a handmade version.

makes two 13-ounce balls of dough

PREP TIME: 8 minutes, plus 45 minutes rising time

1¼ cups lukewarm water (110° to 115°F)

2 teaspoons honey

1 packet (2¼ teaspoons) active dry yeast

3 cups unbleached all-purpose flour, plus more for dusting

1 teaspoon fine sea salt

1 tablespoon olive oil

1 In a small bowl or a 2-cup measuring cup whisk the warm water, honey, and yeast to blend. Set aside for about 5 minutes, or until foamy. Stir to dissolve the yeast.

2 In a food processor, pulse the flour and salt to combine. With the machine running, pour in the yeast mixture and olive oil and process until the dough forms a ball. Transfer the dough to a work surface and knead for about 3 minutes, or until it is smooth and elastic. Do not add too much flour. The dough will be tacky but should release cleanly from your hands.

3 Divide the dough in half and gently form each half into a ball. Place on a floured rimmed baking sheet and dust the tops with flour. Cover with plastic wrap. Let stand in a warm, draft-free place for about 45 minutes, or until the dough doubles in volume.

VARIATION: **HANDMADE PIZZA DOUGH**

To make the dough without a food processor, whisk the warm water, honey, and yeast together in a large bowl to blend. Let stand for about 5 minutes, or until foamy. Stir to dissolve the yeast. Stir in 1 cup of the flour and the salt. Gradually stir in as much of the remaining flour as needed to make a stiff dough that can no longer be stirred. Turn the dough out onto a well-floured work surface. Knead, adding flour as necessary, until the dough is smooth and elastic but still tacky, about 8 minutes. Proceed as directed above.

W hile the salmon in this dish is delicious, the real star is the orange. The simple orange reduction, which is sweet and sour at the same time, makes a delicious sauce for the salmon and broccolini. The juicy segments add a burst of freshness. For an easier variation, just peel the oranges and cut them into wedges.

PANFRIED SALMON WITH BROCCOLINI AND ORANGE SAUCE

serves
4

PREP TIME: 15 minutes
COOKING TIME: 20 minutes

8 navel oranges

12 ounces broccolini, trimmed

2 tablespoons unsalted butter

2 tablespoons olive oil

Kosher salt and freshly ground black pepper

Four 6-ounce skinless salmon fillets

1. Cut off the tops and bottoms of two oranges. Using a small sharp knife, cut away the peel and white pith from the oranges, following the curve of the oranges from top to bottom. Holding one orange in your hand, and working over a bowl, make 2 cuts along the membranes on either side of a segment, then lift the segment out of the membranes and drop it into the bowl. Repeat to remove all the segments from both oranges. Squeeze the membranes over the bowl to release as much juice as possible and discard them. Pour the accumulated juices into a 2-cup measuring cup; set the segments aside. Squeeze enough juice from the remaining 6 oranges to make 2 cups total juice.

2. Pour the orange juice into a wide heavy saucepan and boil over medium-high heat for about 10 minutes, or until reduced to ½ cup. Remove from the heat and cover to keep warm.

3. Meanwhile, bring a large saucepan of salted water to a boil over high heat. Add the broccolini and cook for about 2 minutes, or just until it is bright green and tender. Drain and transfer to a bowl of ice water to cool completely. Drain well and pat dry with paper towels.

4. Heat a large heavy skillet over medium-high heat. Melt 1 tablespoon of the butter with 1 tablespoon of the olive oil in the pan, add the broccolini, and cook, stirring occasionally, for about 5 minutes, or until heated through. Season to taste with salt and pepper.

5. Meanwhile, sprinkle the salmon fillets with salt and pepper. Heat a large heavy nonstick skillet over medium-high heat. Add the remaining 1 tablespoon olive oil, then add the salmon and cook, turning the salmon over halfway through cooking, for about 3 minutes per side, or until it is mostly opaque, with a rosy center when pierced in the thickest part with the tip of a small knife. Transfer to a platter and let rest for 2 minutes.

6. Divide the broccolini among four dinner plates and top with the salmon fillets. Whisk the remaining 1 tablespoon butter into the orange juice reduction and drizzle over and around the salmon. Garnish with the orange segments and serve.

ave this for when you see a big heap of freshly picked green peas for sale. Make this a group-effort recipe, and enlist some help to shuck the peas. If you would like a side dish, serve Mashed Potatoes (page 226).

SEARED SCALLOPS AND PEAS WITH BACON AND MINT

serves
4

PREP TIME: 15 minutes
COOKING TIME: 15 minutes

2½ cups shelled fresh peas (from 2 pounds peas in the pod)

3 slices thick-sliced bacon, cut crosswise into ¼-inch-wide strips

½ cup coarsely chopped shallots

2 tablespoons coarsely chopped fresh mint

Kosher salt and freshly ground black pepper

12 large sea scallops, tough side muscle removed and patted dry

2 tablespoons olive oil

1. Bring a large saucepan of salted water to a boil over high heat. Add the peas and cook for about 2 minutes, or just until they are bright green and tender. Drain and transfer the peas to a bowl of ice water to cool. Drain well.

2. Heat a large heavy skillet over medium-high heat. Add the bacon and cook, stirring occasionally, for about 5 minutes, or until golden and crisp. Using a slotted spoon, transfer the bacon to paper towels to drain. Pour off all but a thin layer of fat from the skillet.

3. Add the shallots to the skillet and cook, stirring often, for about 2 minutes, or until softened. Add the peas and cook, stirring often, for about 3 minutes, or until they are heated through. Stir in the bacon and mint. Season to taste with salt and pepper. Keep warm over very low heat.

4. Meanwhile, season the scallops with salt and pepper. Heat another large heavy skillet over high heat until it is very hot. Add the olive oil, then add the scallops and cook for about 2 minutes, or until the underside is golden brown. Turn the scallops and cook for about 2 minutes more, or until the other side is golden brown but the scallops are still translucent when pierced in the center with the tip of a small knife. Transfer the scallops to paper towels to drain briefly.

5. Divide the pea mixture and scallops among four dinner plates and serve.

HEAT IT UP Whenever I take novices into a professional kitchen, they are surprised at how hot it is. The high heat of the burners and ovens gives food a nice, even browning, and that caramelized surface translates into delicious flavor. To promote a good sear, I always heat my skillets over medium-high heat until they are good and hot before adding the oil and then the food. After adding the meat, don't move it for at least 2 minutes, to allow a crust to form on the underside. This crust will release the meat from the skillet, but if you poke and mess around with it too soon, it will only stick . . . so pour yourself a glass of wine; you have a few minutes.

y young son, Hudson, knows a good thing when he tastes it, and grilled asparagus is his favorite finger food. This recipe is not only made with just five ingredients, it also cooks from start to finish in just 15 minutes. It can be served, if you like, with your favorite rice—long-grain, basmati, or jasmine (page 9). I've included an oven-roasted variation for when you want to make this indoors.

GRILLED SHRIMP AND ASPARAGUS WITH LEMON-SHALLOT VINAIGRETTE

serves
4

PREP TIME: 10 minutes
COOKING TIME: 5 minutes

1 lemon

2 tablespoons finely chopped shallots

¼ cup extra-virgin olive oil

Kosher salt and freshly ground black pepper

1 pound medium-thin asparagus, woody ends trimmed

1 pound large (21 to 30 count) shrimp, peeled, tails left on, and deveined

⅓ cup shaved Pecorino Romano cheese (optional; see page 103)

1 Prepare an outdoor grill for medium-high cooking over direct heat.

2 Grate the zest from the lemon into a small bowl. Squeeze 2 tablespoons of juice from the lemon and add to the bowl. Add the shallots and whisk together. Gradually whisk in 2 tablespoons of the olive oil and season to taste with salt and pepper.

3 Spread the asparagus and shrimp on a large rimmed baking sheet. Coat with the remaining 2 tablespoons olive oil and season with salt and pepper. Transfer the shrimp and asparagus to the grill and cook, turning the asparagus and shrimp occasionally, for about 4 minutes, or until the shrimp are almost opaque throughout when pierced with the tip of a sharp knife and the asparagus are crisp-tender. Remove from the grill.

4 In a large bowl, toss the asparagus with enough vinaigrette to coat. Season to taste with salt and pepper. Divide the asparagus among four dinner plates and top with the shrimp. Drizzle more vinaigrette over the shrimp. Sprinkle the Pecorino Romano cheese over the shrimp, if desired, and serve hot.

VARIATION: OVEN-ROASTED SHRIMP AND ASPARAGUS
The key to this high-roast cooking technique is to use a large half sheet pan (a rimmed baking sheet measuring 18 x 13 inches) and to spread the ingredients out well so they brown lightly (for caramelized flavor) and don't steam. Preheat the oven to 450°F. Toss the asparagus with 2 tablespoons of the olive oil on the baking sheet and season with salt and pepper. Spread the asparagus on one side of the baking sheet, separating the spears. Roast until they turn a brighter shade of green, about 3 minutes. Meanwhile, in a large bowl, toss the shrimp with the remaining 2 tablespoons olive oil and season with salt and pepper. Remove the pan from the oven and arrange the shrimp on the empty side. Return to the oven and roast until the shrimp are almost opaque throughout and the asparagus are crisp-tender, about 5 minutes. Proceed with the recipe as directed.

Brown butter is butter that is cooked until it takes on an amber brown color and nutty flavor. There's nothing to it, but you'll be amazed at what this extra step does for a simple pasta dish. Of course, the basil—which has the ability to take a good recipe and make it better—doesn't hurt, either. Cooked shrimp or chicken can be added to the pasta.

ORECCHIETTE WITH BROWN BUTTER, BROCCOLI, PINE NUTS, AND BASIL

serves
4

PREP TIME: 5 minutes
COOKING TIME: 15 minutes

13 ounces broccoli florets with 1-inch stems (about 6 cups)

1 pound orecchiette

8 tablespoons (1 stick) unsalted butter

½ cup lightly packed fresh basil leaves, coarsely chopped

½ cup pine nuts, toasted (see Kitchen Note, page 20)

2 tablespoons fresh lemon juice

Kosher salt and freshly ground black pepper

Extra-virgin olive oil, for serving

1. Bring a large pot of salted water to a boil over high heat. Add the broccoli and cook for about 2 minutes, or just until bright green. Using a mesh spoon or sieve, scoop the broccoli out of the water, draining it well, and transfer to a rimmed baking sheet. Set aside.

2. Return the water to a boil. Add the orecchiette and cook, stirring often to ensure it doesn't stick together, for about 8 minutes, or until tender but still firm to the bite. Scoop out and reserve ½ cup of the pasta cooking water. Drain the orecchiette.

3. Meanwhile, heat a large heavy skillet over medium-high heat. Add the butter and stir for about 2 minutes, or until it has turned hazelnut brown. Add the broccoli and cook, stirring often, for about 1 minute, or until hot.

4. Add the pasta to the broccoli mixture and stir gently to combine. Stir in the basil, pine nuts, and lemon juice. Season to taste with salt and pepper. Stir in enough of the reserved cooking water to moisten the pasta as necessary.

5. Divide the pasta among four pasta bowls, drizzle with olive oil, and serve.

DELICATE HERBS Using a large knife, chop herbs just before using, because the more delicate ones, like basil, will oxidize and turn brown soon after chopping. Make sure your knife is sharp—a dull one will bruise the herbs.

What strikes me every time I go to Italy is how simple real Italian cooking is. This pasta doesn't need meat, because the kale has so much character. Any kale will do, but I am partial to the black kale (*cavolo nero* or dinosaur kale), as it is an Italian variety. If you would like to add some protein to this dish, see the variation.

SPAGHETTI WITH GARLIC, LEMON, KALE, AND PARMESAN

serves
4

PREP TIME: 10 minutes
COOKING TIME: 15 minutes

1 pound kale, well washed, tough stems removed, leaves thinly sliced

1 pound spaghetti

¾ cup extra-virgin olive oil

6 garlic cloves, finely chopped

2 tablespoons grated lemon zest (from about 4 lemons)

Kosher salt and coarsely ground black pepper

2 tablespoons fresh lemon juice

3 ounces Parmesan cheese, shaved or freshly grated

1 Bring a large pot of salted water to a boil over high heat. Add the kale and cook for about 5 minutes, stirring occasionally, or until tender. Using a mesh spoon or sieve, scoop the kale out of the water, draining it well, and transfer to a bowl.

2 Return the water to a boil. Add the spaghetti and cook, stirring often to ensure it doesn't stick together, for about 8 minutes, or until tender but still firm to the bite. Scoop out and reserve ½ cup of the pasta cooking water. Drain the spaghetti.

3 Heat a large heavy skillet over medium heat. Add ½ cup of the olive oil and the garlic and cook for about 30 seconds, or just until fragrant. Stir in the kale, add the lemon zest, and season with salt and pepper. Add the spaghetti and the remaining ¼ cup olive oil and toss to coat. Stir in the lemon juice, followed by half of the Parmesan cheese. Season to taste with salt and pepper. Stir in enough of the reserved cooking water to moisten the pasta as necessary.

4 Divide the pasta among four pasta bowls, top with the remaining Parmesan cheese, and serve.

VARIATION: SPAGHETTI WITH KALE AND SAUSAGE
In step 3, heat the skillet over medium heat, then add 8 ounces Italian sausage, casings removed, and cook, breaking up the sausage with the side of a spoon, for about 8 minutes, or until browned. Using a slotted spoon, transfer the sausage to a plate. Discard the fat in the pan. Proceed as directed, scraping up the browned bits in the pan when you cook the kale.

hai red curry paste typically has more than eight different ingredients, including hot red pepper and lemongrass, so buying it ready-made is certainly easier than making your own. Look for it in the ethnic foods section of your supermarket or at Asian grocers. You can add 1 pound large shrimp, peeled and deveined, to the curry during the last few minutes of cooking, if you wish. Serve the curry over Perfect Jasmine Rice (page 9).

THAI RED CURRY WITH
BUTTERNUT SQUASH AND CHICKPEAS

serves
4

PREP TIME: 10 minutes
COOKING TIME: 35 minutes

1 small butternut squash (about 2 pounds)

2 tablespoons canola oil

⅓ cup Thai red curry paste

One 15-ounce can chickpeas (garbanzo beans), drained and rinsed

Kosher salt

One 13-ounce can unsweetened coconut milk

⅓ cup fresh cilantro, plus more for garnish

1 Peel the squash, cut it lengthwise in half, and scoop out the seeds. Cut off the top where it meets the bulbous bottom. Cut the bulb end into ¾-inch-wide wedges. Cut the neck end into ½-inch-thick half-moons.

2 Heat a large heavy pot over medium-high heat. Add the canola oil, then add the curry paste and stir for about 1 minute, or until fragrant. Add the squash and stir to coat with the curry paste. Stir in the chickpeas and season with salt. Add the coconut milk and ¾ cup water and bring to a simmer. Reduce the heat to medium-low, cover, and simmer gently for about 10 minutes, or until the squash just begins to soften.

3 Stir in the cilantro and simmer, uncovered, stirring occasionally, for about 20 minutes, or until the squash is tender but not falling apart and the sauce has reduced slightly. Season to taste with salt.

4 Divide the curry among four soup bowls, top with cilantro, and serve.

SPICE IT UP Have you noticed the number of new spices on the market? Seasonings that you used to have to bring back home from a trip abroad are now for sale at the local grocer. Spice blends, which can come in powdered or paste form, are made up of a long list of ingredients, so you get a huge amount of flavor in every spoonful. Two of my favorites are Morocco's harissa (a fiery paste made from chilies, garlic, cumin, coriander, caraway, and olive oil) and Thai red curry paste (containing red chilies, lemongrass, cilantro, and more). Refrigerate these in their containers after opening, and they will keep for at least 6 months.

Celebrate the arrival of Friday with a glass of bubbly. Can't decide between Champagne or a cocktail? Combine the two in this festive drink. The addition of sorbetto (Italian for sorbet) gives it a touch of sweetness and acidity.

BUBBLES AND SORBETTO

serves
6

PREP TIME: 5 minutes

About ½ cup good-quality lemon sorbet

⅓ cup St-Germain elderflower liqueur

One 750-ml bottle Champagne or Prosecco, chilled

6 wide strips lemon zest, removed with a vegetable peeler

1 Place a small scoop (about 2 teaspoons) of the sorbet into each of six Champagne flutes. Pour the liqueur over the sorbet. Gently pour the Champagne into the glasses. Garnish with the lemon zest and serve immediately.

DINNER PARTY
SATURDAYS

WHETHER YOU'RE CELEBRATING A BIRTHDAY or catching up around the table with your favorite people, Saturday night is made for entertaining. This chapter gives you all you need to throw the ultimate dinner party.

Having friends over for dinner is one of my biggest pleasures. Food has an incredible ability to bring people closer together, and to me, there's no better gift than a home-cooked meal. I know many people panic at the thought of cooking for others—but trust me, you don't need to. The secret to a successful dinner party is organization. Shop and prep a few things a day or two ahead; each of these recipes includes elements that can be made in advance. Get out the candles, set the table, and chill the wine early in the day. With the small tasks out of the way, you can focus on cooking an extraordinary meal.

Many of the recipes in this chapter feature luxurious ingredients such as lobster, crab, or scallops, which speak for themselves. Others are such crowd-pleasers that you can't go wrong. And while some may require longer cooking times or stretch your culinary comfort zone a bit, the recipes were written with all the details you need to cook with confidence.

Keep in mind that a festive atmosphere is as important as the masterful dishes you serve. **What makes a dinner party special isn't perfectly browned scallops or a sky-high soufflé: It's you.** So put on your favorite music, pour yourself a glass of wine, and when the oven timer dings, feel free to take a bow.

his is one of my favorite ways to serve rib-eye steak. The richness of the blue cheese butter melting into the grilled steaks is balanced by the tangy vinaigrette. Roasting the tomatoes enhances their sweetness, and grilling the green beans brings a new twist to these dinnertime favorites. Place them crosswise on the cooking grate or use a grill basket to contain them. Baked potatoes make a classic side dish.

GRILLED RIB-EYE STEAKS AND GREEN BEANS WITH ROASTED TOMATO VINAIGRETTE AND CHILI-GORGONZOLA BUTTER

serves
4

PREP TIME: 15 minutes

COOKING TIME: 45 minutes

MAKE-AHEAD: The butter can be made up to 1 day ahead, covered, and refrigerated; bring to room temperature before using. The vinaigrette can be made up to 8 hours ahead and set aside at room temperature.

Gorgonzola Butter

3½ ounces Gorgonzola cheese, crumbled (1 scant cup), at room temperature

3 tablespoons unsalted butter, at room temperature

1 teaspoon chili powder

Kosher salt and freshly ground black pepper

Roasted Tomato Vinaigrette

8 ounces cherry or grape tomatoes, halved

1 tablespoon olive oil

Kosher salt and freshly ground black pepper

½ cup extra-virgin olive oil

¼ cup red wine vinegar

¼ cup coarsely chopped fresh basil

2 tablespoons finely chopped shallots

2 teaspoons finely grated lemon zest

2 bone-in rib-eye steaks (each about 1 pound 6 ounces and 1½ inches thick)

¼ cup olive oil

Kosher salt and freshly ground black pepper

8 ounces green beans, trimmed

1 To make the Gorgonzola butter: In a medium bowl, gently stir the Gorgonzola cheese, butter, and chili powder together. Season to taste with salt and pepper.

2 Preheat the oven to 400°F.

3 To make the vinaigrette: In a medium bowl, toss the tomatoes with the 1 tablespoon olive oil to coat. Spread on a rimmed baking sheet and season with salt and pepper. Roast for about 25 minutes, or until they are golden brown. Let cool.

4 Drain the tomato cooking juices into a medium bowl. Transfer the tomatoes to a cutting board and finely chop them. Add to the cooking juices, then stir in the extra-virgin olive oil, vinegar, basil, shallots, and lemon zest. Season to taste with salt. Cover and set aside.

5 Prepare an outdoor grill for medium-high cooking over direct heat.

6 Coat the steaks with 2 tablespoons of the olive oil and season with salt and pepper. Grill the steaks, turning them over halfway through cooking, for a total of about 15 minutes, or until an instant-read thermometer inserted horizontally into the center of a steak reads 130°F for medium-rare. Transfer to a platter and let rest for about 5 minutes.

7 Meanwhile, in a large bowl, toss the green beans with the remaining 2 tablespoons olive oil and season with salt and pepper. Grill the beans, turning them occasionally, for about 3 minutes, or until seared with grill marks and crisp-tender.

8 Mound the beans around the steaks and top each steak with a generous dollop of Gorgonzola butter. Spoon some of the vinaigrette over the beans and around the steaks. To serve, cut the steaks across the grain into ½-inch-thick slices and serve the remaining Gorgonzola butter and vinaigrette on the side.

had never had short ribs until I came to America, and I fell hard for their velvety deliciousness. The bones enrich the braising liquid, so be sure to buy bone-in ribs, not boneless ones. The slowly simmered sauce, rich with dry red wine and herbs, is truly incredible.

WINE-BRAISED SHORT RIBS WITH CELERY ROOT PUREE, CARROTS, AND SHALLOTS

serves
8

PREP TIME: 15 minutes

COOKING TIME: 3 hours 45 minutes, plus 30 minutes standing time

MAKE-AHEAD: The short ribs can be cooked through step 4 up to 2 days ahead, cooled, covered, and refrigerated in the Dutch oven; discard the fat from the surface of the cooking liquid and reheat over medium-low heat before proceeding.

8 meaty bone-in beef short ribs (about 10 ounces each)

1 teaspoon kosher salt

1¼ teaspoons freshly ground black pepper

2 tablespoons olive oil

1 large carrot, cut into 4 pieces

2 celery ribs, cut into 4 pieces

3 large shallots (about 6 ounces total), quartered

6 large garlic cloves, coarsely chopped

3 cups dry red wine

6 cups reduced-sodium beef broth

5 large sprigs of fresh thyme

1 large sprig of fresh rosemary

1 bay leaf

2 tablespoons unsalted butter

Celery Root Puree (recipe follows)

Slow-Cooked Carrots and Shallots (recipe follows)

1 Preheat the oven to 275°F.

2 To make the short ribs: Season the beef with the salt and pepper. Heat a large Dutch oven (at least 6 quarts) over medium-high heat. Add the olive oil and then, working in batches, add the short ribs and cook, turning the ribs over occasionally, for about 12 minutes per batch, or until browned on all sides. Transfer the beef to a large bowl.

3 Reduce the heat to medium, add the carrots, celery, and shallots to the pot, and cook, stirring occasionally, for about 5 minutes, or until the vegetables soften slightly. Stir in the garlic, followed by the wine. Raise the heat to medium-high and boil for about 5 minutes, or until the wine is reduced by half. Stir in the broth, thyme, rosemary, and bay leaf.

4 Return the beef to the pot. Bring to a simmer over high heat, cover the Dutch oven, and transfer to the oven. Bake for about 2 hours, or until the meat is just tender. Uncover the Dutch oven and continue baking for about 30 minutes, or until the meat is fork-tender. Remove the pot from the oven, uncover, and let stand for at least 30 minutes.

5 Using a slotted spoon, gently transfer the ribs to a large platter. Tent with aluminum foil to keep warm. Spoon off any fat from the surface of the cooking liquid, then strain the liquid through a fine-mesh sieve into a wide heavy saucepan. Bring to a boil over high heat and cook for about 45 minutes, or until reduced enough to very thinly coat the back of a spoon (you should have about 1¼ cups). Remove from the heat and whisk in the butter, then return the ribs to the sauce and baste them with the sauce to rewarm them.

6 Spoon the celery root puree into the center of eight plates. Place the short ribs atop the puree so that they are offset. Place the carrots and shallots alongside. Spoon the sauce over the short ribs and around the puree and serve immediately.

Celery Root Puree

Celery root (also called celeriac) is a rather unassuming vegetable, but underneath its knobbly beige exterior is beautiful creamy white flesh that tastes like a cross between potato and celery. Pureed, it makes a delicious side dish to meats and poultry.

serves 8

PREP TIME: 10 minutes

COOKING TIME: 40 minutes

MAKE-AHEAD: Can be made up to 1 day ahead, cooled, covered, and refrigerated; reheat over low heat.

2 tablespoons unsalted butter

3 pounds celery root, peeled and cut into 1-inch cubes

3 cups whole milk

1 cup heavy cream

½ cup coarsely chopped shallots

1½ teaspoons kosher salt

1 In a large heavy saucepan, melt the butter over medium heat. Add the celery root, milk, cream, shallots, and salt and bring to a gentle simmer. Reduce the heat to medium-low and simmer very gently, uncovered, stirring occasionally, for about 35 minutes, or until the celery root is tender enough to mash with a spoon.

2 Working in batches, using a slotted spoon, transfer the celery root and shallots to a blender (preferably a high-powered one) and blend until smooth, adding enough of the cooking liquid to form a very thick, creamy, and completely smooth puree.

Slow-Cooked Carrots and Shallots

To coax out the sweetness from the carrots and shallots, cook them slowly in a skillet, without any parboiling first. I add a little sherry vinegar at the end to brighten the flavor.

serves 8

PREP TIME: 10 minutes

COOKING TIME: 35 minutes

MAKE-AHEAD: The vegetables can be made up to 2 hours ahead and set aside at room temperature; reheat over low heat.

2 tablespoons olive oil

1¾ pounds carrots, cut into 1-inch pieces

4 large shallots (about 7 ounces total), halved lengthwise

1½ teaspoons coarsely chopped fresh thyme

1 tablespoon sherry vinegar

2 tablespoons unsalted butter

Kosher salt and freshly ground black pepper

1 Heat a large heavy skillet over medium heat. Add the olive oil, then add the carrots in a single layer and cook, without stirring, for about 10 minutes, or until they are golden brown on the bottom. Stir in the shallots and cook, stirring occasionally, for about 20 minutes, or until the carrots are caramelized and firm-tender.

2 Stir in the thyme, add the vinegar, and simmer for about 1 minute, or until evaporated. Add the butter and toss until the butter melts and coats the vegetables. Season to taste with salt and pepper.

This incredible dish will bring out your inner chef. Implementing various techniques, it is one that will no doubt impress your guests with its complex and intoxicating flavors, aromas, and textures; it is worthy of the best restaurants I've worked in. It takes some time, but it is worth every minute. You may have to order the lamb shoulder ahead of time from your butcher. If you like, serve the Cumin-Cilantro Couscous on page 51, to soak up every bit of the luscious sauce.

MOROCCAN BRAISED LAMB SHOULDER WITH GOLDEN RAISIN–LEMON PUREE

serves
6

PREP TIME: 15 minutes

COOKING TIME: 3 hours and 50 minutes, plus 1 hour 30 minutes cooling time

MAKE-AHEAD: The puree can be made up to 2 days ahead, covered, and refrigerated; bring to room temperature before serving. The lamb can be cooked through step 5 up to 2 days ahead, cooled, covered, and refrigerated in the Dutch oven; discard the fat from the surface of the cooking liquid and rewarm over medium-low heat before proceeding.

Lamb

4 pounds boneless lamb shoulder, trimmed of excess fat

Kosher salt and freshly ground black pepper

3 tablespoons olive oil

1 yellow onion, coarsely chopped

3 carrots, cut into 1-inch pieces

2 heads garlic, halved horizontally

1½ cups dry red wine

¾ cup red wine vinegar

5 cups reduced-sodium beef broth

5 sprigs of fresh rosemary

8 whole star anise

2 cinnamon sticks

Golden Raisin–Lemon Puree

1 teaspoon olive oil

½ cup finely chopped shallots

½ teaspoon ground cumin

1 cup golden raisins

½ cup dry white wine

½ cup champagne vinegar or white wine vinegar

½ cup reduced-sodium chicken broth

1. To cook the lamb: Preheat the oven to 300°F.

2. Cut the lamb along its natural divisions into 6 large serving pieces. Season the lamb with salt and pepper. Heat a large Dutch oven over medium-high heat. Add the olive oil and then, working in batches, add the lamb and cook, turning occasionally, for about 8 minutes per batch, or until well browned. Transfer to a bowl and set aside.

3. Add the onions and carrots to the Dutch oven and cook for about 8 minutes, or until the onions are tender and beginning to brown. Stir in the garlic, followed by the wine and vinegar, and bring to a boil, stirring with a wooden spoon to scrape up the browned bits on the bottom of the pot. Add the broth, rosemary, star anise, and cinnamon and bring to a simmer. Return the lamb to the pot.

4. Cover the pot, transfer to the oven, and bake for about 2 hours and 30 minutes, or until the meat is very tender. Remove from the oven, uncover, and let the lamb cool in the liquid for about 1 hour and 30 minutes, or until lukewarm.

5. Meanwhile, make the raisin puree: Heat a small heavy saucepan over medium-low heat. Add the olive oil, then add the shallots and cook, stirring often, for about 2 minutes, or until tender. Add the cumin and stir for about 30 seconds, or until fragrant. Add the raisins, wine, vinegar, broth, ginger, and lemon zest and bring the liquid to a simmer. Reduce the heat to medium-low and simmer gently for about 18 minutes, or until the liquid reduces by about half and the raisins are plump and tender. Remove the pan from the heat, cover, and let stand for 30 minutes.

(continues on next page)

1 tablespoon finely chopped peeled fresh ginger

Zest of 1 lemon, removed in wide strips with a vegetable peeler

½ teaspoon ground turmeric

Kosher salt

6 Using a slotted spoon, transfer the raisins, lemon zest, shallots, and ginger to a food processor. Add the turmeric and puree, adding enough of the cooking liquid to thin the mixture slightly to a thin puree consistency. Season to taste with salt.

7 When the lamb has cooled to lukewarm, using a slotted spoon or tongs, carefully transfer the lamb to a rimmed baking sheet and set aside. Skim off the fat on the surface of the cooking liquid, then simmer the liquid over medium-high heat for about 30 minutes, or until it is reduced by about half.

8 Strain the cooking liquid through a sieve into a bowl, pressing on the solids to extract as much liquid as possible. For a smoother sauce, strain the liquid again through a fine-mesh sieve. You should have about 2½ cups. Spoon off the excess fat that rises to the top of the cooking liquid, then return the cooking liquid and lamb pieces to the pot and simmer over medium-low heat for about 12 minutes, or until the juices have reduced to about 2 cups and the lamb is heated through.

9 Transfer the lamb pieces and ¾ cup of the cooking liquid to a large heavy nonstick skillet; keep the cooking liquid remaining in the pot hot. Bring the liquid to a simmer in the sauté pan over high heat and simmer, constantly spooning the liquid over the lamb, for about 5 minutes, or until the liquid reduces enough to glaze the lamb. Season carefully (the reduced sauce may be already salty enough) to taste with salt and pepper.

10 Smear some of the raisin puree over the bottom of six shallow soup plates and top each with a piece of lamb offset at an angle. Ladle a few tablespoons of the reserved cooking liquid over each piece and serve, passing any remaining puree on the side.

TECHNIQUES OF THE TRADE In the braised lamb, I use a few professional techniques that can elevate your home cooking in general. First, allow braised meats to cool in their cooking liquid to help them retain their moisture. Next, reduce the braising liquid to create an intensely flavored sauce. Never season reduced sauces until just before serving, because as the liquid reduces, the salt will remain constant—so it's easy to accidentally overdo it. Finish the dish with the *poêle* pan technique of glazing the meat in some of the sauce in a skillet; it's another way to deepen the flavor.

There are three elements to this dish that you can use with other grilled meats: the gremolata, pickled onions, and spice rub with its aromatic mix of star anise, coriander, and smoked paprika. These boldly seasoned condiments would also go well with any cut of beef or pork.

SPICED LAMB CHOPS WITH GRILLED ZUCCHINI, FETA, AND OLIVE GREMOLATA

serves
4

PREP TIME: 15 minutes

COOKING TIME: 20 minutes

MAKE-AHEAD: The gremolata can be made up to 1 day ahead, covered, and refrigerated; bring to room temperature. The lamb can be coated with the spice mixture up to 1 day ahead, covered and refrigerated.

Gremolata

6 tablespoons extra-virgin olive oil

3 tablespoons finely chopped shallots

3 tablespoons finely chopped pitted kalamata olives

3 tablespoons sherry vinegar

2 tablespoons finely grated lemon zest

1 tablespoon finely chopped fresh tarragon

Kosher salt and freshly ground black pepper

Lamb

3 tablespoons olive oil

4 whole star anise, toasted and finely ground (use a mortar and pestle or a spice grinder)

2 tablespoons coriander seeds, toasted (see Kitchen Note, page 68) and finely ground

2 teaspoons sweet smoked paprika

1 frenched 8-rib rack of lamb (about 2½ pounds, such as one from Colorado; see Kitchen Note, page 182), cut into 4 double chops

Kosher salt and freshly ground black pepper

Zucchini

2 medium zucchini, cut crosswise on a very sharp diagonal into ¾-inch-thick slices

2 tablespoons olive oil

Kosher salt

Pickled Onions (recipe follows)

½ cup very coarsely crumbled feta cheese (2 ounces)

Flaky sea salt, such as Maldon or fleur de sel, for garnish

1 To make the gremolata: In a small bowl, combine the olive oil, shallots, olives, vinegar, lemon zest, and tarragon. Season lightly to taste with salt and pepper. Cover the gremolata and set aside at room temperature.

2 To prepare the lamb: In a small bowl, stir 2 tablespoons of the olive oil with the star anise, coriander, and paprika. Season the lamb chops with salt and pepper and then with the spice mixture. Let stand at room temperature while you prepare the grill.

3 Prepare an outdoor grill for medium-high cooking over direct heat.

4 Coat the lamb chops with the remaining 1 tablespoon olive oil. Grill the chops, turning occasionally, for about 15 minutes, or until an instant-read thermometer inserted horizontally into the center of a chop registers 125°F for medium-rare. Transfer the chops to a platter and let stand for 10 minutes.

5 Meanwhile, grill the zucchini: In a medium bowl, toss the zucchini with the olive oil and season with salt. Grill the zucchini, turning halfway through cooking, for about 6 minutes, or until charred with grill marks and crisp-tender.

6 When ready to serve, drain the pickled onions. Place a lamb chop on each of four dinner plates. Arrange the zucchini and pickled onions alongside the lamb, then sprinkle with the feta cheese. Spoon the gremolata around the lamb. Sprinkle with sea salt and serve.

(continues on next page)

Pickled Onions

Pickled onions give a kick to even the simplest dishes. Add them to tacos, sandwiches, burgers, and Mediterranean wraps. Here I've used star anise, but feel free to experiment with your favorite spices.

serves 4

PREP TIME: 5 minutes

COOKING TIME: 5 minutes plus 1 hour cooling time

MAKE-AHEAD: The onions can be made up to 5 days ahead, covered, and refrigerated; bring to room temperature.

1 cup dry red wine

½ cup red wine vinegar

½ cup sugar

3 whole star anise

1 teaspoon kosher salt

1 small red onion, halved lengthwise and sliced into ½-inch-wide wedges

In a small heavy nonreactive saucepan, bring the wine, vinegar, sugar, star anise, and salt to a boil over medium heat, stirring to dissolve the sugar and salt. Put the red onion wedges in a small bowl and pour in the hot wine mixture. Cover and let cool to room temperature, about 1 hour.

DOMESTIC RACKS OF LAMB are larger than imported lamb racks from Australia or New Zealand. Colorado lamb is especially meaty, and the racks weigh in at about 2½ pounds. The smaller imported racks run about 1¼ pounds each. If you can only find the smaller racks, buy an extra rack, cut each rack into 4 double chops, giving a total of 8 chops (2 per person), and grill the smaller chops for a couple of minutes less.

Any time a gratin is served at dinner, it's the first thing I dig into. I feel like I struck gold with this combination of cauliflower and Camembert. The cauliflower gives the gratin a subtle layer of flavor while Camembert makes it more luxurious. The simply grilled pork chops are great too—I can't resist nibbling the sweetest bits off the bone.

GRILLED PORK CHOPS WITH POTATO, CAULIFLOWER, AND CAMEMBERT GRATIN

serves
8

PREP TIME: 15 minutes

COOKING TIME: 1 hour 30 minutes, plus 10 to 20 minutes

MAKE-AHEAD: The cauliflower-cream mixture can be made up to 1 day ahead, cooled, covered, and refrigerated; reheat over low heat before assembling the gratin.

Gratin

2 tablespoons unsalted butter, plus more for the baking dish

1 yellow onion, thinly sliced

3 garlic cloves, finely chopped

4 large sprigs of fresh thyme

2 cups finely chopped cauliflower

2 cups heavy cream

2 cups whole milk

4 ounces Camembert cheese, with rind, cut into large pieces

Kosher salt and freshly ground black pepper

2¾ pounds baking potatoes, such as russets, peeled and sliced into ⅛-inch-thick slices

Pork Chops

8 pork loin chops (about 9 to 10 ounces and 1 inch thick)

Kosher salt and freshly ground black pepper

1 Preheat the oven to 325°F. Lightly butter a 3-quart shallow baking dish.

2 To make the gratin: Heat a large pot over medium heat. Add the butter and stir until melted. Add the onions, garlic, and thyme and sauté for about 5 minutes, or until the onions are tender but have not taken on any color. Add the cauliflower and cook for about 6 minutes, stirring often, or until softened. Add the cream and milk and bring to a simmer. Add the cheese and stir until it melts, then remove from the heat and discard the thyme stems.

3 Working in batches, puree the mixture in a blender; return to the pot. Season generously to taste with salt and pepper.

4 Stir the potato slices into the hot cream mixture to coat. Spoon 1 cup of the cream mixture into the baking dish. Spread the potatoes and the remaining cream mixture evenly in the dish. Cover with aluminum foil and put on a rimmed baking sheet. Bake for about 1 hour, or until a knife can be inserted easily into the potatoes. Uncover the dish, raise the oven temperature to 400°F, and continue baking for about 10 minutes, or until golden brown on top. Remove from the oven and let stand for 10 to 20 minutes.

5 Meanwhile, to cook the pork: Prepare an outdoor grill for medium-high cooking over direct heat.

6 Season the pork chops with salt and pepper. Grill for about 5 minutes per side, or until the pork shows only the barest hint of pink when pierced at the bone with the tip of a sharp knife. Transfer to a platter and let stand for 5 minutes before serving with the gratin.

Halibut is a white fish that's meaty and delicate at the same time. It works beautifully with the leeks and asparagus in this dish, but feel free to use any white fish or salmon in its place. The leeks become so tender they virtually melt into the creamy sauce.

GRILLED HALIBUT AND ASPARAGUS WITH MELTED LEEKS

serves
4

PREP TIME: 10 minutes

COOKING TIME: 45 minutes

MAKE-AHEAD: The leeks can be cooked up to 1 day ahead, cooled, covered, and refrigerated; reheat over low heat.

Leeks

1 tablespoon unsalted butter

1 tablespoon olive oil

½ large yellow onion, cut into ½-inch pieces

Kosher salt

3 garlic cloves, finely chopped

2 large leeks (white and pale green parts only), well rinsed and cut into ½-inch pieces (about 4 cups)

1 cup heavy cream

Asparagus

1½ pounds asparagus, woody ends trimmed

3 tablespoons extra-virgin olive oil

2 tablespoons finely chopped shallots

1 teaspoon sweet smoked paprika

Halibut

Four 7-ounce skinless halibut fillets

2 tablespoons olive oil

Kosher salt and freshly ground black pepper

1 lemon, quartered

1 To cook the leeks: Heat a medium heavy saucepan over medium-low heat. Add the butter and olive oil and swirl the pan to melt the butter. Stir in the onions with a generous pinch of salt and cook, stirring occasionally, for about 5 minutes, or until they begin to soften but do not take on any color. Stir in the garlic and cook, stirring occasionally, for about 2 minutes, or until fragrant. Stir in the leeks, add another pinch of salt, and reduce the heat to low. Cook, stirring often, for about 15 minutes, or until the leeks are translucent.

2 Add the cream and raise the heat to medium-low. Simmer very gently for about 12 minutes, or until the leeks are very tender and the cream has thickened slightly. Season with salt. Cover and keep hot over very low heat.

3 Meanwhile, to prepare the asparagus: Spread the asparagus on a small rimmed baking sheet. Drizzle with the extra-virgin olive oil, sprinkle with the shallots and paprika, and toss well. Set aside for about 15 minutes.

4 To cook the halibut: Prepare an outdoor grill for medium-high cooking over direct heat.

5 Coat the halibut with 1 tablespoon of the olive oil and season with salt and pepper. Place the halibut fillets on the grill with the top right corners at the 2-o'clock position. Grill, without moving the halibut, for 4 minutes. (This will help give the fillets a good sear of nice grill marks and make it easier to move.) Add the asparagus and grill, turning occasionally, for about 4 minutes, or until crisp-tender and slightly charred, then transfer to a plate when the fish is ready. Starting at the corner of the fillet nearest to you, slide a long metal spatula under each fillet, and turn it over. Cook for about 2 minutes, or until the fish is just cooked through and all but the very center is opaque when flaked with the tip of a knife. Transfer to a platter.

6 Divide the leeks among four dinner plates. Top each with a halibut fillet and the asparagus. Add a lemon quarter to each plate and serve hot.

almon's richness makes it a good match for earthy flavors, such as the cauliflower and mushrooms in this dish. A sweet dried currant vinaigrette is an unexpected divine touch to bring all of the players together.

OVEN-ROASTED SALMON
WITH CAULIFLOWER AND MUSHROOMS

serves
4

PREP TIME: 10 minutes

COOKING TIME: 40 minutes

MAKE-AHEAD: The vinaigrette can be made up to 8 hours ahead and set aside at room temperature.

Currant–Red Wine Vinaigrette

½ cup dry red wine

¼ cup dried currants

3 tablespoons finely chopped shallots

3 tablespoons red wine vinegar

2 tablespoons light brown sugar

1 tablespoon extra-virgin olive oil

Kosher salt and freshly ground black pepper

Cauliflower and Mushrooms

1 head cauliflower, cored and cut into small florets

¼ cup olive oil

Kosher salt

1¼ pounds assorted mushrooms, such as cremini, oyster, and stemmed shiitakes, large mushrooms halved lengthwise

¼ cup very finely chopped shallots

2 garlic cloves, finely chopped

3 tablespoons thinly sliced fresh sage leaves

Salmon

Four 5-ounce salmon fillets with skin

Kosher salt and freshly ground black pepper

1 tablespoon olive oil

¼ cup hulled pumpkin seeds, toasted (see Kitchen Note, page 68; optional)

1 Preheat the oven to 450°F.

2 To make the vinaigrette: In a small heavy saucepan, bring the wine, currants, shallots, vinegar, and brown sugar to a simmer over medium heat. Reduce the heat to low and simmer gently until the currants are plump and the liquid is reduced to ¼ cup, about 5 minutes. Remove the pan from the heat and whisk in the olive oil. Season to taste with salt and pepper. Transfer to a small bowl.

3 To prepare the cauliflower and mushrooms: In a large bowl, toss the cauliflower with 2 tablespoons of the oil to coat. Season to taste with salt. Spread on a large, rimmed baking sheet. Roast, stirring occasionally, for about 30 minutes, or until the cauliflower is tender and lightly browned. Remove from the oven. Reduce the oven temperature to 400°F.

4 Meanwhile, heat a large heavy nonstick skillet over high heat. Add the remaining 2 tablespoons oil, then add the mushrooms and cook, without stirring, for about 4 minutes, or until golden on the bottom. Stir the mushrooms and cook for about 4 minutes more, or until tender and well browned.

5 Stir the roasted cauliflower, shallots, and garlic into the mushrooms and cook until the shallots soften, about 1 minute. Stir in the sage. Season to taste with salt and pepper. Return the cauliflower mixture to the baking sheet and cover to keep warm. Wipe out the skillet.

6 To cook the salmon: Using a sharp knife, score the skin side of the salmon. Season with salt and pepper. Heat the same skillet over medium-high heat. Add the olive oil, then place the salmon skin side down in the skillet and cook, for about 5 minutes, or until the skin is golden brown. Turn the salmon over, transfer the skillet to the oven, and roast for 3 to 5 minutes, or until the salmon is mostly opaque with a rosy center when flaked in the thickest part with the tip of a small knife. Meanwhile, if necessary, uncover the cauliflower mixture and rewarm in the oven.

7 Transfer the salmon to a platter or four dinner plates. Spoon the cauliflower mixture around the salmon and drizzle with some vinaigrette. Sprinkle with the pumpkin seeds, if using. Serve the remaining vinaigrette on the side.

These Southeast Asian–inspired crab cakes make such a great impression and I love that I can make them ahead with just a little last-minute cooking. I like to serve them with a simple salad of avocado, red onion, and butter lettuce, tossed with lime juice and olive oil.

ASIAN CRAB CAKES WITH MANGO CHUTNEY

serves
6

PREP TIME: 45 minutes

COOKING TIME: 15 minutes

MAKE-AHEAD: The chutney can be made up to 1 week ahead. The crab cakes can be made through step 3 up to 8 hours ahead, covered and refrigerated.

Mango Chutney

½ cup sugar

1 mango, pitted, peeled, and cut into ¼-inch dice

¼ cup unseasoned rice wine vinegar

2 tablespoons fresh lime juice

Kosher salt

Crab Cakes

½ cup mayonnaise

1 large egg

2 tablespoons Thai or Vietnamese fish sauce

1 tablespoon peeled and minced fresh ginger

1 tablespoon finely chopped fresh cilantro

1 teaspoon toasted sesame oil

1 to 2 teaspoons seeded and finely chopped red jalapeño pepper

½ teaspoon kosher salt

Finely grated zest of 1 lime

¼ cup finely chopped green onions, white and green parts

1 pound jumbo lump crabmeat, picked over for cartilage and shells, well drained

1½ cups panko (Japanese bread crumbs)

6 tablespoons canola oil

4 tablespoons (½ stick) unsalted butter

½ English cucumber, sliced into thin rounds, and then into matchstick-size strips

Fresh cilantro sprigs, for garnish

Flakey sea salt, such as Maldon, for garnish

1 To make the chutney: Heat a medium heavy saucepan over medium heat for 2 minutes. Add the sugar and cook without stirring, tilting the pan as needed so that the sugar cooks evenly, for about 5 minutes, or until it melts into an amber caramel. Do not stir or the caramel will crystallize. Remove from the heat and stir in the mango (the caramel will seize), then the rice vinegar and lime juice. Return to medium heat and stir constantly for about 5 minutes, or until the mango is translucent and the caramel is dissolved and syrupy. Transfer to a bowl and let cool. Season with salt.

2 To prepare the crab cakes: In a large bowl, whisk the mayonnaise, egg, fish sauce, ginger, cilantro, sesame oil, jalapeños, salt, and lime zest together, then whisk in the green onions. Add the crabmeat and stir to coat, coarsely breaking apart the crabmeat, leaving small whole chunks in the mixture. Fold in the panko. Cover and refrigerate the crab mixture for 30 minutes so that the mixture is easier to form.

3 Using about ⅓ cup of the crab mixture for each cake, shape into twelve ¾-inch thick crab cakes and place on a baking sheet.

4 To cook the crab cakes: Preheat the oven to 200°F. Line a baking sheet with paper towels. Heat a large nonstick sauté pan over medium-high heat. Add 3 tablespoons of the oil and 2 tablespoons of the butter and heat until hot but not smoking. Working in two batches, fry 6 crab cakes for about 2 minutes on each side, or until crisp and golden, adjusting the heat as needed to brown evenly without scorching. Transfer to the baking sheet and keep warm in the oven. Wipe out the skillet with paper towels and repeat with the remaining 3 tablespoons canola oil, 2 tablespoons butter, and 6 crab cakes.

5 To serve, place 2 crab cakes on each of six plates. Spoon some of the mango chutney over and alongside the crab cakes. Top each with the cucumber and garnish with the cilantro sprigs and sea salt.

The coconut-lime sauce in this dish looks mild, but don't let the creamy white color fool you. It packs an intense blend of flavors from the jalapeños, lemongrass, ginger, lime, and garlic. It brings together the fresh ocean flavor of the caramelized scallops and the crispness of the lightly sautéed vegetables.

SEARED SCALLOPS AND SPRING VEGETABLES WITH COCONUT-LIME SAUCE

serves
4

PREP TIME: 15 minutes, plus 10 minutes standing time

COOKING TIME: 25 minutes

MAKE-AHEAD: The sauce can be made 1 day ahead, cooled, covered, and refrigerated; reheat over low heat.

Coconut-Lime Sauce

1 tablespoon olive oil

3 shallots, thinly sliced

1 stalk lemongrass, woody top discarded, bottom split lengthwise and crushed under the side of a heavy knife

1 red jalapeño pepper, seeded and coarsely chopped

3 garlic cloves, sliced

One 1-inch piece of fresh ginger, peeled and thinly sliced

2 cups unsweetened coconut milk

1 tablespoon Thai or Vietnamese fish sauce (nam pla or nuoc mam)

Finely grated zest of 1 lime

1 tablespoon fresh lime juice

Vegetables and Scallops

3 tablespoons olive oil

6 baby bok choy, trimmed and halved lengthwise

6 baby carrots, halved lengthwise

12 sugar snap peas, trimmed

Kosher salt

12 large sea scallops, tough side muscle removed and patted dry

Freshly ground black pepper

¼ cup slivered almonds, toasted (Kitchen Note, see page 113)

Sprigs of fresh cilantro, for garnish

1 To make the sauce: Heat a medium heavy saucepan over medium-low heat. Add the olive oil, then add the shallots, lemongrass, and jalapeños and cook, stirring often, for about 3 minutes, or until the shallots are translucent. Stir in the garlic and ginger and cook for about 2 minutes, or until fragrant. Add the coconut milk, bring to a simmer, and cook gently for about 3 minutes to infuse the flavors. Stir in the fish sauce, lime zest, and lime juice. Return the sauce to a simmer, then remove from the heat, cover, and steep for 10 minutes.

2 Strain the sauce through a fine-mesh sieve into a small saucepan. Cover and keep warm over very low heat.

3 To cook the vegetables: Heat a large heavy skillet over medium-high heat. Add 1 tablespoon of the olive oil, then place the bok choy cut side down in the skillet and cook for about 1 minute, or until golden brown on the bottom. Turn the bok choy over and cook for about 2 minutes to lightly brown the other side. Move the bok choy to one side of the pan. Add the carrots to the empty side of the pan and cook for about 1 minute, or until they begin to soften slightly. Add the sugar snap peas and 3 tablespoons water, reduce the heat to medium-low, and cook, stirring occasionally, for about 3 minutes, or until the peas are crisp-tender. Season to taste with salt.

4 Meanwhile, to cook the scallops: Season the scallops with salt and pepper. Heat another large heavy skillet over high heat until very hot. Add the remaining 2 tablespoons olive oil, then add the scallops and cook for about 2 minutes, or until the underside is golden brown. Turn the scallops and cook for about 2 minutes more, or until the other side is golden brown but the scallops are still translucent when pierced in the center with the tip of a small knife. Transfer the scallops to paper towels to drain briefly.

5 Divide the scallops and vegetables among four dinner plates. Spoon the coconut sauce over and around the scallops. Sprinkle with the almonds, garnish with the cilantro, and serve.

I created this elegant dish for a cooking demonstration at the New York City Wine and Food Festival. While lobster is always a showstopper, the corn butter holds its own. Sweet, creamy, and lighter than straight butter, it's unlike anything you've tried. This dish is also sensational with colossal shrimp standing in for the lobsters (see the variation).

GRILLED LOBSTER WITH SWEET CORN BUTTER AND BACON MARMALADE

serves
6

PREP TIME: 15 minutes

COOKING TIME: 1 hour

MAKE-AHEAD: The corn butter can be made up to 1 day ahead and the bacon marmalade can be made up to 5 days ahead. Cover them separately and refrigerate; bring to room temperature before using. The lobsters can be prepared through step 6 up to 6 hours ahead, covered and refrigerated.

Corn Butter

3 cups fresh corn kernels (cut from 4 large ears yellow corn)

1 tablespoon fresh thyme leaves, finely chopped

8 tablespoons (1 stick) salted butter, cut into ½-inch pieces and softened

Bacon Marmalade

4 slices bacon, cut into ½-inch pieces

½ cup chopped shallots

2 teaspoons finely chopped fresh thyme

½ cup sherry vinegar

1 cup dry sherry

¼ cup extra-virgin olive oil

Kosher salt and freshly ground black pepper

6 live Maine lobsters (1½ pounds each)

About 1 tablespoon olive oil

3 large ears yellow corn, husked and cut in half

Kosher salt

Chopped fresh chives, for garnish

1. To make the corn butter: Run the corn kernels through an electric juicer to extract the corn juice; discard the solids. You should get at least 1½ cups of corn juice. Or, if you don't have a juicer, puree the kernels in a blender. Strain the juice through a fine-mesh sieve set over a bowl, pressing hard on the solids to extract all the juice.

2. In a small heavy nonaluminum saucepan, bring the corn juice to a boil over medium heat, whisking constantly, then whisk for about 10 minutes, or until it thickens to a pudding-like consistency. (The natural starch in the corn will cause the juice to thicken.) Transfer to a small bowl.

3. Whisk the thyme into the corn juice. Whisk in the butter, a few pieces at a time. Press a sheet of plastic wrap on the surface of the butter and let cool to room temperature.

4. To make the bacon marmalade: Heat a large heavy saucepan over medium-high heat. Add the bacon and cook, stirring occasionally, for about 5 minutes, or until it is nearly crisp. Add the shallots and thyme and sauté for about 2 minutes, or until the shallots are tender. Add the vinegar and cook for about 5 minutes, or until reduced by half. Add the sherry and cook for about 10 minutes, or until reduced by half. Transfer to a small bowl and set aside to cool slightly, then stir in the extra-virgin olive oil and season to taste with salt and pepper. Set aside at room temperature for up to 2 hours.

5. Bring a large pot of salted water to a boil over high heat. Add 1 lobster and immediately turn off the heat. Let the lobster cook gently in the hot water for 3 minutes. The lobster will be medium-rare at this point, which is what you want, since it will be grilled later. Remove the lobster from the hot water and immediately place it in a large bowl of ice water to cool. Repeat with the remaining 5 lobsters, returning the water to a boil before placing each lobster in the water. Once they are cool, drain the lobsters.

(continues on page 196)

6. Remove the claws from the lobsters. Using a very sharp chef's knife, cut the lobster bodies lengthwise in half; remove and discard the intestines.

7. Prepare an outdoor grill for high cooking over direct heat.

8. Brush the lobster tail meat generously with some of the corn butter. Grill the lobster halves, cut side down, with the claws for about 4 minutes, or until grill marks appear on the meat, then turn over the lobster halves and claws and cook for about 2 minutes longer, until cooked through. Meanwhile, lightly oil the corn, season it with salt, and grill for about 8 minutes, turning occasionally, or until slightly charred.

9. To serve: Transfer the corn and lobster to six dinner plates or platters. Spoon more corn butter and some bacon marmalade over the lobster meat. Garnish with the chives. Serve the remaining corn butter and bacon marmalade alongside.

VARIATION: **GRILLED SHRIMP WITH SWEET CORN BUTTER AND BACON MARMALADE**

Substitute 16 colossal (U–16) shrimp for the lobsters. Split them down the back but leave them in their shell. Skip the parcooking and preparation procedure in steps 5 and 6. In step 8, brush the shrimp with some of the corn butter. Place the corn on the cob on the grill and grill for 3 minutes. Add the shrimp and continue grilling, turning as needed, until the shrimp is firm and opaque and the corn is lightly charred, about 5 minutes. Transfer 4 shrimp and a corn cob half to each plate, spoon some of the corn butter and bacon marmalade over the shrimp, and serve the rest on the side.

quash blossoms are such a rare treat; when you can find them, they're worth serving to guests. You will see them at farmers' markets in midsummer when zucchini flowers are in bloom. They are a staple in Mexican cooking, and are sometimes available at Latin markets. If you have a vegetable garden, plant zucchini and you can pick the blossoms off the vines. Here I grill them very briefly to heighten their delicate flavor.

GRILLED SQUASH BLOSSOM SALAD WITH PESTO CROUTONS

serves
4

PREP TIME: 10 minutes
COOKING TIME: 5 minutes

12 ounces cherry tomatoes (preferably assorted colors), halved

1 teaspoon coarsely chopped fresh thyme

2 tablespoons fresh lemon juice

8 tablespoons extra-virgin olive oil

Kosher salt and freshly ground black pepper

24 squash blossoms

Four 1-inch-thick slices ciabatta bread

⅓ cup Pesto (page 40)

5 ounces mixed baby greens (about 8 cups not packed)

1. Prepare an outdoor grill for medium-high cooking over direct heat.

2. In a medium bowl, toss the tomatoes, thyme, lemon juice, and 4 tablespoons of the olive oil together. Season with salt and pepper. Set aside to allow the tomatoes to exude some juice into the dressing.

3. Remove and discard the pistils from the center of each squash blossom. Drizzle the blossoms with 1 tablespoon of the olive oil and season with salt and pepper. Brush the bread with the remaining 3 tablespoons olive oil.

4. Grill the squash blossoms for about 2 minutes per side, or until they wilt and become slightly charred. At the same time, grill the bread for about 2 minutes per side, or until toasted. Tear the bread into large bite-size pieces and spoon some pesto onto each piece.

5. Divide the baby greens among four plates. Using a slotted spoon, arrange the tomatoes over the greens, then drizzle with the dressing remaining in the bowl. Arrange the grilled blossoms over the salads and season with salt and pepper. Add the pesto croutons and serve immediately.

When the summer is over, and the tomatoes and basil are gone, don't get sad—the mushrooms are on their way. For this deeply flavorful ragout, be sure to buy an interesting assortment of mushrooms in various colors, sizes, and shapes. You may find the best selection at an Asian market. Good old American grits, with their slightly coarse texture, act as the perfect vehicle for the earthy mushrooms. Even quick-cooking grits take about 30 minutes to cook to tenderness, regardless of what the package directions say.

MUSHROOM RAGOUT ON CREAMY GRITS

serves
4

PREP TIME: 15 minutes
COOKING TIME: 40 minutes

Grits

3 cups whole milk

Kosher salt

1 cup quick-cooking grits

2 tablespoons unsalted butter

Ragout

¼ cup extra-virgin olive oil

2 portobello mushrooms, dark gills scraped out with a spoon, cut into ½-inch-thick slices

1¾ pounds assorted mushrooms, such as oyster, cremini, maitake, bunashimeji, and/or king trumpets, trimmed, large mushrooms halved or quartered

5 large sprigs of fresh thyme

1 large shallot, finely chopped

3 garlic cloves, finely chopped

¾ cup dry white wine

1 cup reduced-sodium chicken broth

2 tablespoons finely chopped fresh flat-leaf parsley, plus more for garnish

Kosher salt and freshly ground black pepper

3 tablespoons unsalted butter

1. To make the grits: In a large heavy saucepan, bring the milk, 3 cups water, and 1½ teaspoons salt to a gentle simmer over medium-high heat. Gradually whisk in the grits and continue to whisk until the mixture comes to a boil. Reduce the heat to medium-low and simmer gently, whisking often, for about 15 minutes, or until the grits are thickened. Reduce the heat to low, cover, and continue cooking the grits, stirring often, for about 15 minutes, or until they are the consistency of loose mashed potatoes and no longer have a starchy taste. Whisk in the butter. Season to taste with salt.

2. Meanwhile, to make the ragout: Heat a large deep skillet over medium-high heat. Add the olive oil, then add the mushrooms and thyme and cook, stirring occasionally but letting the mushrooms brown on the bottom each time before stirring, for about 15 minutes, or until they are tender.

3. Stir in the shallots and garlic and cook, stirring often, for about 2 minutes, or until the shallots soften. Stir in the wine and cook for about 1 minute, or until reduced by half. Add the broth and parsley and simmer for about 4 minutes, or until the sauce reduces slightly. Remove and discard the thyme stems. Season to taste with salt and pepper and stir in the butter.

4. Divide the grits among four dinner plates, then top with the mushroom ragout. Sprinkle with parsley and serve hot.

ROUNDING OUT THE MEAL **KALE, ORANGE, AND TOASTED ALMOND SALAD** This salad goes well with Mediterranean flavors, such as this ragout. Remove the center ribs and stems from kale leaves, then very thinly slice the leaves crosswise. In a medium bowl, combine the kale, orange segments, and toasted sliced almonds. Toss with enough Currant–Red Wine Vinaigrette (page 189) to coat. Season to taste with salt and pepper and serve.

any old-fashioned libations have made a comeback, and the bramble is one of the most delicious. Traditionally it was made with gin and blackberries (hence the *bramble* in the name), but I've mixed it up. This version uses blueberries, mint, cucumber, and crème de cassis.

BLUEBERRY GIN BRAMBLE

serves
1

PREP TIME: 5 minutes

3 cups ice cubes

¼ cup fresh blueberries

4 thin slices English cucumber

3 large fresh mint leaves

2 teaspoons agave nectar

1½ teaspoons fresh lemon juice

1 teaspoon crème de cassis

¼ cup dry gin

1. In a food processor, grind the ice so that it is very finely crushed and fluffy, like shaved ice.

2. Put the blueberries, 2 of the cucumber slices, the mint, agave, lemon juice, and crème de cassis in an old-fashioned (rocks) glass and muddle (mash) with a muddler or a pestle. Add the gin and stir. Add the remaining 2 cucumber slices to the glass. Stir in ½ cup of the crushed ice, and pack more ice into the glass, mounding it well above the rim. Serve immediately.

FAMILY SUPPER SUNDAYS

SUNDAYS ARE ALL ABOUT FAMILY. SOME FAM-
ilies spend long, leisurely hours sharing stories, while others camp in
front of the TV to savor every minute of the big game. There are endless ways to enjoy the day, but one thing is certain: On Sunday, the
meal matters. Rich aromas fill the house, growing more intense
throughout the afternoon, and the food is slow-cooked and served
family-style, the way Sunday dinners were meant to be.

When I was growing up, my grandparents used to roast a chicken
on Sundays. I still think of them whenever I smell chicken cooking in
the oven or see that particular golden-brown skin that can come only
from patiently roasting a bird. There were other favorites too, such as
pot roast and honey-glazed ham, which turned into delicious sandwiches the next day. Since moving to the States, I've fallen in love
with pulled pork. It's quintessential Sunday fare, because the slow-
and-low cooking makes the meat melt-in-your-mouth tender.

I hope the dishes in this chapter will become some of your family's standards. **With the extra time and everyone close by, this
is the day to create new traditions, pass on family recipes,
and share stories with your kids.** Show them how your grand-
mother used to mash potatoes and how your dad grills the perfect
steak. Teach them to caramelize onions and fry the crispiest fish and
chips. After all, Sunday dinners make memories.

The key to this dish are the roasted tomatoes. They take a bit of time, so you might want to make a large batch. They'll keep in the fridge for one week and you can use them in salads or a panini. You can make the butter a week ahead—even months if you freeze it—then all you'll need to do is roast the chicken. In a pinch, chop up sun-dried tomatoes and stir them into softened butter.

WHOLE ROASTED CHICKEN
WITH TOMATO-BASIL BUTTER

serves
4

PREP TIME: 15 minutes

COOKING TIME: 2 hours 25 minutes, plus 15 minutes resting time

Tomato-Basil Butter

4 plum tomatoes (about 12 ounces total), quartered

4 large sprigs of fresh thyme

3 garlic cloves, very coarsely chopped

2 tablespoons olive oil

Kosher salt and freshly ground black pepper

¼ cup coarsely chopped fresh basil

8 tablespoons (1 stick) unsalted butter, at room temperature

Chicken

One 4½-pound chicken

3 carrots, coarsely chopped

3 celery ribs, coarsely chopped

1 yellow onion, cut into 8 wedges

1 head garlic, halved horizontally

Kosher salt and freshly ground black pepper

½ cup reduced-sodium chicken broth

1 Preheat the oven to 375°F.

2 To make the tomato-basil butter: In a large bowl, toss the tomatoes, thyme, and garlic with the olive oil. Season with salt and pepper. Arrange the tomatoes, with the thyme and garlic, on a large rimmed baking sheet. Roast for about 1 hour, or until the tomatoes are lightly browned. Remove from the oven and cool slightly; discard the thyme stems. Leave the oven on.

3 On a cutting board or in a food processor, finely chop the tomatoes and garlic. Transfer the tomato jam to a small bowl and mix in the basil.

4 In a medium bowl, mix the butter and half of the tomato jam to blend. Season to taste with salt and pepper. Reserve the remaining tomato jam.

5 To roast the chicken: Using your fingers, starting at the neck end of the chicken, carefully make a pocket between the flesh and skin of the chicken breasts and top of the legs. Gently slide enough of the tomato butter under the skin to coat the breasts and legs evenly. Spread some tomato butter inside the cavity of the chicken, then stuff the cavity with some of the carrots, celery, and onions and half of the garlic. Using kitchen twine, tie the legs of the chicken together. Tuck the wing tips behind the shoulders.

6 Place the remaining chopped vegetables in a medium roasting pan. Spread the remaining tomato butter all over the chicken; set the chicken on the vegetables. Season the chicken with salt and pepper. Roast the chicken for about 1 hour and 20 minutes, or until an instant-read thermometer inserted into a thigh reads 160°F. Transfer the chicken to a carving board to rest for about 15 minutes.

7 Meanwhile, discard the vegetables in the pan. Pour the pan juices into a measuring cup and spoon off the fat. Heat the pan over medium heat and add the broth and pan juices. Bring to a boil, scraping up the browned bits with a wooden spoon. Season with salt and pepper. Pour into a sauceboat.

8 Carve the chicken and serve with the pan juices and tomato jam passed on the side.

You aren't going to eat fried chicken every night (even if you might want to), so when you do indulge, it had better be bloody good! To me one of the most important things about fried chicken is a super-crunchy coating. So I've got a trick: I add a little cornstarch into my flour and spice mixture for extra crispiness. A soak in buttermilk brine seasons the chicken from the inside out. For a down-home chicken dinner, serve this with Mashed Potatoes (page 226) and "Fireworks" Coleslaw (page 231).

SOUTHERN FRIED CHICKEN

serves
4

PREP TIME: 15 minutes, plus at least 2 hours brining time
COOKING TIME: 35 to 50 minutes

3 cups buttermilk

4 teaspoons kosher salt

One 4-pound chicken, cut into 8 serving pieces

Canola oil, for deep-frying

1¾ cups all-purpose flour

½ cup cornstarch

1½ tablespoons dry mustard

1½ tablespoons garlic powder

1½ tablespoons onion powder

1½ tablespoons sweet paprika

1 teaspoon freshly ground black pepper

1 In a large bowl, whisk the buttermilk and 1½ teaspoons of the salt together. Add the chicken and turn to coat. Cover and refrigerate for at least 2 hours, and up to 12 hours.

2 Preheat the oven to 300°F.

3 Set a large deep cast-iron or other heavy skillet over medium-high heat, pour in enough canola oil to reach about halfway up the sides of the skillet, and heat until it reaches 350°F on a deep-frying thermometer.

4 Meanwhile, in a shallow dish, whisk the flour, cornstarch, mustard, garlic powder, onion powder, paprika, pepper, and 2 teaspoons of the remaining salt together. Working with one piece at a time, lift the chicken from the marinade, allowing the excess marinade to drip back into the bowl. Roll the chicken in the flour mixture to coat completely, and transfer to a large rimmed baking sheet. When all of the chicken has been floured, coat it a second time with the flour mixture.

5 Working in two or three batches, carefully place the chicken in the hot oil and cook, turning occasionally and adjusting the heat as necessary to maintain a temperature of about 350°F, for about 12 minutes, or until the chicken is golden and almost cooked through. Using a wire skimmer, transfer the chicken to a wire cooling rack set on a rimmed baking sheet to drain.

6 Bake the chicken on the baking sheet, on the rack, for about 10 minutes, or until a chicken thigh shows no sign of pink when pierced at the bone with the tip of a small sharp knife. Sprinkle the chicken with the remaining ½ teaspoon salt and serve.

y nieces and nephews love it when they come to visit Uncle Curtis. My wife, Lindsay, says it is for the swimming pool, but I think that these Parmesan-crusted chicken tenders might have something to do with it. I promise the kids won't be the only ones having seconds. If you want a sauce for dipping the tenders, try the Marinara Sauce on page 12, the Apple-Bourbon Barbecue Sauce on page 230, or even the Herb Aïoli on page 67.

PARMESAN-CRUSTED CHICKEN TENDERS WITH STRING BEANS

serves
4

PREP TIME: 15 minutes

COOKING TIME: 15 minutes

½ cup all-purpose flour

Kosher salt

3 large eggs

1¾ cups panko (Japanese bread crumbs)

1¼ cups finely grated Parmesan cheese (about 5 ounces)

12 chicken tenders (about 1¼ pounds total)

7 tablespoons unsalted butter

5 tablespoons olive oil

8 ounces thin green beans, trimmed

8 ounces yellow wax beans, trimmed

3 tablespoons finely chopped shallots

1. Preheat the oven to 200°F.

2. In a pie plate or wide shallow bowl, mix the flour and 1½ teaspoons salt. Lightly whisk the eggs in a second pie plate or wide shallow bowl to blend. In a third pie plate or wide shallow bowl, mix the panko and Parmesan cheese together.

3. Line a large plate or rimmed baking sheet with wax paper. Generously season the chicken tenders with salt. One at a time, roll the chicken tenders in the flour to coat lightly, shaking off the excess flour, then dip into the eggs to coat and roll in the panko mixture, patting firmly to help the mixture adhere. Transfer to the plate.

4. Place a wire cooling rack on a large, rimmed baking sheet. Heat a large non-stick skillet over medium-high heat, then add 3 tablespoons of the butter with 2 tablespoons of the olive oil and heat until the butter melts. Add 6 chicken tenders and cook for about 3 minutes per side, or until they are golden brown and show no sign of pink when pierced with the tip of a small sharp knife. Transfer the chicken tenders to the rack and keep warm in the oven. Wipe out the skillet. Repeat with 3 tablespoons more butter and 2 tablespoons more olive oil and the remaining 6 chicken tenders.

5. Meanwhile, heat a large heavy sauté pan over medium heat. Add the remaining 1 tablespoon butter and 1 tablespoon olive oil, then add the green and yellow beans, season with salt, and toss to coat. Cover and cook, stirring occasionally, for about 5 minutes, or until the green beans are bright green. Stir in the shallots and cook, uncovered, for about 3 minutes, or until the beans are crisp-tender and the shallots are tender. Season with salt.

6. Serve the chicken tenders hot with the beans.

ROUNDING OUT THE MEAL **CRISPY ROASTED POTATOES** You'll want to make these over and over. Cut potatoes into wedges, toss with olive oil to coat, and season with salt and pepper. Roast them on a baking sheet at 450°F, turning as needed, for about 45 minutes, or until tender and golden brown.

Great chicken soup takes time, and you can really taste the time spent to make this deeply flavored broth, which gets an underlying spiciness from star anise, cinnamon, and coriander seeds. Part of the fun of pho (pronounced "fah") is the accompaniments, so let diners choose their own bean sprouts, scallions, chilies, and more. Like most chicken soups, this makes a big batch, but leftovers are always welcome.

VIETNAMESE-STYLE CHICKEN SOUP WITH NOODLES (PHO)

serves
8

PREP TIME: 20 minutes

COOKING TIME: 2 hours 30 minutes

MAKE-AHEAD: The broth and chicken can be made up to 2 days ahead, cooled, transferred to separate covered containers, and refrigerated.

Broth

6 whole star anise

1 cinnamon stick

1 tablespoon coriander seeds

½ teaspoon whole cloves

1 tablespoon canola oil

2 yellow onions, thinly sliced

One 3-ounce piece of fresh ginger (about 5 inches long), peeled and thinly sliced

One 4½-pound chicken

4 ounces rice vermicelli (mai fun noodles) or angel hair pasta

½ cup Thai or Vietnamese fish sauce (nam pla or nuoc mam), or to taste

2 tablespoons sugar

Kosher salt

Accompaniments

6 scallions (white and green parts), thinly sliced

2 limes, cut into wedges

1½ cups fresh bean sprouts

1 cup fresh cilantro

1 cup fresh Thai or Italian basil

2 fresh red chilies, thinly sliced into rounds

Hoisin sauce

Sriracha sauce

1 To make the broth: Heat a 12-quart stockpot over medium-high heat. Add the star anise, cinnamon, coriander, and cloves and stir for about 4 minutes, or until the spices are fragrant and the coriander seeds are a shade darker. Pour the spices onto a plate and let cool, then wrap in cheesecloth and tie with kitchen twine to make a sachet.

2 Return the stockpot to medium heat. Add the canola oil, then add the onions and ginger and cook, stirring often, for about 10 minutes, or until the onions are golden brown. Place the chicken, breast side up, in the pot. Add enough cold water to cover the chicken (about 5 quarts), then add the spice sachet and bring to a gentle simmer over high heat, being sure the water does not boil. Reduce the heat to medium-low and simmer gently, uncovered, for 2 hours, skimming off any foam that rises to the top.

3 Remove the pot from the heat and discard the sachet. Carefully transfer the chicken to a large plate and let stand until cool enough to handle. Remove the chicken meat, discarding the skin, bones, and cartilage, then coarsely shred the meat.

4 Skim off and discard the fat from the top of the broth, then bring the broth to a boil. Add the noodles and cook, stirring, for about 3 minutes, or until just tender. Stir in the fish sauce, adding it to taste, followed by the sugar, and season with salt. Return the meat to the simmering broth.

5 Using kitchen tongs, transfer the chicken and noodles to deep soup bowls. Ladle in the soup. Serve hot, with the accompaniments passed on the side to add to the soup as desired.

R oast turkey is too good to save for only big holiday dinners. A turkey breast is perfect for smaller gatherings, and it is much easier to cook perfectly than a whole bird. It also makes for super-simple carving. A soak in a lemon-and-herb-flavored brine is insurance against dry turkey, as the brine works itself into the meat and adds moisture.

ROAST TURKEY BREAST
WITH LEMON AND SAGE BROWN BUTTER

serves
6

PREP TIME: 20 minutes, plus at least 2 hours brining time
COOKING TIME: 1 hour 30 minutes

Turkey

4 cups cold water

¼ cup sugar

2 tablespoons kosher salt

1 teaspoon black peppercorns

Finely grated zest of 3 lemons

¼ cup fresh lemon juice

2 garlic cloves, crushed and peeled, plus 1 head garlic, halved horizontally

¼ cup lightly packed fresh sage leaves

¼ cup lightly packed fresh thyme sprigs

1 sprig of fresh rosemary

One 3¼-pound boneless turkey breast (see Kitchen Note, page 216)

1 large carrot, cut into 1½-inch chunks

2 large celery ribs, cut into 1½-inch lengths

1 yellow onion, cut into 8 wedges

½ cup reduced-sodium turkey or chicken broth

Sage Brown Butter

½ pound (2 sticks) unsalted butter, at room temperature

2 tablespoons finely chopped fresh sage

2 tablespoons finely chopped shallots

1 large garlic clove, finely chopped

Kosher salt and freshly ground black pepper

Leek and Herb Stuffing (recipe follows)

1. To brine the turkey: In a large bowl, combine the water, sugar, salt, peppercorns, lemon zest, lemon juice, and crushed garlic cloves. Using the side of a heavy knife, lightly crush the sage, thyme, and rosemary on a cutting board, then stir them into the brine.

2. Submerge the turkey breast, meaty side down, in the brine. Cover and refrigerate for at least 2 hours, and up to 8 hours.

3. Meanwhile, make the sage brown butter: In a medium skillet, stir 6 tablespoons of the butter over medium heat for about 4 minutes, or until it melts and turns a nutty brown. Add the sage, shallots, and garlic and stir for about 1 minute, or until the shallots soften. Pour the butter into a medium bowl and let cool.

4. Add the remaining 10 tablespoons butter to the brown butter and blend well. Season to taste with salt and pepper.

5. To roast the turkey: Preheat the oven to 350°F.

6. Remove the turkey from the brine; discard the brine. Rinse the turkey under cold running water. Pat it dry with paper towels. Place the turkey on a cutting board. Using your fingers, carefully make a pocket between the skin and the breast meat. Spread about ⅓ cup of the butter under the skin to cover the breast meat completely, then rub ⅓ cup of the remaining butter all over the outside of the turkey breast. Tie the breast crosswise in a couple of places with kitchen twine to help it hold its shape.

7. Spread the carrots, celery, onions, and garlic halves on a large, rimmed sheet. Set the turkey breast on top and roast for about 1 hour and 20 minutes, or until an instant-read thermometer inserted into the thickest part of the turkey reads 155°F (see Kitchen Note). Transfer the turkey and vegetables to a platter and let rest for 10 minutes.

8. Meanwhile, pour any pan juices into a small saucepan. Let stand for 3 minutes, then spoon off the fat that has risen to the surface of the juices. Set the baking sheet over medium heat, then pour in the broth and bring to a simmer, scraping up the browned bits in the pan with a wooden spoon. Add to

(continues on page 216)

the skimmed juices in the saucepan. Bring to a simmer and season with salt and pepper. Transfer to a sauceboat.

9 In a small saucepan, melt the remaining sage brown butter over medium-low heat; transfer to a bowl. Using a large sharp knife, cut the turkey crosswise into slices. Return the turkey to the platter and serve with the stuffing, melted sage brown butter, and pan juices.

TURKEY TALK Some large single turkey breasts weigh 3 pounds or so. Or you may find two small turkey breast halves, still connected where the breastbone was, rolled together to make a turkey breast roast. After stuffing the butter under the skin, tie the double breast crosswise in a few places to hold its shape.

Since turkey breasts are lean and can become tough and dry if overcooked, I prefer to cook them to an internal temperature no higher than 155°F, and allow the temperature of the turkey to rise slightly as it rests at room temperature when removed from the oven. This, I assure you, results in meat that's juicy and tender. However, I realize more standard guidelines indicate 165°F as the recommended temperature. So, feel free to choose the temperature that you prefer.

Leek and Herb Stuffing

The true name for a stuffing that is not actually stuffed into food is dressing. I don't want to break any rules, but *stuffing* sounds so much more appetizing to me. The great thing about this style of stuffing is that it gets crispy and golden brown on top. This recipe makes a generous amount to allow for seconds.

serves 6 to 8

PREP TIME: 15 minutes

COOKING TIME: 1 hour 25 minutes, plus cooling time

MAKE-AHEAD: The stuffing can be assembled 6 hours ahead and refrigerated; add 10 minutes to the baking time.

½ pound (2 sticks) unsalted butter, cut into ½-inch cubes, plus butter for the baking dish

1 pound French or Italian bread, cut into ¾-inch cubes

¼ cup olive oil

1 large yellow onion, finely chopped

4 medium leeks (white and pale green parts only), well rinsed and finely chopped

5 celery ribs, cut into ¼-inch pieces

6 large sprigs of fresh thyme

2 sprigs of fresh rosemary

6 garlic cloves, finely chopped

¾ cup dry white wine

2 cups reduced-sodium chicken broth

⅓ cup finely chopped fresh flat-leaf parsley

Kosher salt and freshly ground black pepper

2 large eggs, lightly beaten

1 Preheat the oven to 350°F. Butter a 13 × 9 × 2-inch baking dish.

2 Spread the bread on a large, rimmed baking sheet. Bake for about 15 minutes, or just until dried but not browned. Let cool.

3 Meanwhile, heat a large deep skillet over medium-high heat. Add the olive oil, then add the onions and cook, stirring occasionally, for about 3 minutes, or until they soften. Add the leeks, celery, thyme, and rosemary and cook, stirring often, for about 4 minutes, or until the leeks are translucent. Stir in the garlic and continue cooking, stirring often, for about 5 minutes, or until the vegetables begin to brown. Add the wine and cook for about 2 minutes, or until the wine has evaporated but the vegetables are still very moist.

4 Add the broth and butter, bring to a simmer, and simmer for about 5 minutes, or until the liquid is reduced by half. Transfer to a large bowl and let cool slightly; remove and discard the rosemary and thyme stems.

5 Stir the parsley into the leek mixture. Add the bread cubes and mix well. Season to taste with salt and pepper. Mix in the eggs. Spread the stuffing in the baking dish and cover with aluminum foil.

6 Bake for about 30 minutes, or until the stuffing is heated through and puffed. Remove the foil and continue baking the stuffing for about 40 minutes longer, or until golden brown. Serve hot.

I t's impossible not to love a pot roast that you can carve with a spoon. I get it that way by placing it in the oven, where a low steady heat simmers it gently for a longer period of time. The olives add a nice salty kick to this tender dream of a supper.

POT ROAST WITH CHERRY TOMATOES, FINGERLING POTATOES, AND OLIVES

serves
6

PREP TIME: 15 minutes

COOKING TIME: 4 hours, plus 30 minutes resting time

MAKE-AHEAD: The beef can be made through step 4 up to 2 days ahead, cooled, covered, and refrigerated; remove the hardened fat on the surface of the cooking liquid, and reheat gently until simmering before proceeding.

One 4-pound boneless beef chuck roast

Kosher salt and freshly ground black pepper

2 tablespoons olive oil

2 yellow onions, chopped

12 garlic cloves, coarsely chopped

1 cup dry red wine

4 cups reduced-sodium beef broth, or as needed

4 large sprigs of fresh thyme

1 sprig of fresh rosemary

1½ pounds fingerling potatoes, halved lengthwise

12 ounces cherry tomatoes (preferably assorted colors)

¾ cup pitted green olives

1 Preheat the oven to 350°F.

2 Pat the beef dry with paper towels. Season with salt and pepper. Heat a large Dutch oven (at least 6 quarts) over medium-high heat. Add the olive oil, then add the beef and cook, turning occasionally, for about 12 minutes, or until browned on all sides. Transfer the beef to a bowl.

3 Reduce the heat to medium, add the onions to the pot, and cook, stirring occasionally and scraping up the brown bits on the bottom of the pot with a wooden spoon, for about 5 minutes, or until the onions are tender. Stir in the garlic and cook for about 1 minute, or until fragrant. Stir in the wine, bring to a boil, and boil for 1 minute. Stir in the broth, thyme, and rosemary.

4 Return the beef to the pot and scatter the potatoes, tomatoes, and olives around it. You should have enough liquid to cover all but about the top 1 inch of the beef; add broth or water if needed. Bring to a simmer over high heat, cover tightly, and transfer the pot to the oven. Bake for about 2 hours and 30 minutes, turning the beef over after the first 1½ hours, or until it is just tender. Uncover and continue baking for about 30 minutes, or until the beef is fork-tender. Set aside to rest for 30 minutes.

5 Using a slotted spoon, transfer the beef, vegetables, and olives to a platter. Gently pull the beef into large chunks along its natural separations. Cover the beef, vegetables, and olives with aluminum foil to keep warm. Skim off the fat that has risen to the surface of the cooking liquid and remove and discard the herb stems. Bring the liquid to a boil and boil for about 20 minutes, or until slightly reduced.

6 Return the beef, vegetables, and olives to the pot and simmer for about 5 minutes, or just until reheated. Divide the beef, vegetables, and olives among six dinner plates. Spoon a few tablespoons of the cooking liquid over each serving. Pour the remaining cooking liquid into a sauceboat. Serve hot, with the cooking liquid on the side.

I've never understood why you don't see savory cobblers more often. They get their name from the biscuit topping, which resembles cobblestones on a street. Here the cheese-flavored biscuit topping crumbles into the succulent stew.

STEAK AND MUSHROOM COBBLER WITH GRUYÈRE BISCUIT TOPPING

serves
6

PREP TIME: 15 minutes

COOKING TIME: 55 minutes

MAKE-AHEAD: The filling can be made up to 1 day ahead, cooled, covered, and refrigerated; reheat over medium heat until simmering before proceeding.

Filling

1¾ pounds flank steak, cut into 1-inch cubes

Kosher salt and freshly ground black pepper

4 tablespoons olive oil

1 yellow onion, chopped

3 garlic cloves, finely chopped

1 pound white button mushrooms, small mushrooms halved, large mushrooms quartered

3 carrots, cut into ¾-inch pieces

2 tablespoons all-purpose flour

2½ cups reduced-sodium beef broth

½ cup dry red wine

1 tablespoon Dijon mustard

1 tablespoon finely chopped fresh thyme

Biscuits

1 cup all-purpose flour

2 teaspoons baking powder

½ teaspoon baking soda

½ teaspoon fine sea salt

⅔ cup shredded Gruyère cheese (about 2 ounces)

4 tablespoons (½ stick) cold unsalted butter, cut into ½-inch pieces

¾ cup heavy cream

2 tablespoons freshly grated Parmesan cheese

2 tablespoons unsalted butter, melted

1. To make the filling: Season the steak with salt and pepper. Heat a large heavy skillet over high heat. Add 1 tablespoon of the olive oil, then add the steak pieces and cook, turning occasionally, for about 5 minutes, or until browned. Transfer the beef to a bowl and set aside.

2. Reduce the heat to medium. Add 1 tablespoon of the olive oil to the skillet, then add the onions and garlic and cook, stirring occasionally with a wooden spoon to scrape up the browned bits on the bottom of the skillet, for about 2 minutes, or until the onions soften. Transfer the onion mixture to the bowl with the beef. Heat the remaining 2 tablespoons olive oil in the skillet over medium-high heat. Stir in the mushrooms and cook, stirring occasionally, for about 4 minutes, or until tender and beginning to brown. Add the carrots and cook for about 1 minute. Sprinkle in the flour and stir well.

3. Return the beef and onion mixture, with any juices, to the skillet. Stir in the broth, wine, mustard, and thyme and bring to a simmer. Reduce the heat to medium-low and simmer gently, stirring occasionally, for about 15 minutes, or until the liquid has thickened into a light sauce. Season with salt and pepper. Transfer the beef mixture to a 13 × 9 × 2-inch baking dish and set aside.

4. Preheat the oven to 400°F.

5. To make the biscuits: In a large bowl, whisk the flour, baking powder, baking soda, and salt together. Using a pastry cutter, cut half of the Gruyère cheese and the 4 tablespoons butter into the flour until the mixture is crumbly, with pea-size pieces of butter.

6. Pour the cream over the flour mixture and stir with a fork just until moistened but still lumpy. Fold in the remaining Gruyère cheese with the Parmesan cheese. Divide the dough into 6 equal mounds and place the mounds over the steak and mushroom filling, spacing them evenly, and press the tops to flatten slightly. Brush the tops of the mounds generously with some of the melted butter; set the remaining butter aside.

7. Bake for about 25 minutes, or until the biscuits are dark golden brown on top and the filling is bubbling. Remove from the oven. Brush the biscuits with the reserved butter. Let stand for 5 minutes before serving.

Whole dried red chilies make this chili like none other. I first made it in Santa Fe, New Mexico, where chilies are a cooking staple, for *Take Home Chef*. Replace the ground beef with cubes of pork shoulder and simmer the chili for an additional 30 minutes to make a classic *carne adovada*.

SOUTHWESTERN CHILI

serves
8

PREP TIME: 20 minutes, plus 20 minutes soaking time

COOKING TIME: 1 hour 40 minutes

MAKE-AHEAD: The chili can be made up to 3 days ahead, cooled, covered, and refrigerated; reheat gently until simmering before serving.

9 dried red New Mexico or California chilies, stems and seeds removed

8 garlic cloves, crushed and peeled

4 cups reduced-sodium beef broth

Kosher salt

2 tablespoons canola oil

2 pounds lean ground beef

2½ teaspoons ground cumin

1½ teaspoons freshly ground black pepper

½ teaspoon cayenne pepper (optional)

2 medium white onions, finely chopped

One 28-ounce can crushed tomatoes

1 tablespoon white wine vinegar

Two 15-ounce cans red kidney beans, drained and rinsed

Accompaniments

Grated white Cheddar cheese

Chopped scallions

Plain Greek yogurt or sour cream

Corn tortillas or corn chips

1 In a large saucepan, bring 4 cups water to a boil over high heat. Remove the pan from the heat and add the chilies. Weigh down the chilies with a plate and soak for about 20 minutes, or until they soften slightly. Drain.

2 In a blender, puree the chilies and garlic with the broth. Season to taste with salt and set the sauce aside.

3 Heat a large Dutch oven over high heat. Add the canola oil, then add the ground beef and cook, stirring occasionally and breaking up the meat with the side of the spoon, for about 8 minutes, or until the beef is browned. Stir in the cumin, black pepper, and cayenne pepper, if using. Add the onions and cook, stirring occasionally, for about 10 minutes, or until tender.

4 Stir in the reserved chili sauce, the tomatoes, and the vinegar and bring to a gentle simmer. Reduce the heat to medium-low and simmer gently, uncovered, stirring occasionally, for about 1 hour, or until the sauce thickens slightly.

5 Stir in the beans. Cover and simmer very gently, stirring occasionally, for about 15 minutes, or until the chili has thickened a little more. Season to taste with salt.

6 Ladle the chili into bowls and serve with the Cheddar cheese, scallions, yogurt, and tortillas or chips on the side.

eat loaf is another food that I never had until I arrived in the States. Since then, I have experienced the good, the bad, and the ugly. I prefer to cook mine free-form, not in a loaf pan. This exposes more surface to the oven heat, making a crusty, browned exterior that adds flavor and texture.

CLASSIC MEAT LOAF WITH MASHED POTATOES

serves
6

PREP TIME: 10 minutes

COOKING TIME: 1 hour, plus 10 minutes resting time

1 cup cubed (½-inch) French baguette

⅓ cup whole milk

1½ pounds lean ground beef

⅓ cup finely chopped fresh flat-leaf parsley

⅓ cup coarsely grated yellow onion (use the large holes on a box grater)

½ cup freshly grated Parmesan cheese

⅓ cup tomato paste

2 large eggs, beaten to blend

1 tablespoon chopped fresh thyme

1 teaspoon chopped fresh rosemary

2 teaspoons kosher salt

1½ teaspoons freshly ground black pepper

½ cup Homemade Ketchup (recipe follows)

2 tablespoons light brown sugar

1 tablespoon Worcestershire sauce

Mashed Potatoes (recipe follows)

1. Position a rack in the middle of the oven and preheat the oven to 350°F. Line a large rimmed baking sheet with aluminum foil (for easy cleanup). Place a wire cooling rack on the foil.

2. In a large bowl, stir the bread cubes and milk together. Soak for about 10 minutes, or until the bread is very soft.

3. Mash the bread with your hands. Add the ground beef, parsley, onions, Parmesan cheese, tomato paste, eggs, thyme, rosemary, salt, and pepper. Using your hands, mix just until all of the ingredients are thoroughly combined. Shape the meat mixture into a 9½ x 4½-inch oval loaf and place on the rack on the baking sheet. Bake for 40 minutes.

4. Meanwhile, in a small bowl, mix the ketchup, brown sugar, and Worcestershire sauce together.

5. Spread half of the ketchup mixture over the meat loaf and continue baking for about 20 minutes more, or until an instant-read thermometer inserted into the center of the loaf reads 150°F. Let stand at room temperature for 10 minutes.

6. Remove the meat loaf from the rack, slice, and serve with the mashed potatoes and the remaining ketchup mixture.

Mashed Potatoes

You know when you eat in a restaurant and get those perfect, creamy, velvety mashed potatoes? Here's how they make them. First, you want starchy baking potatoes. Then, after they are cooked until tender and drained, place the strainer over the hot, steamy pot to dry them out a little. For the smoothest results, I like a food mill or ricer, but you can just crush the potatoes with a handheld masher.

serves 6

PREP TIME: 10 minutes
COOKING TIME: 20 minutes

2½ pounds large baking potatoes, such as russets, peeled and quartered

5 tablespoons unsalted butter, at room temperature

¾ cup whole milk, or as needed

Kosher salt and freshly ground black pepper

1 Place the potatoes in a large saucepan and add enough cold salted water to cover them by 1 inch. Bring the water to a simmer over high heat, then reduce the heat to medium and simmer for about 15 minutes, or until the potatoes are tender.

2 Drain the potatoes in a strainer and set the strainer over the hot saucepan to evaporate the excess steam. Put the potatoes in the saucepan, and reduce the heat to low, then add 4 tablespoons of the butter and mash the potatoes until they are nearly smooth. Whisk in enough of the milk to form a creamy consistency. Season to taste with salt and pepper. Spoon the potatoes into a serving bowl and top with the remaining 1 tablespoon butter.

Homemade Ketchup

Have some fun and make homemade ketchup. It will have a fresh, zesty flavor that's hard to resist.

makes about 1½ cups

PREP TIME: 10 minutes
COOKING TIME: 1 hour 15 minutes
MAKE-AHEAD: The ketchup can be made up to 2 weeks ahead and stored in an airtight container in the refrigerator.

3 ripe medium tomatoes (about 1¼ pounds total), quartered

1 tablespoon Worcestershire sauce

1 tablespoon olive oil

1 small yellow onion, finely chopped

⅓ cup packed dark brown sugar

1 tablespoon tomato paste

½ cup cider vinegar

Kosher salt

1 In a blender, puree the tomatoes with the Worcestershire sauce until smooth.

2 Heat a small heavy saucepan over medium heat. Add the olive oil, then add the onions and cook, stirring occasionally, for about 6 minutes, or until tender. Stir in the brown sugar and tomato paste, then stir in the pureed tomatoes and vinegar. Bring the mixture to a boil over high heat, stirring often. Reduce the heat to medium-low and simmer, stirring occasionally to prevent the ketchup from scorching, for about I hour, or until thickened to the desired consistency.

3 Season the ketchup to taste with salt. Serve warm or cold.

When I was a kid, my dad would take us for fish and chips every Friday night. The only other thing that you can buy at an Australian fish and chips shop is a steak sandwich, and I would have a dilemma every week about which to order. That's why I put both recipes in this book! These days I like to make the sandwich with Cheddar cheese, beef, and horseradish sauce. They're a terrific trio and the caramelized onions cap this off.

STEAK SANDWICHES WITH CARAMELIZED ONIONS AND CHEDDAR

serves
6

PREP TIME: 10 minutes

COOKING TIME: 30 minutes

MAKE-AHEAD: The onions can be made up to 1 day ahead, cooled, covered, and refrigerated; reheat over low heat before serving. The horseradish sauce can be made up to 1 day ahead, covered, and refrigerated.

Caramelized Onions

2 tablespoons olive oil

2 large yellow onions (about 1¾ pounds total), halved lengthwise and cut into thin half-moons

4 large sprigs of fresh thyme

1 bay leaf

2 garlic cloves, finely chopped

¼ cup sherry vinegar

1 cup reduced-sodium beef broth

Kosher salt and freshly ground black pepper

Horseradish Sauce

½ cup prepared horseradish

¼ cup mayonnaise

¼ cup sour cream

Kosher salt and freshly ground black pepper

Sandwiches

3 New York (top loin) steaks (each about 12 ounces and 1 inch thick)

Kosher salt and freshly ground black pepper

5 tablespoons olive oil

Twelve ½-inch-thick slices whole-grain bread

8 ounces sharp Cheddar cheese, thinly sliced

2 bunches watercress, tough stems removed

1. To caramelize the onions: Heat a large heavy skillet over medium-high heat. Add the olive oil, then add the onions, thyme, and bay leaf and cook, stirring often, for about 15 minutes, or until the onions are tender and golden brown.

2. Add the garlic and sauté for about 2 minutes, or until beginning to soften. Add the vinegar and cook for about 1 minute, or until reduced by half. Add the broth, bring to a boil, and cook for about 2 minutes, or until reduced by half. Remove and discard the thyme stems and bay leaf. Season to taste with salt and pepper. Remove from the heat and cover tightly to keep warm.

3. Meanwhile, make the horseradish sauce: In a small bowl, mix the horseradish, mayonnaise, and sour cream to blend. Season to taste with salt and pepper.

4. To cook the steaks: Prepare an outdoor grill for medium-high cooking over direct heat.

5. Season the steaks with salt and pepper. Coat the steaks with 1 tablespoon of the olive oil. Brush both sides of the bread slices with the remaining 4 tablespoons olive oil. Grill the steaks for about 3 minutes on each side, or until the meat feels only slightly resilient when pressed with a fingertip for medium-rare. Transfer the steaks to a carving board and let rest for 5 minutes.

6. Meanwhile, grill the bread on one side for about 2 minutes. Turn the bread over and divide the Cheddar cheese among 6 slices. Close the grill and cook until the Cheddar cheese has melted and the bread is toasted, about 2 minutes.

7. To assemble the sandwiches: Spread about 1½ tablespoons of the horseradish sauce over each of the 6 slices without cheese. Trim the excess fat and sinew from the steaks, then thinly slice the steaks across the grain. Divide the steak slices among the sauce-topped bread. Spoon the onions and their jus over the steak. Drizzle 1 tablespoon of the sauce over each. Top with the watercress and remaining toasted bread slices, cheese side down, cut the sandwiches in half, and serve.

I f I was forced to choose one sandwich above all others, pulled pork would win the contest. The classic version of this sandwich uses a slow-cooked barbecued pork shoulder. Mine is braised in the oven so it's easier to make, and you can enjoy it any time of year. The result is a perfect combination of juicy, tender pork, soft bun, tangy sauce, and crunchy slaw. There is no polite way to eat a pulled pork sandwich, so grab a napkin and enjoy every messy mouthful.

SLOW-COOKED PULLED PORK SANDWICHES WITH "FIREWORKS" COLESLAW

serves
6

PREP TIME: 15 minutes

COOKING TIME: 3 hours, plus 30 minutes cooling time

MAKE-AHEAD: The pork can be made up to 1 day ahead, cooled, covered, and refrigerated; reheat over medium heat before serving.

Pulled Pork

One 4-pound boneless pork shoulder roast

Kosher salt and freshly ground black pepper

2 tablespoons olive or canola oil

2 medium red onions, quartered

2 large carrots, cut into 1-inch chunks

3 celery ribs, cut into 1-inch chunks

1 head garlic, halved horizontally

1 cup dry red wine

4 cups reduced-sodium chicken broth

½ cup cider vinegar

1 navel orange, quartered

4 large sprigs of fresh thyme

1 bay leaf

½ teaspoon black peppercorns

About 3 cups Apple-Bourbon Barbecue Sauce (recipe follows), warm

Sandwiches

6 kaiser rolls with poppy seeds, split

"Fireworks" Coleslaw (page 231)

1   Preheat the oven to 275°F.

2   To cook the pork: Season the pork with salt and pepper. Heat a large Dutch oven over medium-high heat. Add the olive or canola oil, then add the pork and cook, turning occasionally, for about 15 minutes, or until golden brown all over. Transfer to a rimmed baking sheet and pour off all but 2 tablespoons of fat from the Dutch oven.

3   Add the onions, carrots, celery, and garlic to the pot and cook, stirring occasionally, for about 5 minutes, or until the onions are golden brown. Return the pork to the pot, add the wine, and bring to a simmer, scraping up the browned bits on the bottom of the pot with a wooden spoon. Boil for about 3 minutes, or until the wine is reduced by half. Add the broth, vinegar, orange, thyme, bay leaf, and peppercorns and bring to a simmer.

4   Cover the pot and transfer to the oven. Bake for about 2½ hours, or until the pork is fork-tender. Remove from the oven, uncover, and let cool for 30 minutes.

5   Transfer the pork to a baking dish. Using a fork and knife, pull the meat apart into large chunks. Moisten the shredded pork with some of the braising liquid and then toss with some of the warm barbecue sauce. Cover with aluminum foil to keep warm.

6   To make the sandwiches: Heat a grill pan or griddle over medium-high heat. Grill the rolls, cut side down, until lightly toasted. Pile the pork on the bottoms of the buns. Top with more of the sauce, the coleslaw, and the tops of the buns. Serve hot.

Apple-Bourbon Barbecue Sauce

I am very proud of this barbecue sauce, with its spicy, hot, sweet, sour, and salty notes. The flavors blend together into a delicious slather for grilled spareribs, chicken, pork chops, or pulled pork sandwiches. This makes a big batch, but it keeps well.

makes about 5½ cups

PREP TIME: 15 minutes

COOKING TIME: 1 hour 15 minutes

MAKE-AHEAD: The sauce can be made up to 2 weeks ahead, cooled, covered, and refrigerated; reheat before using.

2 tablespoons unsalted butter

1 yellow onion, chopped

2 garlic cloves, finely chopped

1 teaspoon sweet paprika

½ teaspoon dry mustard

½ cup bourbon whiskey

1 cup cider vinegar

2 cups reduced-sodium chicken broth

2 cups ketchup

¾ cup packed light brown sugar

2 canned chipotle chilies in adobo sauce, finely chopped

2 tablespoons Worcestershire sauce

1 teaspoon kosher salt

½ teaspoon freshly ground black pepper

2 Granny Smith apples, peeled, cored, and finely chopped

¼ cup fresh lemon juice

1 In a large saucepan, melt the butter over medium heat. Add the onions and cook, stirring often, for about 5 minutes, or until tender. Stir in the garlic and cook for about 3 minutes, or until the garlic is tender.

2 Stir in the paprika and dry mustard, then stir in the bourbon and vinegar, bring just to a simmer, and simmer for 3 minutes. Stir in the broth, ketchup, brown sugar, chilies and their sauce, Worcestershire sauce, salt, and pepper. Add the apples and lemon juice and bring the sauce to a simmer over high heat. Reduce the heat to medium-low and simmer uncovered, stirring often to prevent scorching, for about 1 hour, or until the sauce reduces and thickens slightly. Remove from the heat.

"Fireworks" Coleslaw

While this slaw was created for the pulled pork sandwiches, it can be put into service any time you need a great-looking salad to dress up the table. It got its name from the colorful array of vegetables in the bowl, but it also bursts with flavor.

serves 6

PREP TIME: 20 minutes, plus at least 10 minutes standing time

Poppy Seed Dressing

1½ cups mayonnaise

¼ cup finely chopped shallots

2 tablespoons cider vinegar

1 tablespoon poppy seeds

Finely grated zest of 1 lemon

2 teaspoons fresh lemon juice

2 teaspoons kosher salt

Slaw

½ head napa cabbage, cored, cut in half, and then cut crosswise into ⅛-inch-wide slices (about 3 cups)

½ head red cabbage, cored, quartered, and then cut crosswise into ⅛-inch-wide slices (about 2 cups)

1 large carrot, cut into thin matchstick-size strips

8 scallions (white and green parts), thinly sliced

½ cup lightly packed fresh cilantro

1 To make the dressing: In a medium bowl, whisk all the ingredients to combine. Cover and refrigerate for at least 10 minutes to develop the flavors.

2 To make the slaw: Using your hands, gently toss the napa cabbage, red cabbage, carrots, scallions, and cilantro in a large bowl to combine. Toss the coleslaw with enough dressing to coat (reserve any remaining dressing for another use). Serve immediately.

There is no way to rush great barbecued ribs, which is one of the reasons why the very best ones turn out juicy and fall-off-the-bone tender. These hickory-smoked beauties start off with an overnight spicing, then are slowly cooked for a few hours. Be flexible with the cooking time, as there are a lot of variables when barbecuing (see Grilling Versus Barbecuing, page 235). Serve with corn on the cob and your favorite potato salad.

BARBECUED SPARERIBS
WITH APPLE-BOURBON BARBECUE SAUCE

serves
6

PREP TIME: 10 minutes, plus at least 12 hours marinating time
COOKING TIME: 3 hours 30 minutes

Spice Rub

¼ cup packed light brown sugar

3 tablespoons sweet paprika

2 teaspoons freshly ground black pepper

1 teaspoon ground cumin

½ teaspoon cayenne pepper

Two 3½-pound racks pork spareribs

¾ cup cider vinegar

2 tablespoons kosher salt

Apple-Bourbon Barbecue Sauce (page 230), warm

Special Equipment

One 13 × 9-inch (or larger) disposable aluminum foil pan

3 cups hickory wood chips, soaked in cold water to cover for 1 hour

Clean spray bottle

1. The day before you cook the ribs, make the spice rub: In a medium bowl, mix the brown sugar, paprika, black pepper, cumin, and cayenne pepper together. Place the ribs on a large baking sheet and rub the ribs with the spice mixture. Cover and refrigerate for at least 12 hours, and up to 24 hours.

2. Prepare an outdoor grill for low cooking over indirect heat: *For a gas grill,* place the foil pan over one or two unlit burners and half-fill the pan with water. Turn on the remaining burner(s) and heat the grill to 300°F. Spread 1 cup of the drained wood chips on a piece of heavy-duty aluminum foil. Place the foil directly on the lit burner and wait until the chips are smoking before you add the ribs to the grill.

   For a charcoal grill, place the foil pan on the charcoal grate on one side of the grill and half-fill the pan with water. Build a charcoal fire on the other side and let it burn until the coals are covered with white ash and you can hold your hand just above the cooking grate for 4 to 5 seconds. (To check the temperature more accurately, cover the grill and drop a long-stemmed metal candy thermometer through the top vent; it should register about 300°F.) Sprinkle 1 cup of the drained wood chips over the coals.

3. Combine the vinegar and ¾ cup water in the spray bottle. Season the ribs with the salt. Place the ribs on the cooking grate over the water-filled pan. (Don't worry if the ribs extend over the pan, as the pan will still catch the majority of the dripping juices.) Grill, with the lid closed, turning the ribs over and spraying them every 45 minutes or so with the vinegar mixture, adding another cup of drained wood chips at the same intervals, for about 3 hours, or until the meat is just tender. *For a charcoal grill,* you will need to add 12 ignited charcoal briquettes (or the equivalent in hardwood charcoal) to the fire along with the chips every 45 minutes to maintain the grill temperature. (Light the charcoal in a chimney starter on a fire-safe surface, or use a small portable grill or hibachi.)

(continues on page 234)

For either grill, do not add more wood chips after the 1 hour and 30 minute point, as too much smoke will give the ribs a bitter flavor.

4   Once the ribs are tender, begin brushing them lightly with the barbecue sauce every few minutes or so, allowing the sauce to set before applying the next coat. Continue brushing the ribs with the sauce, turning occasionally, for about 30 minutes, or until the meat has shrunk from the ends of the bones. Transfer the ribs to a carving board and let rest for 5 minutes.

5   Using a large sharp knife, cut the racks into individual ribs. Transfer to a large bowl and toss with enough of the remaining warm barbecue sauce to coat. Arrange the ribs on a platter and serve with the remaining sauce on the side.

GRILLING VERSUS BARBECUING

Cooking outdoors is one of life's great pleasures. There's something primal about making dinner with the sun shining on your face—or even with the stars twinkling above you. And the flavor! Whether it's grilled or barbecued, the taste of food that has been kissed by flames is hard to beat. But, let's get something straight: there's a big difference between barbecuing and grilling. Here's how they differ:

Temperature and Time

Barbecuing uses low heat levels and longer cooking times (we're talking hours), whereas grilling uses high heat levels and shorter cooking times (we're talking minutes).

For grilling high and fast, I use a medium-high heat level of about 500°F for most of the recipes in this book. That's easy to set on a gas grill. For grilling on a charcoal grill, let the charcoal or briquettes burn until they're covered in white ash, then let them burn down for 5 minutes or so. The grill is ready when you're barely able to hold your hand an inch above it. For grilling, the lid can be open or closed.

For barbecuing low and slow, the optimal temperature is 300°F. For a charcoal grill, heap the coals on one side of the grill and let them burn down for at least 30 minutes. The heat is ready for the low and slow cooking if you can hold your hand just above the grate for about 4 seconds. For barbecuing, the lid must be kept closed to maintain the internal heat of the barbecue, just as an oven door must be kept closed to keep it hot for baking or roasting.

Direct or Indirect

When grilling, the meat should lie directly over the flames of the charcoal or gas flames, which will sear the outside of the meat while just cooking it through to the desired doneness (I prefer my steaks medium rare).

When barbecuing, however, the meat should be placed away from the hot coals. Pile the charcoal on one side of the barbecue grill and cook the meat on the opposite side of the grill. This will ensure the meat doesn't burn during the long cooking time.

Meat Choices

Ideal foods for grilling—steak, burgers, sausages, fish, shrimp, and pork chops—are naturally tender, so they cook fast and the high heat sears the outside, while keeping the inside of the meat tender and juicy.

On the other hand, your best bets for barbecuing are the larger or tougher and more flavorful cuts of meat—spareribs, baby back ribs, beef brisket, and whole chickens. The longer cooking time of barbecuing will ensure these meats end up deliciously tender.

Fueling Your Fire

Gas grills work great for high and fast grilling (which comes in handy on a busy weeknight). They're easy to prepare, and although gas grills don't impart the smoky richness of barbecue, you can get some of that flavor by adding wood chips. Soak the wood chips first (so they'll smoke and not flare up) then drain them and place them in an aluminum foil broiler pan. Set the pan directly on the gas burners until they smoke before grilling your food.

Charcoal barbecues are best for the low and slow method of barbecuing since the smoke from coals imparts the quintessential smoky flavor of good barbecue. Lump charcoal is my preferred choice of fuel for barbecuing, as they burn clean and provide steady, long-lasting heat.

Spice It Right

A dry rub or marinade can be used for both grilling and barbecuing. Grilling's high temperatures and the lengthy cooking time of barbecuing tend to burn sweet marinades and sauces, such as barbecue sauces and pesto, so add them only during the final moments of cooking.

Keep It Clean

Remember to keep your grill clean. The junk on the grates will not burn off, and if the grates aren't clean, the food (especially delicate fish) will stick. So, after preheating the grill, give the cooking grates a thorough scrub with a sturdy grill brush before adding the food.

I couldn't write about fabulous family suppers without a sensational glazed ham. It is the holiday roast of choice for many cooks, because it feeds a lot of people with very little effort. I also like the idea of having leftover ham for making sandwiches, tossing into fried rice and omelets, and turning into soup.

HONEY-GLAZED HAM

serves
8

PREP TIME: 10 minutes

COOKING TIME: 2 hours and 40 minutes, plus 20 minutes standing time

Glaze

1 cup honey

½ cup cider vinegar

½ cup coarsely chopped peeled fresh ginger

½ cup fresh lemon juice

½ cup packed light brown sugar

½ cup bourbon whiskey

⅓ cup Dijon mustard

Zest of 2 oranges, removed in wide strips with a vegetable peeler

2 cinnamon sticks

10 whole cloves

2 whole star anise

2 garlic cloves, crushed and peeled

Ham

2 carrots, cut into 2-inch chunks

2 celery ribs, cut into large chunks

1 yellow onion, cut into large chunks

1 navel orange, cut into 4 wedges

One 7- to 9-pound smoked cured ham

1 To make the glaze: In a medium heavy saucepan, combine all the ingredients and bring to a simmer over medium-high heat, stirring to dissolve the sugar. Remove from the heat and let stand for 15 minutes.

2 Meanwhile, to bake the ham: Preheat the oven to 350°F.

3 Strain the glaze through a sieve into a small bowl; discard the solids.

4 Spread the carrots, celery, onions, and orange wedges in a heavy roasting pan. Place the ham on the vegetable-orange mixture. Brush some of the glaze over the ham. Cover the ham (not the roasting pan) with aluminum foil.

5 Bake for about 2 hours, or until an instant-read thermometer inserted into the thickest part of the ham reads 115°F.

6 Remove the foil and brush the ham with more glaze. Continue to bake, uncovered, for another 30 minutes, brushing the ham with the glaze every 10 minutes (you should have leftover glaze). The glaze should be golden and caramelized and the ham should read at least 130°F on the thermometer. Transfer the ham to a carving board and let it rest for 10 minutes.

7 Strain any pan juices into a small saucepan and let stand for 3 minutes, then skim off the fat that has risen to the surface. Stir the remaining glaze into the pan juices and bring to a simmer over medium heat, stirring often. Transfer to a sauceboat.

8 Carve the ham and serve warm, with the glaze mixture alongside to drizzle over the ham slices.

ROUNDING OUT THE MEAL WHIPPED SWEET POTATOES Try these Southern-style yams (also known as red-skinned sweet potatoes) with this ham or Succulent Pork and Greens (page 91). In a saucepan of boiling salted water, cook chunks of peeled yams for about 15 minutes, or until tender. Drain. In a food processor, blend the hot yams until smooth, adding enough milk, cream, and butter to create the consistency of creamy mashed potatoes. Season with nutmeg, if desired, and salt to taste.

fficially known as Lancashire hot pot, this dish comes from northern England, where it has fed hardworking folk for centuries. I've lavished lots of tender loving care on my version. You'll see everyone at the table fighting to get at the crusty potato topping. If your market doesn't carry lamb shoulder cubes (these are common at halal butchers), ask to have a 4-pound roast trimmed, boned, and cubed. Although not traditional, there is no reason why this wouldn't also be good with beef chuck.

LAMB AND POTATO HOT POT

serves
6 to **8**

PREP TIME: 15 minutes

COOKING TIME: 3 hours, plus 20 minutes standing time

2½ pounds well-trimmed boneless lamb shoulder, cut into 1½-inch pieces

Kosher salt and freshly ground black pepper

¼ cup all-purpose flour

3 tablespoons olive oil, or as needed

2 pounds yellow onions, thinly sliced

2 large turnips (about 1 pound total), peeled and cut into ¾-inch pieces

2 carrots, cut into ¾-inch pieces

3 large garlic cloves, finely chopped

1 sprig of fresh rosemary

2 large sprigs of fresh thyme

1 cup dry sherry

4 cups reduced-sodium chicken broth

2 pounds medium baking potatoes, such as russets, peeled and cut into ¼-inch-thick rounds

3 tablespoons unsalted butter, melted

1 tablespoon chopped fresh chives

1 Preheat the oven to 350°F.

2 Season the lamb with salt and pepper. In a large bowl, toss the lamb with the flour to coat lightly. Shake off the excess flour and transfer the lamb to a plate. Heat a large deep heavy skillet over medium-high heat. Add 2 tablespoons of the olive oil and then, working in two batches, add the lamb and cook, turning occasionally and adding more olive oil if needed, for about 8 minutes per batch, or until golden brown. Transfer the lamb to a bowl.

3 Add the onions to the skillet, along with the remaining 1 tablespoon olive oil, and cook, stirring occasionally with a wooden spoon and scraping up any browned bits in the bottom of the pan, for about 8 minutes, or until the onions have softened and begin to color slightly. (It will look like a lot of onions when you first add them to the pan, but they will cook down considerably.) Stir in the turnips, carrots, garlic, rosemary, and thyme and cook for 3 minutes. Add the sherry and cook for about 10 minutes, or until the liquid has completely evaporated. Season the vegetables to taste with salt and pepper and spread evenly in a 13 × 9 × 2-inch baking dish. Arrange the lamb evenly over the vegetables and drizzle with any juices from the bowl.

4 Return the skillet to medium-high heat, add the broth, and bring to a simmer. Carefully pour enough of the hot broth over the lamb and vegetables to almost cover the lamb. Arrange half the potato slices in rows in a single tight, even layer, slightly overlapping, over the meat. Brush with some of the melted butter and season with salt and pepper. Repeat with another layer of potatoes, brush with the remaining butter, and season with salt and pepper.

5 Cover the baking dish with a lid or aluminum foil. Bake for about 1 hour, or until the meat is almost tender.

6 Remove the lid or foil and continue baking for about 1 hour and 30 minutes longer, or until the potatoes are golden brown and the cooking liquid has reduced and formed a sauce. Let stand for 20 minutes before serving.

7 Sprinkle the chives over the potatoes and serve hot.

When winter rolls around, I could make this every night. As the lamb shanks cook slowly to tenderness, the house becomes filled with an intoxicating aroma—don't be surprised if neighbors knock at your door and invite themselves over for dinner. Look for naan (thick flatbread) at Indian grocers and larger supermarkets.

CURRIED LAMB SHANKS WITH CARROTS, CHICKPEAS, AND POTATOES

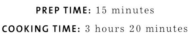

serves
4

PREP TIME: 15 minutes
COOKING TIME: 3 hours 20 minutes

4 lamb shanks (about 1 pound each)

Kosher salt and freshly ground black pepper

2 tablespoons olive oil

1 yellow onion, coarsely chopped

1 large leek (white and pale green parts only), well rinsed and cut into ½-inch pieces

4 large garlic cloves, coarsely chopped

4 teaspoons curry powder

1 teaspoon ground cumin

½ teaspoon red pepper flakes, or to taste

Four 3-inch-long strips of lemon zest, removed from a large lemon with a vegetable peeler

4 large sprigs of fresh thyme

1 bay leaf

½ cup red wine vinegar

5 cups reduced-sodium beef broth, or as needed

3 small Yukon Gold potatoes (about 14 ounces total), scrubbed and cut into ¾-inch pieces

5 medium carrots, cut into 1-inch pieces

One 15-ounce can chickpeas (garbanzo beans), drained and rinsed

2 scallions (white and green parts), thinly sliced on the diagonal

⅓ cup very coarsely chopped fresh cilantro

Warm naan, for serving

Plain low-fat or whole milk yogurt, for serving

1 Preheat the oven to 325°F.

2 Season the lamb with salt and pepper. Heat a large Dutch oven or other wide heavy pot over medium-high heat. Add the olive oil, then add the lamb shanks and cook, turning occasionally, for about 10 minutes, or until browned. Transfer to a large bowl.

3 Add the onions and leeks to the Dutch oven and cook, stirring occasionally, for about 5 minutes, or until tender. Add the garlic, curry powder, cumin, red pepper flakes, lemon zest, thyme, and bay leaf and stir for about 1 minute, or until fragrant. Stir in the vinegar and cook, stirring to scrape up the browned bits, for about 3 minutes, or until reduced by half.

4 Return the lamb shanks and their juices to the Dutch oven. Add enough broth to nearly cover the shanks, bring to a simmer, and cover. Transfer the pot to the oven and bake for about 2 hours, or until the meat is just tender.

5 Return the Dutch oven to medium-low heat on the stovetop. Add the potatoes and carrots and season lightly with salt. Cook at a gentle simmer, uncovered, for about 30 minutes, or until the vegetables are nearly tender and the liquid has reduced slightly. Using a slotted spoon or tongs, carefully transfer the lamb shanks to a plate (try to keep them intact) and cover with aluminum foil to keep warm. Discard the thyme stems and bay leaf.

6 Stir the chickpeas into the braising liquid and cook for about 15 minutes, or until the potatoes and carrots are tender. Stir in the scallions and half of the cilantro and season to taste with salt and pepper. Return the lamb shanks and their juices to the pot and simmer for 5 minutes to reheat the shanks.

7 Divide the lamb shanks and braising mixture among four wide shallow bowls. Sprinkle with the remaining cilantro. Serve hot, with naan and yogurt on the side.

In Australia, fish and chip stands are the equivalent of American hamburger joints—they are everywhere. There are three things that ensure this recipe comes out just right: Make sure your fish is fresh; use a great recipe for a crispy batter (you're about to read one); and serve them as they come out of the fryer.

HOMEMADE FISH AND CHIPS

serves
4

PREP TIME: 15 minutes, plus 1 hour standing time
COOKING TIME: 25 minutes
MAKE-AHEAD: The tartar sauce can be made up to 3 days ahead. The potatoes can be parcooked up to 2 hours ahead, covered with plastic wrap, and set aside at room temperature.

Tartar Sauce

1 cup mayonnaise

¼ cup finely chopped cornichons or dill pickles

2 tablespoons finely chopped fresh flat-leaf parsley

2 tablespoons coarsely chopped drained nonpareil capers

1 tablespoon fresh lemon juice

Kosher salt and freshly ground black pepper

Batter

One 12-ounce bottle lager beer, at room temperature

1 teaspoon active dry yeast

¼ teaspoon sugar

About 1¼ cups all-purpose flour, plus more for dredging

Fish and Chips

3 large baking potatoes, such as russets (about 1 pound each)

Canola oil, for deep-frying

Four 6-ounce skinless cod fillets

Kosher salt and freshly ground black pepper

Lemon wedges, for serving

1 To make the tartar sauce: In a small bowl, stir all the ingredients together. Season with salt and pepper. Cover and chill for at least 1 hour.

2 Meanwhile, to prepare the batter: In a large bowl, whisk the lager, yeast, and sugar to combine. Let stand in a warm place for about 10 minutes, or until the yeast dissolves. Gradually whisk enough flour into the yeast mixture to form a thick but fluid batter (when you dip your finger in the batter, the bubbles in the batter should fall slowly off your finger). Cover with a moistened kitchen towel and let stand in a warm place for 45 minutes.

3 Meanwhile, to prepare the chips: Line a large, rimmed baking sheet with paper towels. Bring a large pot of water to a boil over high heat. Peel the potatoes and cut them lengthwise into 5-inch-long by ½-inch-thick sticks. Add the potatoes to the boiling water. Once the water returns to a boil, cook for 2 minutes; drain the potatoes well. Spread them in a single layer on the baking sheet and let cool.

4 To fry the fish and chips: Heat a large wide Dutch oven over medium-high heat. Add enough canola oil to come halfway up the sides of the pot and heat to 375°F on a deep-frying thermometer. Place a large cooling rack on a large rimmed baking sheet.

5 Season the cod with salt and pepper. Spread about ½ cup flour in a shallow dish. Roll 1 cod fillet in the flour and shake off the excess. Dip in the batter, let the excess drip back into the bowl, and gently add the cod to the hot canola oil. Add one-fourth of the potatoes to the canola oil. Fry the cod and potatoes, adjusting the heat to keep the canola oil at about 350°F, for about 6 minutes, or until golden brown. Using a wire skimmer, transfer the cod and potatoes to the rack to drain. Immediately sprinkle the fish and chips with salt. Serve hot with the tartar sauce and lemon. Repeat to cook the remaining fish and chips, returning the canola oil to 375°F before frying each batch.

How do you make the world's best mac and cheese? I think that the combination of Cheddar and Gruyère cheese puts this one over the top. A mac and cheese doesn't need to be baked. If the sauce and pasta are hot, popping it under the broiler is all you need to get a cheesy crust and gooey center. I often make the sauce and cook the mac and cheese in the same skillet to save on cleanup. When I serve this to company, I divide it among individual casseroles before broiling.

MAC AND CHEESE WITH GRUYÈRE, CHEDDAR, AND BACON

serves
8

PREP TIME: 15 minutes
COOKING TIME: 30 minutes

6 slices bacon, cut crosswise into ¼-inch-wide strips

½ cup chopped shallots

2 garlic cloves, finely chopped

2 tablespoons all-purpose flour

3½ cups whole milk, or as needed

1½ cups heavy cream, or as needed

1½ cups shredded Gruyère cheese (about 6 ounces)

1½ cups shredded white Cheddar cheese (about 6 ounces)

Kosher salt and freshly ground black pepper

1 pound penne

2 tablespoons unsalted butter, melted, plus butter for the baking dish

⅔ cup panko (Japanese bread crumbs)

⅓ cup freshly grated Parmesan cheese

2 tablespoons finely chopped fresh flat-leaf parsley

1. Heat a large heavy saucepan over medium-high heat. Add the bacon and cook, stirring often, for about 5 minutes, or until golden brown. Using a slotted spoon, transfer the bacon to paper towels to drain, leaving the drippings in the saucepan. Add the shallots to the saucepan and cook, stirring often, for about 2 minutes, or until translucent. Add the garlic and sauté for about 1 minute, or until fragrant.

2. Reduce the heat to medium-low, whisk in the flour, and cook, whisking, for about 1 minute. Gradually whisk in the milk and cream, then bring the sauce to a gentle simmer over medium heat and simmer, whisking often, for about 10 minutes (do not allow the sauce to boil). Reduce the heat to medium-low and gradually whisk in the Gruyère and Cheddar cheeses. Remove the pan from the heat and season the sauce to taste with salt and pepper; it will seem thin at this point.

3. Meanwhile, bring a large pot of salted water to a boil over high heat. Stir in the penne and cook, stirring often to prevent it from sticking together, for about 8 minutes, or until tender but still firm to the bite. Drain well.

4. Stir the penne into the hot cheese sauce. If the sauce becomes too thick, thin it as desired with more milk or cream. Stir in the reserved bacon. Season to taste again with salt and pepper.

5. Position the broiler rack about 8 inches from the heat source and preheat the broiler. Butter a 3-quart baking dish or individual crocks. Spread the penne mixture in the baking dish.

6. In a small bowl, toss the panko, Parmesan cheese, parsley, and melted butter to mix well. Season with salt and sprinkle evenly over the penne. Broil, watching closely, for about 2 minutes, or until the topping is golden brown. Let stand at room temperature for 5 minutes before serving.

indsay is crazy about lasagna, and I am always looking for ways to bring a smile to her face with a new version. We love this one with grilled vegetables, which just happens to be lighter than most, but without any trade-off in flavor. You can assemble this before anyone arrives, then toss it in the oven an hour and fifteen minutes before you're ready to eat.

GRILLED VEGETABLE LASAGNA
WITH RICOTTA-TOMATO SAUCE

serves
8 to **10**

PREP TIME: 30 minutes

COOKING TIME: 2 hours and 20 minutes, plus 35 minutes standing time

MAKE-AHEAD: The sauce and grilled vegetables can be made up to 1 day ahead, cooled, covered separately, and refrigerated; reheat the sauce before using.

Ricotta-Tomato Sauce

2 tablespoons olive oil

1 large yellow onion, finely chopped

6 garlic cloves, minced

5 large sprigs of fresh thyme

2 bay leaves

1 teaspoon dried oregano

½ teaspoon red pepper flakes

2 cups dry white wine

3½ pounds ripe plum tomatoes, cut into ½-inch pieces

Kosher salt

1 cup whole-milk ricotta cheese

½ cup very coarsely chopped fresh basil

Freshly ground black pepper

Grilled Vegetables

1 medium eggplant (about 1¼ pounds), stem end trimmed and sliced lengthwise into ¼-inch-thick slabs

Kosher salt

3 tablespoons balsamic vinegar

3 tablespoons olive oil

Freshly ground black pepper

3 zucchini, sliced lengthwise into ¼-inch-thick slabs

2 red bell peppers, cored, seeded, and quartered

1 To make the ricotta-tomato sauce: Heat a large heavy saucepan or Dutch oven over medium heat. Add the olive oil, then add the onions and garlic and cook, stirring occasionally, for about 5 minutes, or until the onions are tender. Add the thyme, bay leaves, oregano, and red pepper flakes and cook, stirring often, for about 2 minutes, or until fragrant. Add the wine, raise the heat to high, and boil for about 12 minutes, or until reduced by half.

2 Stir in the tomatoes and season with salt. Bring to a simmer, then reduce the heat to medium-low and simmer gently, uncovered, stirring occasionally, for about 50 minutes, or until the tomatoes are very tender and have broken down to form a chunky sauce.

3 Meanwhile, prepare the vegetables: Lay the eggplant slices on a baking sheet and sprinkle with 1 tablespoon salt. Let stand for about 20 minutes, or until the salt begins to draw out moisture from the eggplant.

4 Rinse the eggplant under cold running water, then drain well. Place on a dry baking sheet and pat dry with paper towels.

5 Prepare an outdoor grill for medium-high cooking over direct heat.

6 In a small bowl, whisk the vinegar and olive oil together and season with salt and pepper. Lay the zucchini and bell peppers on a large rimmed baking sheet and brush both sides of the vegetables with ¼ cup of the balsamic mixture. Brush the remaining balsamic mixture over both sides of the eggplant slices.

7 Transfer the vegetables to the grill, in batches if necessary, and grill until just tender and slightly charred, about 3 minutes per side for the eggplant and zucchini, and about 4 minutes per side for the bell peppers. Return the vegetables to the baking sheets as they are cooked and let cool. Cut the bell pepper quarters in half.

8 When the sauce is done, remove the pan from the heat, then remove and

(continues on page 246)

12 dried lasagna noodles (about 12 ounces)

1 pound mozzarella cheese, shredded (about 4 cups)

discard the bay leaves and thyme stems. Stir in the ricotta cheese. Puree half of the sauce in a blender. Return the puree to the sauce remaining in the pan and stir in the basil. Season the sauce to taste with salt and pepper.

9 Preheat the oven to 350°F.

10 To assemble and bake the lasagna: Spread 1 cup of the tomato sauce over the bottom of a 13 × 9 × 2-inch baking dish. Lay 4 uncooked lasagna noodles over the sauce, breaking them to fit (don't worry if there's space around the noodles, since they will expand as they cook). Lay one-third of the grilled vegetables over the noodles, then spoon 1½ cups of the sauce over the vegetables and sprinkle one-third of the mozzarella cheese over the sauce. Repeat layering the noodles, vegetables, sauce, and mozzarella cheese one more time. Top with the remaining 4 noodles, then spread with 1½ cups of the sauce. Arrange the remaining vegetables on top. Spoon the remaining sauce over the vegetables.

11 Cover the baking dish with aluminum foil. Bake for 45 minutes. Remove the foil and sprinkle the remaining mozzarella cheese over the lasagna. Bake, uncovered, for about 30 minutes, or until the cheese has melted and the lasagna is golden brown on top and heated through (if you insert a knife into the center of the lasagna for 10 seconds, it should feel hot after you pull it out). Let the lasagna stand for 15 minutes before serving.

CURTIS'S KITCHEN NOTE

LET VEGETABLES SHINE More and more, vegetables are getting their due as important components of dinner, not just side dishes or afterthoughts. I often find myself inspired by beautiful produce at the market, and I bring a big bag home to cook a vegetarian meal. Vegetables should be loved for the flavor and color they bring to our cooking as well as for their nutritional benefits.

I bet that you never thought of actually firing up an outdoor grill for a grilled cheese, but this sandwich is a perfect balance of char, cheese, tomato, and spice. My friend Rochelle, a respected food professional, says that this is the best sandwich she has ever had. When she recommends something so strongly, you listen!

OUTDOOR GRILLED CHEESE SANDWICHES WITH TOMATOES AND PESTO

serves
6

PREP TIME: 10 minutes
COOKING TIME: 10 minutes

1½ pounds ripe tomatoes, cut into ¾- to 1-inch pieces

1 tablespoon balsamic vinegar

Kosher salt and freshly ground black pepper

1 loaf ciabatta bread

1 cup Pesto (page 40)

2 cups shredded Gruyère cheese (about 8 ounces)

4 ounces double-cream Brie cheese, rind trimmed and cut into ¼-inch-thick slices

1. Prepare an outdoor grill for high cooking over indirect heat: *For a gas grill,* heat one burner on high and leave the other burner(s) off. *For a charcoal grill,* build a fire on one side of the charcoal grate, leaving the other side of the grill empty, and let burn just until the coals are covered with white ash. Do not spread out the coals.

2. Meanwhile, in a large bowl, toss the tomatoes with the vinegar and season to taste with salt and pepper. Let stand, stirring occasionally, while you prepare the sandwiches.

3. Using a large serrated knife, cut the ciabatta horizontally in half. Spread the pesto over both cut sides of the ciabatta. Top with the Gruyère cheese, followed by the Brie cheese.

4. Place the ciabatta halves over the unlighted (empty) side of the grill. Cook, with the lid closed, for about 10 minutes, or until the cheese is melted and the bread is toasty. Transfer to a cutting board.

5. Using a slotted spoon, scatter the tomatoes in a thick layer over the bottom half of the ciabatta; discard the juices in the bowl. Cover with the top half of the ciabatta, cheese side down, and press gently. Using the serrated knife, cut the sandwich into 6 pieces and serve immediately.

hen my family comes over, I make a big pitcher of these upside-down tequila sunrises and let them help themselves. You can easily leave out the tequila so the kids can have some too, then let the grown-ups add the booze to taste.

TANGERINE TEQUILA SUNSET

serves
6

PREP TIME: 10 minutes, plus cooling time

COOKING TIME: 10 minutes

MAKE-AHEAD: The ginger–star anise syrup and cranberry reduction can be made
1 week ahead, covered separately, and refrigerated; bring the reduction to room temperature before using.

Ginger–Star Anise Syrup

1 cup agave nectar

5 whole star anise

2 tablespoons chopped peeled fresh ginger

Cranberry Reduction

1 cup cranberry juice

Cocktails

3 small tangerines, quartered

15 fresh mint leaves

1½ cups añejo tequila

Ice cubes

1 cup chilled club soda, or as needed

1 To make the syrup: In a small heavy saucepan, bring the agave nectar, star anise, and ginger to a boil over medium-high heat. Remove from the heat and let cool completely, then strain into a small bowl.

2 To make the cranberry reduction: In a small heavy nonaluminum saucepan, bring the cranberry juice to a boil over medium-high heat. Cook for about 7 minutes, or until reduced to ½ cup. Transfer to a small bowl and let cool completely; the cooled reduction will be quite thick.

3 To make the cocktails: In a large glass pitcher, combine the tangerine quarters and mint leaves. Using a muddler or the handle of a long wooden spoon, muddle (mash) the tangerines and mint for 15 seconds. Add the tequila and ¾ cup of the ginger–star anise syrup and stir well. Fill the pitcher with ice cubes. Stir, then add club soda to taste. Pour ⅓ cup of the cranberry reduction over the mixture in the pitcher, pour into ice-filled glasses, and serve.

SOMETHING SWEET

I'VE NEVER MET A DESSERT I DIDN'T LIKE.
Whether it's as simple as a bowl of berries or as decadent as a pot de crème, ending your dinners with a touch of sweetness always makes them special. When eating in a restaurant, I like to try fancy desserts, but at home, I make the classics: cheesecakes, pies, bread puddings, and cookies. **All of the recipes in this chapter are time-honored desserts that I've recrafted slightly to add elegance to their rustic goodness.**

When making desserts, remember these few tips: First, fresh seasonal fruits are always better than frozen or canned. They're sweet and ripe and won't need as much sugar to heighten their flavor. Feel free to swap in what's in season for your fruit-based cobblers and pies. Second, desserts can be satisfying without being naughty. A traditional Italian olive oil cake is butter-free and deceptively rich, and dark chocolate—my favorite has at least 70 percent cacao—is packed with antioxidants. And, finally, don't skip the salt in your dessert recipes. Just a pinch will enhance flavors and make sweets like cakes and custards even more tempting.

Strawberries and rhubarb are the epitome of spring cooking, and I love them equally. This compote—which can be served hot, warm, or chilled—shows how well they work together. Olive oil gives the cake a moist, pound-cake-like texture, and lemon, orange, and rosemary provide fragrant flavors and aromas. Use a fruity extra-virgin olive oil for the best results.

OLIVE OIL CAKE WITH STRAWBERRY-RHUBARB COMPOTE

serves
8

PREP TIME: 15 minutes

COOKING TIME: 35 minutes, plus 15 minutes cooling time

STORING: The cake can be stored, wrapped in plastic wrap, at room temperature for up to 2 days.

Cake

Nonstick olive oil cooking spray

1½ cups all-purpose flour

2 teaspoons baking powder

½ teaspoon fine sea salt

1 cup granulated sugar

1½ teaspoons minced fresh rosemary

Finely grated zest of 1 orange

Finely grated zest of 1 lemon

3 large eggs

¼ cup whole milk

¾ cup extra-virgin olive oil

Compote

12 ounces slender rhubarb stalks (about 3), cut into 2- by ⅓-inch-thick sticks

1 pound fresh strawberries, halved

¾ cup granulated sugar

3 tablespoons fresh lemon juice

Confectioners' sugar, for dusting

Extra-virgin olive oil, for drizzling

1 To make the cake: Position a rack in the center of the oven and preheat the oven to 350°F. Spray a 9-inch round cake pan with nonstick olive oil cooking spray. Line the bottom of the pan with parchment paper and spray the paper with nonstick olive oil spray.

2 In a medium bowl, whisk the flour, baking powder, and salt together.

3 In a large bowl, combine the sugar and rosemary. Add the orange and lemon zest, then rub the mixture between your fingertips until it is moist and fragrant. Add the eggs and, using an electric mixer, beat on medium-high speed for about 5 minutes, or until pale and thick. Beat in the milk. Gradually beat in the olive oil. Using a wooden spoon, stir in the flour mixture just until blended. Spread the batter in the pan.

4 Bake for about 35 minutes, or until a wooden toothpick inserted into the center of the cake comes out with moist crumbs attached. Let cool in the pan on a wire cake rack for 15 minutes, then invert the cake onto the rack and remove and discard the paper. Invert the cake, right side up, onto a cake plate.

5 Meanwhile, make the compote: In a large heavy skillet, bring the rhubarb, strawberries, sugar, and lemon juice to a simmer over medium-high heat, stirring often. Continue to cook, stirring often, for about 5 minutes, or until the juices thicken slightly and the rhubarb is falling apart. Let cool.

6 Sift confectioners' sugar over the cake. Cut the cake into wedges, place on dessert plates, and spoon the compote on top. Drizzle a little olive oil around the cake and serve.

anana bread is the perfect thing to have on standby. Serve it to guests who pop in, pack it into the kids' lunches, or treat yourself to a slice as a snack with a cup of tea. This one is full of walnuts to give it an extra burst of toasty flavor.

BANANA BREAD WITH LOTS OF TOASTED WALNUTS

serves
8

PREP TIME: 15 minutes

COOKING TIME: 1 hour 25 minutes, plus at least 15 minutes cooling time

STORING: The banana bread can be stored, wrapped in plastic wrap, at room temperature for up to 3 days.

Nonstick cooking spray

2 cups walnuts

1²⁄₃ cups all-purpose flour

1 teaspoon baking soda

½ teaspoon fine sea salt

½ teaspoon freshly grated nutmeg

¼ teaspoon ground cinnamon

1¼ cups sugar

2 large eggs

½ cup canola oil

1⅓ cups coarsely mashed ripe bananas (about 3 large)

2 tablespoons plain whole-milk yogurt

1 teaspoon pure vanilla extract

1 Position a rack in the center of the oven and preheat the oven to 350°F. Spray a 9 × 5 × 3-inch loaf pan with nonstick cooking spray.

2 Spread 1½ cups of the walnuts on a large heavy baking sheet. Bake, stirring occasionally, for about 8 minutes, or until the walnuts are toasted and a nut broken in half is golden brown in the center. Let cool, then coarsely chop.

3 In a medium bowl, whisk the flour, baking soda, salt, nutmeg, and cinnamon together to blend.

4 In a large bowl, using an electric mixer on medium-high speed, beat the sugar and eggs for about 8 minutes, or until pale and thick. Gradually beat in the canola oil. Beat in the bananas, yogurt, and vanilla. Reduce the speed to low, add the flour mixture, and mix just until blended. Using a large flexible spatula, fold the toasted walnuts into the batter.

5 Spread the batter in the loaf pan. Sprinkle the top with the remaining ½ cup walnuts. Bake for about 1 hour and 15 minutes, or until the top is browned and a wooden toothpick inserted into the center of the loaf comes out clean. If the bread is browned before it tests done, tent the top with aluminum foil. Let cool in the pan on a wire cake rack for 15 minutes.

6 Invert the banana bread onto the rack and turn right side up. Slice and serve warm, or let cool completely before serving.

BANANAS FOR BAKING Many bakers wait until banana skins are black-ripe before using the bananas in baked goods. This actually isn't a great idea, because blackened bananas will have developed a fermented flavor. The best bananas for baking have skins that are just flecked with brown spots. When bananas reach this state and you have no immediate use for them, they can be frozen. Pop them into the freezer, right in their skins, for up to 2 months. The skin will turn dark brown, but the flesh won't be affected.

ere's my lemony New York–style cheesecake. Fresh summer cherries are ideal spooned over it. Don't bother to cook the cherries, just macerate them with lemon juice and sugar to bring out the juices.

NEW YORK CHERRY CHEESECAKE

serves
12

PREP TIME: 15 minutes

COOKING TIME: 1 hour 45 minutes, plus 1 hour cooling time and at least 8 hours refrigerating time

STORING: The cheesecake can be refrigerated for up to 2 days.

Butter for the pan

Crust

12 whole graham crackers

3 tablespoons sugar

5 tablespoons unsalted butter, melted

Filling

Four 8-ounce packages cream cheese, at room temperature

1¼ cups sugar

2 teaspoons finely grated lemon zest

1 tablespoon fresh lemon juice

1 teaspoon pure vanilla extract

4 large eggs

Sour Cream Topping

2 cups sour cream

3 tablespoons sugar

Cherry Topping

1 pound fresh Bing cherries, halved and pitted

3 tablespoons sugar

1 tablespoon fresh lemon juice

1. Position a rack in the center of the oven and preheat the oven to 350°F. Lightly butter a 9-inch springform pan with 3-inch-high sides.

2. To make the crust: In a food processor, grind the graham crackers into very fine crumbs (you should have 1⅓ cups). Add the sugar and melted butter and pulse until moistened. Press the crumb mixture evenly onto the bottom and 1½ inches up the sides of the pan. Bake for about 12 minutes, or until the crust is a shade darker. Cool on a rack, then wrap three layers of wide heavy-duty foil around the outside of the pan.

3. To make the filling: Clean the food processor bowl, then blend the cream cheese and sugar until smooth, occasionally scraping down the sides of the bowl with a flexible spatula. Add the lemon zest, lemon juice, and vanilla; pulse to combine. Add the eggs and pulse until blended.

4. Pour the filling into the crust-lined pan. Place the pan in a large roasting pan. Pour in enough hot water to come halfway up the sides of the springform pan. Bake for about 1 hour 15 minutes, or until the filling is set except for the very center when the pan is gently shaken (the cake will become firm when chilled).

5. Meanwhile, prepare the sour cream topping: In a medium bowl, stir the sour cream and sugar to blend.

6. Spoon the sour cream mixture onto the hot baked cheesecake and smooth it over the top. Continue baking the cheesecake for about 15 minutes, or until the topping is set. Let the cheesecake cool in the pan on a rack for 1 hour.

7. Run a sharp paring knife around the edges of the cheesecake to loosen it from the pan sides (leave the sides in place). Cover loosely with plastic wrap and refrigerate for at least 8 hours, or until thoroughly chilled.

8. To make the cherry topping: In a medium bowl, combine the cherries with the sugar and lemon juice and toss to coat. Let stand at room temperature, tossing occasionally, for about 30 minutes, or until juices form.

9. Remove the pan sides from the cheesecake. Cut the cake with a large sharp knife (dip the knife in hot water after each cut to moisten it and wipe it clean) and transfer to plates. Spoon the cherry topping over and serve.

These cookies should come with a warning: With oversized chocolate chunks and crunchy pecans, they are truly addictive. While I love 70 percent cacao chocolate for eating and some recipes, it tends to melt and spread too much when used in these cookies. I prefer a sweeter chocolate with 60 percent cacao, here.

CHOCOLATE CHUNK COOKIES WITH PECANS

makes
18

PREP TIME: 15 minutes

COOKING TIME: 30 minutes

STORING: The cookies are best eaten warm.

2 cups all-purpose flour

1 teaspoon baking soda

½ pound (2 sticks) unsalted butter, at room temperature

1 cup granulated sugar

¾ cup packed light brown sugar

2 teaspoons pure vanilla extract

¾ teaspoon fine sea salt

2 large eggs

12 ounces bittersweet chocolate (60% cacao), very coarsely chopped into chunks

2 cups pecan halves, toasted (see Kitchen Note, page 113)

1. Position racks in the top third and center of the oven and preheat the oven to 375°F. Line two large (18 × 13 × 1-inch) heavy rimmed baking sheets with parchment paper.

2. In a small bowl, whisk the flour and baking soda together.

3. In a large bowl, using an electric mixer, beat the butter, granulated sugar, brown sugar, vanilla, and salt on medium-high speed for about 4 minutes, or until creamy. One at a time, add the eggs, beating well after each addition. Reduce the mixer speed to low and gradually beat in the flour mixture just until combined. Add the chocolate chunks and pecans and mix just until the pecans break up a bit.

4. Using about ⅓ cup dough for each cookie, drop the dough, spacing it evenly and placing only 6 cookies on each sheet, onto the prepared baking sheets. These cookies will spread, so don't place them too close together. (The shaped cookies can be frozen until firm, then stored in a freezer bag for up to 1 month. Bake the frozen cookies without thawing, but allow a few additional minutes of baking time.)

5. Bake the cookies, switching the positions of the sheets from top to bottom and front to back halfway through baking, for about 13 minutes, or until the edges and tops are golden brown but the centers are still soft and moist. Let the cookies cool on the baking sheets for 5 minutes. Using a metal spatula, transfer the cookies to wire racks. Repeat with the remaining dough, being sure that the baking sheets are completely cooled before adding the dough. Serve the cookies warm.

CHOCOLATE AND CACAO Chocolate is made from roasted and ground cacao beans. The only other main ingredients are usually sugar, vanilla (natural or artificial vanillin), and lecithin (an emulsifier). Cocoa butter, a by-product of grinding cacao beans, is sometimes added for extra smoothness, and dried milk is added to make milk chocolate. The cacao content you see nowadays on packages refers to the percentage of ground beans in each bar. The higher the cacao content, the lower the sugar, and the more bitter the chocolate.

This is an ANZAC (Australian and New Zealand Army Corps) biscuit, the most popular cookie Down Under. People used to send these long-keeping treats to members of the army. History aside, this oatmeal coconut cookie belongs in your cookie jar too.

OATMEAL COCONUT BUTTER COOKIES

makes
36

PREP TIME: 15 minutes

COOKING TIME: 30 minutes

STORING: The cookies can be stored in an airtight container at room temperature for up to 5 days.

1 cup old-fashioned (rolled) oats

¾ cup unsweetened shredded coconut

1 cup all-purpose flour

1 cup sugar

12 tablespoons (1½ sticks) unsalted butter

3 tablespoons golden syrup, such as Lyle's (see Kitchen Note)

2 tablespoons boiling water

1½ teaspoons baking soda

1. Position racks in the top third and center of the oven and preheat the oven to 300°F. Line two large (18 × 13 × 1-inch) heavy rimmed baking sheets with parchment paper.

2. In a large bowl, mix the oats, coconut, flour, and sugar to combine.

3. In a medium heavy saucepan, stir the butter and syrup over low heat until the butter is melted. Remove the saucepan from the heat. In a small bowl, stir the water and baking soda together, and stir into the butter mixture. Stir into the flour mixture.

4. Using 1 tablespoon dough for each cookie, drop 12 mounds of dough onto each baking sheet, spacing them evenly. Do not crowd the cookies, as they will spread considerably.

5. Bake the cookies, switching the positions of the sheets from top to bottom and front to back halfway through baking, for about 15 minutes, or until golden brown. Let cool on the baking sheet for 5 minutes.

6. Transfer the cookies to wire racks and let cool completely. The cookies will become slightly crisp and chewy once cooled. Repeat with the remaining dough, being sure that the baking sheets are completely cooled before adding the dough.

LYLE'S GOLDEN SYRUP is a British product that is sweet and sticky, like corn syrup, but made purely from sugar. Partly because it is now owned by an American firm, Lyle's syrup is available at most supermarkets here, but you can also order it online. The plastic squeeze bottle is a lot easier to use than the can, though the can looks very cool in your pantry.

The power of apple pie is awesome: This simple dessert has been making grannies famous for generations. There is something about the smell of cinnamon, cloves, and apples baking in a buttery crust that makes you feel good. I use different varieties of apples to get the best qualities of each, but feel free to use your favorite type. I always make my pastry dough in a food processor, because it is so fast, but I provide a handmade version as a variation here.

SPICED APPLE PIE

serves
8

PREP TIME: 20 minutes, plus at least 30 minutes chilling time
COOKING TIME: 1 hour 15 minutes, plus at least 1 hour cooling time
STORING TIME: The pie is best served warm, but will keep, covered and at room temperature, for up to 1 day.

Crust

2½ cups all-purpose flour

2 tablespoons granulated sugar

1 teaspoon fine sea salt or table salt

½ pound (2 sticks) cold unsalted butter, cut into ½-inch cubes

½ cup ice-cold water

Filling

⅔ cup packed light brown sugar

3 tablespoons all-purpose flour

1 teaspoon ground cinnamon

½ teaspoon freshly grated nutmeg

Pinch of ground cloves

¼ teaspoon fine sea salt

3 Granny Smith apples, peeled, cored, and cut into ½-inch wedges

2 Golden Delicious apples, peeled, cored, and cut into ½-inch wedges

2 Gala apples, peeled, cored, and cut into ½-inch wedges

⅓ cup dark raisins

2 tablespoons unsalted butter, thinly sliced

About 1 teaspoon whole milk

2 teaspoons raw or granulated sugar

Vanilla ice cream, for serving

1. To make the crust: In a food processor, pulse the flour, sugar, and salt to blend. Add the butter and pulse about 10 times, until the butter is in pea-size pieces. While pulsing the food processor, drizzle the ice water through the feed tube and process just until moist clumps form. Transfer the dough to a work surface, divide it in half, making one half slightly larger than the other, and form into 2 thick disks. Wrap each one in plastic wrap and refrigerate for at least 30 minutes, and up to 1 day.

2. Position a rack on the lowest rung of the oven and preheat the oven to 425°F. (Being near the source of heat helps the bottom crust of the pie to bake and brown properly.)

3. To make the filling: In a large bowl, whisk the brown sugar, flour, cinnamon, nutmeg, cloves, and salt together. Add the apple wedges and raisins and mix to combine.

4. Unwrap the larger disk of dough and set it on a floured surface, then lightly dust the top of the dough. (If the dough is too cold and firm to roll out, let it stand at room temperature, covered, until it softens slightly.) Starting from the center of the dough and rolling toward the edges, roll out the dough into a 13-inch round, occasionally rotating the dough and dusting the surface with flour to prevent the dough from sticking. Brush away excess flour. Place the rolling pin on the edge of the dough that's farthest away from you and gently and loosely roll the dough up around the pin until you have half of it on the pin. Hold the pin over the edge of a 9- to 9½-inch glass pie plate and unroll the dough, draping and centering it over the pie plate. Lightly press the dough into the dish. Trim the overhang to ½ inch. Refrigerate the pie shell. Roll out the other disk of dough on the floured surface into a 12-inch round.

5. Spread the apple mixture in the pie shell, then scatter the sliced butter on top. Cover the pie with the remaining dough round. Trim the overhang to

(continues on next page)

½ inch and press the edges together, fold the dough under itself so it is flush with the edge of the pie plate. Crimp the dough edge decoratively.

6 Lightly brush the top of the pie with the milk and sprinkle all over with the raw sugar. Using a small sharp knife, cut 4 steam vents in the top crust. Bake for 20 minutes. Reduce the oven temperature to 350°F and bake the pie for about 55 minutes longer, or until the crust is golden and the filling is bubbling through the steam vents. Let the pie cool on a wire rack until warm.

7 Cut the pie into wedges and serve with ice cream.

VARIATION: **HANDMADE PIE DOUGH**

In a large bowl, whisk the flour, sugar, and salt together. Add the butter. Using a pastry blender or two forks, cut the butter into the flour until the butter is in pea-size pieces. Drizzle the ice water over the flour and gently toss the mixture together to moisten. Turn the mixture out onto a work surface and gently gather it to form a dough.

COOKING IN SEASON No wonder it's so difficult to know what produce is in season when so many fruits and vegetables are available year-round at the grocery store. But Mother Nature has a time for everything, and it benefits you to eat according to her schedule. Produce is more flavorful as well as more abundant in season, which makes it less expensive, and it's a great chance to try something new. I'm always a little sad at the end of a season to see some of my favorites go away, but then the new season's offerings come along and I'm inspired again. Take a stroll through your farmers' market and get familiar with the season's bounty.

reamy custard, sweet ripe bananas, and crunchy streusel—I'm in heaven. There are two ways to serve this: either in a large bowl, family style, or in individual dessert glasses for when guests come over. If you have yet to make your first caramel sauce, give it a shot. It is so delicious. Whip up a double batch and refrigerate the extra to pour over ice cream.

BANANA CREAM PARFAIT WITH GINGERSNAP STREUSEL

serves
8

PREP TIME: 15 minutes

COOKING TIME: 30 minutes, plus 1 hour cooling time

STORING: The caramel sauce can be refrigerated in an airtight container for up to 1 week; reheat just until fluid before serving. The parfait can be refrigerated, covered with plastic wrap, for up to 4 hours.

Ginger Caramel Sauce

½ cup sugar

¾ cup heavy cream

One 1½-inch-long piece of fresh ginger, peeled and cut into 6 slices

Streusel

22 crisp gingersnap cookies (about 6 ounces)

1 tablespoon sugar

4 tablespoons (½ stick) unsalted butter, melted

Vanilla Custard

½ cup sugar

⅓ cup cornstarch

¼ teaspoon fine sea salt

2¾ cups heavy cream

1½ cups whole milk

3 large egg yolks

½ vanilla bean, split lengthwise

2 tablespoons unsalted butter

4 large ripe bananas, peeled

1 To make the caramel sauce: In a small heavy saucepan, stir the sugar and ¼ cup water over medium heat for about 2 minutes, or until the sugar dissolves. Brush down the sides of the pan with a moistened pastry brush to remove any sugar granules. Cook, without stirring, for about 7 minutes, or until the caramel turns amber in color, swirling the pan as needed to ensure the sugar caramelizes evenly. Reduce the heat to low and carefully pour in the cream (the caramel will bubble up and harden). Add the ginger and cook, whisking constantly, until all of the caramel is dissolved. Remove the pan from the heat and let cool to warm or room temperature.

2 Strain the caramel through a sieve into a bowl. Let cool.

3 Preheat the oven to 350°F.

4 To make the streusel: In a food processor, grind the gingersnap cookies until they form very fine crumbs (you will have about 1 cup crumbs). Add the sugar and melted butter and pulse until combined. Sprinkle the mixture evenly over a large heavy rimmed baking sheet. Bake, stirring after 5 minutes, for about 10 minutes, or until the crumbs clump together and become a shade darker. Let cool.

5 To make the vanilla custard: Whisk the sugar, cornstarch, and salt together in a medium heavy saucepan. Gradually whisk in 1½ cups of the cream and the milk, followed by the egg yolks. Using the tip of a small sharp knife, scrape the seeds from the vanilla bean, whisk them into the milk mixture, and drop in the vanilla bean too. Set the pan over medium-high heat and whisk for about 6 minutes, or until the custard thickens and large bubbles just begin to burst through the surface. Remove from the heat and whisk in the butter. Remove and discard the vanilla bean. Transfer the custard to a large bowl and cool completely, whisking occasionally, for about 1 hour.

6 In a large bowl, using an electric mixer, beat the remaining 1¼ cups cream

(continues on next page)

until it thickens and forms loose mounds. Stir the custard to loosen it. Fold 1 cup of the whipped cream into the custard.

7   Spoon 1 cup of the custard over the bottom of a 2½-quart glass or other serving bowl. Holding 1 banana over the bowl, cut it into ¼-inch-thick slices, allowing the slices to fall onto the custard, and cover it sparsely. Sprinkle ½ cup of the streusel over the bananas, then spread 1½ cups of the custard over the bananas. Slice 1½ more bananas, allowing the slices to fall onto the custard and cover it evenly. Sprinkle ¾ cup of the streusel over the bananas. Repeat the layering one more time with the remaining custard, streusel, and bananas. Top with the remaining whipped cream. Spoon the parfait into bowls, drizzle with the caramel sauce, and serve.

VARIATION: **INDIVIDUAL PARFAITS**

For a special presentation, layer the custard, caramel sauce, sliced bananas, streusel, and whipped cream among eight parfait glasses, topping each with a dollop of whipped cream and a drizzle of caramel sauce.

When you take delicious ripe seasonal fruit, mix it with some spice and sweetness, and cover it with crunchy goodness, you've won me over. Change the fruit from peach to whatever is in season and tasty—you can't go wrong.

PEACH AND ALMOND COBBLER

serves
8

PREP TIME: 15 minutes

COOKING TIME: 50 minutes, plus at least 15 minutes cooling time

1 tablespoon unsalted butter, at room temperature

Filling

¾ cup sugar

⅓ cup all-purpose flour

1 teaspoon ground cinnamon

1 vanilla bean, split lengthwise

5 pounds ripe peaches

2 tablespoons fresh lemon juice

Biscuit Topping

2¼ cups all-purpose flour

6 tablespoons sugar

1 tablespoon baking powder

¾ teaspoon fine sea salt

8 tablespoons (1 stick) cold unsalted butter, cut into small pieces

1 large egg

¾ cup plus 2 tablespoons heavy cream

¼ cup sliced almonds

Vanilla ice cream, for serving

1. Position one rack in the center of the oven and the second rack in the lower third of the oven and preheat the oven to 400°F. Coat a 13 × 9 × 2-inch rectangular or 10½-inch square baking dish with the butter.

2. To make the filling: In a large bowl, mix the sugar, flour, and cinnamon together. Using the tip of a small sharp knife, scrape the seeds from the vanilla bean, add them to the mixture, and whisk to blend. Gently rub the peaches under cold running water to remove their peach fuzz, then pat dry.

3. Cut the peaches in half, remove the pits, and cut the halves into 1-inch-thick wedges. Add the peaches and lemon juice to the sugar mixture and toss to coat. Set the peaches aside while you prepare the biscuit topping, occasionally tossing the peaches to help release some juices.

4. To make the biscuit topping: In a large bowl, whisk the flour, 4 tablespoons of the sugar, the baking powder, and salt together. Add the butter and use your fingertips to rub it into the mixture until it resembles coarse meal.

5. In a small bowl, whisk the egg and ¾ cup of the cream together. Using a wooden spoon, gently stir into the flour mixture just until combined and a dough forms; do not overmix.

6. Spread the peach mixture in the baking dish. The dish may seem very full, but the peaches will shrink during baking. Using about ¼ cup of dough for each biscuit, gently shape the dough into about 12 disks, placing them, as they are shaped, over the fruit and spacing them evenly. Flatten the biscuits slightly with your fingertips. Sprinkle the almonds over. Brush with the remaining 2 tablespoons cream and sprinkle with the remaining 2 tablespoons sugar.

7. Place an empty baking sheet on the lower oven rack (to catch any juices) and place the cobbler on the center rack. Bake for about 50 minutes, or until the biscuits are golden brown and the juices are bubbling. If the biscuits have browned nicely before the filling bubbles, tent the dish with aluminum foil and continue to bake until the filling bubbles. Cool the cobbler on a wire rack for at least 15 minutes.

8. Spoon into bowls and serve warm, with vanilla ice cream.

If there's a way to improve on smooth and silky chocolate mousse, it's with a bit of cool mint to cut through the richness. But with or without the mint, this recipe will become your go-to chocolate mousse. I make mine with dark chocolate, which allows its flavor to really come through.

BITTERSWEET CHOCOLATE–MINT MOUSSE

serves
6 to **8**

PREP TIME: 10 minutes, plus 15 minutes cooling time and at least 2 hours chilling time
STORING: The mousse can be refrigerated for up to 2 days.

7 ounces bittersweet chocolate (70% cacao), coarsely chopped

2 tablespoons unsalted butter, thinly sliced

½ cup whole milk

3 large eggs, separated

⅔ cup confectioners' sugar

1 cup heavy cream

⅛ teaspoon mint extract

1 Set a large heatproof bowl over a saucepan of barely simmering water. Add the chocolate and butter to the bowl and stir until melted and smooth. Remove the bowl from the saucepan. Whisk in the milk. Let stand for about 15 minutes, stirring occasionally, or until the mixture is cool.

2 In a medium bowl, using an electric mixer, beat the egg yolks and ⅓ cup of the confectioners' sugar on medium-high speed, until light and airy. In another medium bowl, using clean beaters, beat the egg whites with the remaining ⅓ cup confectioners' sugar on medium-high speed until soft peaks form. Using a large flexible spatula, fold the egg yolk mixture into the cooled chocolate mixture. Gently fold in the egg white mixture.

3 Add the cream and the mint extract to the bowl that held the egg whites. Beat with the mixer (no need to clean the beaters) on high speed until thick, soft peaks form. Fold the whipped cream into the chocolate mixture.

4 Divide the mousse among six to eight dessert cups or bowls. Cover each one with plastic wrap. Refrigerate for at least 2 hours to chill and set the mousse.

Bread may be a humble ingredient, but it doesn't take much to turn it into something special. Whenever I have extra bread around I know this dessert is in my future. Feel free to use chocolate chips instead of chopped chocolate. This is at its best when warm.

CHOCOLATE BREAD PUDDING

serves
8

PREP TIME: 10 minutes, plus 20 minutes soaking time
COOKING TIME: 50 minutes

2½ cups heavy cream

1¼ cups whole milk

1¼ cups packed light brown sugar

5 large eggs

1½ teaspoons pure vanilla extract

1 pound day-old French or Italian bread, cut into 1-inch cubes (about 12 cups)

1 tablespoon unsalted butter, at room temperature

8 ounces semisweet chocolate, coarsely chopped

1 tablespoon granulated sugar

1 In a large bowl, whisk the cream, milk, brown sugar, eggs, and vanilla together. Add the bread and gently stir to coat well. Set aside for about 20 minutes to allow the bread to soften and soak up some of the egg mixture.

2 Position a rack in the center of the oven and preheat the oven to 350°F. Coat a 13 × 9 × 2-inch oval baking dish with the butter.

3 Fold the chocolate into the bread mixture. Transfer to the prepared baking dish and sprinkle with the granulated sugar. Bake for about 50 minutes, or until the pudding puffs and is golden brown on top but still moist inside. Cool slightly before serving.

nly my mum would think to combine two of my favorite desserts, sticky toffee pudding and ice cream. What is truly amazing about this dessert is how it tastes extravagant but is so easy to make. This might just become your new favorite ice cream flavor.

LOZZA'S STICKY TOFFEE ICE CREAM

serves
10 to **12**

PREP TIME: 10 minutes

COOKING TIME: 15 minutes, plus 2 hours cooling time and at least 12 hours freezing time

STORING: The ice cream can be frozen for up to 2 days.

8 ounces Medjool dates (about 14), pitted and coarsely chopped

1 cup packed light brown sugar

8 tablespoons (1 stick) unsalted butter

½ cup heavy cream

Nonstick cooking spray

½ gallon vanilla ice cream

1 The day before serving the ice cream, in a small heavy saucepan, bring the dates and ⅔ cup water to a boil over high heat. Reduce the heat to medium and simmer for about 3 minutes, or until the dates are tender and the liquid has evaporated. Remove from the heat.

2 Meanwhile, in a medium heavy saucepan, heat the brown sugar and butter over medium heat, stirring almost constantly, for about 5 minutes, or until the sugar dissolves and the mixture comes to a simmer. Carefully stir in the cream and bring to a boil. Simmer for about 7 minutes, or until the mixture thickens and darkens slightly.

3 Remove the saucepan from the heat and stir in the date mixture. Transfer the mixture to a bowl and refrigerate for about 2 hours, or until cold and sticky.

4 Spray a 9 × 5 × 3-inch loaf pan with nonstick spray. Line the pan with plastic wrap, allowing the wrap to extend over the edges of the pan. Spoon the ice cream into a large bowl and allow it to soften just slightly if necessary. Working quickly, mix the date mixture into the ice cream. You can mix it in completely, or fold it in to create a ripple effect. Pack the ice cream mixture into the prepared loaf pan. Cover with the overhanging plastic wrap and freeze for at least 12 hours.

5 Uncover the ice cream. Rub your warm hands over the pan to help soften the edges of the ice cream and loosen it from the pan. Invert the ice cream onto a rectangular platter and remove the pan and plastic wrap. Cut the ice cream into slices and serve immediately.

Pots de crème are little baked custards with a fancy name. A pinch of salt in these custards heightens the caramel flavor. Cover the baking pan of custard cups with aluminum foil; it makes for the most luxuriously smooth pots de crème you'll ever have.

SALTED CARAMEL POTS DE CRÈME

serves
8

PREP TIME: 10 minutes
COOKING TIME: 1 hour, plus 1 hour cooling time and at least 4 hours chilling time
STORING: The pots de crème can be refrigerated for up to 2 days.

4 tablespoons (½ stick) unsalted butter

¾ cup packed light brown sugar

½ teaspoon kosher salt

½ vanilla bean, split lengthwise

1¾ cups heavy cream

¾ cup whole milk

6 large egg yolks

Flaky sea salt, such as Maldon, for garnish

1 Position a rack in the center of the oven and preheat the oven to 325°F. Place eight ½-cup (4-ounce) ovenproof cups, custard cups, or ramekins in a large baking pan.

2 In a large heavy saucepan, melt the butter over medium heat. Whisk in the brown sugar and kosher salt. Using the tip of a small sharp knife, scrape the vanilla seeds from the bean, add to the butter mixture, and drop in the bean too. Stir for about 5 minutes, or until the mixture has the texture of thick sand and has taken on a nutty, caramel fragrance.

3 Reduce the heat to medium-low and gradually whisk in the cream. The mixture will bubble vigorously and will seize when the cream is added. Whisk for about 5 minutes, or until the hardened sugar bits dissolve and the mixture begins to boil. Remove the pan from the heat and whisk in the milk.

4 In a large bowl, stir the egg yolks to blend. Gradually whisk in the warm caramel mixture. Strain the custard through a fine-mesh sieve into a 4-cup liquid measuring cup or a bowl with a spout. Pour the custard into the cups, dividing it equally. Cover the pan with aluminum foil, leaving one corner uncovered. Place the pan in the oven and carefully pour enough hot water into the pan to come halfway up the sides of the cups, then cover the open corner with the foil. Bake the custards for about 50 minutes, or until they are just set around the edges but still jiggle slightly when the cups are gently shaken. (Be very careful of escaping steam when you uncover the pan.)

5 Remove the cups from the pan and transfer to a wire rack to cool, about 1 hour. Cover each cup with plastic wrap and refrigerate until chilled, at least 4 hours, or up to 2 days.

6 Sprinkle a pinch of sea salt over each pot de crème and serve chilled.

FINISHING SALTS Chefs use different salts for different purposes. "Finishing salts" are not for cooking; rather, they're intended to flavor and add a bit of texture to your food as you're serving it. I am partial to Maldon salt, harvested from the sea near Essex, Britain. It has a pristine white color and very crunchy flakes.

Crisp, buttery, fruity . . . there is a lot to love about strudel, especially this one with juicy pears and tart dried cherries. With or without the amaretto custard sauce, this dessert is a real treat, especially served warm right out of the oven.

PEAR AND DRIED CHERRY STRUDEL WITH AMARETTO CUSTARD SAUCE

serves
6

PREP TIME: 15 minutes

COOKING TIME: 55 minutes, plus 15 minutes cooling time

Strudel

7 tablespoons unsalted butter

¾ cup panko (Japanese bread crumbs)

⅓ cup sugar

¾ teaspoon ground cinnamon

Pinch of fine sea salt or kosher salt

3 Anjou pears (about 1¼ pounds total), peeled, quartered, cored, and cut crosswise into ½-inch-thick slices

¼ cup dried tart cherries

12 sheets frozen filo pastry, thawed overnight in the refrigerator

Confectioners' sugar, for sifting

Amaretto Custard Sauce

¾ cup whole milk

½ cup heavy cream

2 tablespoons sugar

3 large egg yolks

1 to 2 tablespoons amaretto liqueur

1 To make the strudel: Position a rack in the center of the oven and preheat the oven to 375°F. Line a large heavy rimmed baking sheet with parchment paper.

2 In a small heavy skillet, melt 2 tablespoons of the butter over medium heat. Add the panko and stir for about 5 minutes, or until golden. Transfer the panko mixture to a large bowl. Stir in the sugar, cinnamon, and salt. Add the pears and cherries and stir well.

3 Place the remaining 5 tablespoons butter in a small saucepan and melt it over low heat. Lay 1 filo sheet on the work surface with a long side facing you. Brush the filo lightly with some of the melted butter. Layer 5 more sheets of filo over the first sheet in the same manner, brushing each sheet lightly with melted butter. Mound half of the pear mixture evenly along one long side, leaving about a 1½-inch border at both ends. Roll up the strudel tightly, turn it seam side down and fold the ends under to enclose the filling. Transfer the strudel to the baking sheet and brush with some melted butter. Repeat to make a second strudel.

4 Bake the strudels for about 45 minutes, or until dark golden (some juices will spill out of the strudels). Transfer the baking sheet to a wire rack and cool the strudels for 15 minutes.

5 Meanwhile, make the custard sauce: In a small heavy saucepan, bring the milk and cream to a simmer over medium heat. In a medium bowl, whisk the sugar and yolks together. Whisk in the hot milk mixture, then return the hot milk-yolk mixture to the saucepan. Using a heatproof silicone spatula, stir the mixture over medium-low heat for about 5 minutes, or until the custard thickens slightly and reaches 180°F on an instant-read thermometer; do not allow the custard to simmer. Stir in the amaretto to taste. Strain the sauce through a sieve into a bowl and set aside.

6 Lift the warm strudels, on the paper, and transfer to a cutting board. Sift confectioners' sugar over the strudels. Using a large serrated knife, trim the ends, then cut each strudel into 6 slices. Place the slices on plates, spoon some custard sauce alongside, and serve immediately.

We have a fig tree in our backyard, and it always gives us plenty of fruit to enjoy. For all its simplicity, this is a remarkable dessert, and I make it often when the figs are heavy on the tree. You could also serve these over ice cream, if you prefer.

CARAMELIZED FIGS WITH MASCARPONE AND HONEY

serves
4

PREP TIME: 5 minutes
COOKING TIME: 5 minutes

3 tablespoons sugar

¼ teaspoon ground ginger

⅛ teaspoon ground cinnamon

Pinch of ground cloves

8 ripe figs, halved lengthwise

¾ cup mascarpone cheese

½ cup walnut halves and pieces, toasted (see Kitchen Note, page 113)

1 tablespoon honey

1   Position the broiler rack 6 inches from the heat source and preheat the broiler. Line a large heavy rimmed baking sheet with aluminum foil.

2   In a small bowl, mix the sugar, ginger, cinnamon, and cloves together. One at a time, dip the figs, cut side down, in the sugar mixture to coat. Then coat the figs a second time with the sugar mixture and arrange cut side up on the baking sheet. Broil the figs, watching closely, for about 4 minutes, or until the sugar melts and begins to caramelize and the figs soften slightly and begin to ooze their juice.

3   Carefully transfer 4 figs to each dessert plate. Spoon a dollop of mascarpone cheese on top of each fig half. Sprinkle with the walnuts and drizzle with the honey. Serve warm.

At the height of summer, when peaches are flavorful and juicy, I eat them for dessert. Add a soft goat cheese, and it turns a simple pleasure into an elegant way to end a meal. Pair it with a chilled glass of Sauternes or your favorite dessert wine.

PEACHES WITH MELTED BÛCHERON

serves
4

PREP TIME: 5 minutes
COOKING TIME: 1 minute

2 large ripe peaches, halved and pitted

Four ½-inch-thick slices Bûcheron cheese (see Kitchen Note)

1 Position the broiler rack 6 inches from the heat source and preheat the broiler. Line a heavy rimmed baking sheet with aluminum foil.

2 Arrange the peach halves cut side up on the baking sheet and lay 1 slice of Bûcheron cheese over each peach half. Broil the peaches, watching closely, for about 45 seconds, or until the Bûcheron cheese melts and begins to brown. Carefully transfer the hot peaches to four dessert plates and serve immediately.

BÛCHERON Native to France's Loire Valley, Bûcheron is a goat cheese that is unique in its log shape and wide diameter. The rind is edible, even more so when softened by broiling. Slices of Bûcheron are the perfect size to cover the peach halves in this recipe. It is available at just about any cheese shop, as well as many supermarkets.

ACKNOWLEDGMENTS

I was extremely lucky to work with some of the best food professionals in the business on this book. Everyone who pitched in, from my culinary team to the students washing dishes, brought expertise to share and an awe-inspiring amount of joy and dedication.

Steven Fretz, affectionately known as Big Dog, leads my culinary team. He brought his amazing palate and never-ending passion for food to the book's photo shoot, where he worked from dawn to dark to bring my recipes to life. At his side were chefs Jeff Thomas and James Trees and my culinary assistant Tiffany Lewis, who with maturity and grace managed Le Cordon Bleu culinary students Erica Lee, Fara Ramos, and Lynn Exe through all of the washing, peeling, chopping, and prepping necessary to create beautiful food.

When it comes to food editors, Rochelle Palermo is irreplaceable—which is one of the reasons I've asked her to work on my last two books. I feel so fortunate to have her generous spirit in the kitchen, testing and editing my recipes with attention to detail and an unwavering love of delicious food. She was integral to this book from start to finish. Whether she was working with me to handpick the recipes, managing the photo shoot, or putting all the moving parts together, I couldn't have done this cookbook without her.

Quentin Bacon is an amazing photographer and something of a magician who uses only natural lighting to illuminate the food. He's also an incredible foodie, which is another reason his photographs are good enough to eat. He has an unmatched ability to know exactly what the camera wants to see and how to adjust the food perfectly for the lens, while keeping it looking natural and organic. There's no better prop stylist than Kate Martindale, whose passion for the patina on a silver spoon is as impressive as her ability to express my aesthetics so perfectly. Thanks for setting warm and welcoming tables I would eat at any day of the week, and keeping our long days energized with fun and the occasional dirty joke. I love styling my own dishes. It was one of the most gratifying things I did as a chef in fine-dining restaurants and it's something I still love today. It was all the more enjoyable to do it alongside the incredibly talented food stylist Carrie Ann Purcell. I loved how Carrie's unfussy grace lent the food a natural style while her relaxed and cool manner brought calm to our shoot.

A heartfelt thanks to Damien Webster, who rode his bike twenty-seven miles to the set every day to take beautiful behind-the-scenes photos, and Vicky Andrade and Maria Angeles for keeping everything clean and shiny. Thank you to Health Ceramics, Match, and Eclectic Acres for lending their beautiful goods to our photographs.

When creating a cookbook, I love thinking of the concept, dreaming up recipes, and endlessly testing, tasting, and refining the dishes. But when it comes to getting my story on paper, I can use a little help. With this book, I had more than a little from Rachel Dowd, who stayed up far too late night after night with Rochelle and me in order to shape my thoughts into poetic goodness. Thanks to Sasha Arciniega for keeping me in the right place at the right time and tying up the loose ends.

This book could not have come together without the diligence and dedication of my best friend and sometimes boss, Jodie Gatt. We've known each other for a lifetime and I couldn't imagine tackling any endeavor without her clever strategizing, organizing, and championing at every turn.

A huge thanks to my editorial team at Random House. We worked on a wildly tight deadline and my editor, Pamela Cannon, was incomparable at keeping us on track. The hardworking Rick Rodgers dropped everything to jump on board and lend us his excellent food knowledge, and Judith Sutton copyedited the manuscript with truly impressive detail and thoughtfulness.

To my darling wife, Lindsay, who watched without a word of complaint as our home turned into a madhouse during three solid weeks of shooting, thanks for being there for me in every way. You are generous and gracious, no matter what cast of characters is sitting around our dinner table, and I love that my seat is always at your side.

A last special thank-you to my mum, who taught me the beauty of gathering around the dinner table each night. She has a recipe in every cookbook I've written and, hand on my heart, her sticky toffee ice cream is the best I've ever eaten. Thanks for making me a good cook, Mumma.

INDEX

ABOUT THE AUTHOR

CURTIS STONE is the author of five cookbooks and host of *Top Chef Masters* on Bravo. He is also the creator of Kitchen Solutions, a sleek line of cookware sold in retailers worldwide, and writes a monthly column for *Men's Fitness*. Born in Melbourne, Australia, Stone honed his skills in London at Café Royal, under legendary three-star Michelin chef Marco Pierre White, and at Mirabelle and the revered Quo Vadis. He lives in Los Angeles with his wife and son.

www.curtisstone.com

ABOUT THE TYPE

This book is set in Excelsior, a typeface first designed in 1931 by Chauncey H. Griffith. An American printer, compositor and typeface designer, Griffith established Linotype as the industry standard in newspaper and book composition in the early twentieth century. One of five typefaces in "Griffith's Legibility Group," Excelsior is a clear typeface of even color that reads easily in small sizes, producing a calm effect on the page. As such it was widely adopted as a text and display face for newspapers across the United States, and has retained its popularity in Europe.